ALASKA ON THE GO

ALASKA ON THE GO

EXPLORING THE
ALASKA MARINE HIGHWAY SYSTEM
WITH CHILDREN

Erin Kirkland

University of Alaska Press
Fairbanks

University of Alaska Press
P.O. Box 756240
Fairbanks, AK 99775-6240

Library of Congress Cataloging in Publication Data

Names: Kirkland, Erin, author.
Title: Alaska on the go : exploring the marine highway system with children / by Erin Kirkland.
Description: Fairbanks, AK : University of Alaska Press, [2017]
Identifiers: LCCN 2016025132 (print) | LCCN 2016037342 (ebook) |
    ISBN 9781602233157 (pbk. : alk. paper) | ISBN 9781602233164 ()
Subjects: LCSH: Alaska—Guidebooks. | Ferries—Alaska—Guidebooks. |
    Family recreation—Alaska—Guidebooks. | Children—Travel—Alaska—Guidebooks.
Classification: LCC F902.3 .K573 2017 (print) | LCC F902.3 (ebook) | DDC 917.9804/5dc23
LC record available at https://lccn.loc.gov/2016025132

Main cover image: Alaska Marine Highway Ferry *Aurora* travels through Passage Canal on the way to the port town of Whittier, Prince William Sound and Southcentral Alaska. Photo by Patrick Endres, Alaska Stock.

All small images on cover by Erin Kirkland.

All photos credited to the Alaska Marine Highway System are printed with permission.

All other photos, not credited, are by Erin Kirkland.

Cover design: University of Alaska Press
Text design: Paula Elmes, ImageCraft Publications & Design

∞ This paper meets the requirements for ANSI / NISO Z39.48-1992 (R2002)
(Permanence of Paper).

Dedicated to mariners, past and present, who so willingly shared their knowledge of and relationship with the sea. May that be passed on to future generations of Alaska visitors.

———————————————

Some love to roam o're the dark seas foam,
Where the shrill winds whistle free.

–Charles Mackay

CONTENTS

PREFACE

It's easy for me to imagine a life spent exploring the rugged ocean edges of Alaska. Perhaps the blood of my great-great-great-grandfather, a merchant marine captain from Sweden, propels me toward water. Maybe it's my childhood in the Puget Sound area near Seattle and the hours I spent scanning the horizon for whales and ships sliding silently through the briny waterways. As an adult and an Alaskan, I find the sea to be a mysterious extension of the place in which I choose to work, play, and raise a family.

Alaska's coastal communities present a certain conundrum with regard to transportation. Planes are fast but provide only a one-dimensional view of Alaska's topographic personality; trains and cars eventually run out of rail or road due to mountainous terrain and steep shorelines that prevent access. Boats, on the other hand, are ancient modes of getting nearly everywhere. Watercraft of various sizes and styles has played an enormous role in shaping the state's personality, and they help shape its present and future.

The Alaska Marine Highway System is more than just a collection of boats, however. With a colorful history as unique as Alaska herself, these ferries, nicknamed the "blue canoes" by residents, sail thirty-five hundred miles of All-American Road and National Scenic Byway routes all year in all types of weather for all types of people.

As I tossed around and rejected several suggestions for a second *Alaska on the Go* book, the Marine Highway System kept returning to view. Why? Was it the ferries' simplicity in a world where luxury often takes precedence in travel? The crew's personality? Famous Alaska scenery and wildlife? The answers remain as individual as the ferry routes themselves. For our family, travel along the Alaska Marine Highway means capturing one of the reasons we live here in the first place: it's simply unlike any opportunity anywhere else. Your family may have a completely different reason, but I challenge you to discover, explore, and embrace it, whatever "it" might be.

Like *Alaska on the Go: Exploring the 49th State with Children*, this book is meant to be used as a tool to navigate your floating adventure and, like the first guide, strives to be as up-to-date as possible. However, at the time of publication, the state of Alaska was in a frustrating budgetary flux. Funds allocated for many state-funded programs were greatly reduced, including the ferry system. While I have made every effort to research routes, schedules, and fares, Alaska legislators continue their battle for line-item elimination with the resulting changes evolving quickly.

Of course, traveling Alaska with children requires thoughtful planning and careful consideration for the ages and abilities of everyone in your party. Communicate clearly; double-check rates, dates, and availability; and above all, keep exploring. Alaska is worth every mile.

INTRODUCTION: HISTORY LEADS TO INDUSTRY

What a beautiful sight that was. We could take our car, or walk on board, and GO SOMEWHERE! Our highway had arrived!

—Betty J. Marksheffel, describing her first view of the ferry as a historical note in celebration of the Alaska Marine Highway System's fiftieth anniversary in 2013

Imagine living in a place so remote that no road could be built to transport people or supplies. Everything from toilet paper to apples and oranges must be ordered and shipped on an airplane or boat; that is, if the weather cooperates. Services like medical and dental care, education, or law enforcement may be lacking or nonexistent, depending upon the time of year and nature of the need. Yet, this place with no roadways somehow attracts a large number of people, drawn to the temperate climate and endless range of forested land, rich in cultural and economic opportunity.

Welcome to busy, bustling coastal Alaska: an area stretching from the southern panhandle cities of Ketchikan and Juneau, then westward toward Kodiak Island and the Aleutian Islands. While most residents of these communities swear they'd never live anywhere else, making a home with few resources can be complicated at best, especially before the Alaska Marine Highway ferries showed up.

The Alaska Marine Highway story begins just after World War II, when surplus machinery, including boats, could be found extra cheap. Steve Homer and brothers Ray and Gustav Gelotte, residents of the tiny Southeast Alaska town of Haines, decided to capitalize on a lack of coastal transportation options by purchasing an old US Navy landing craft. Christened the MV *Chilkoot*, this fourteen-car vessel required much work before she was deemed worthy to sail the eighty-plus miles between Haines and Tee Harbor near Juneau, which was still seventeen miles northwest of downtown Juneau. Naming their business the Chilkoot Motorship Lines Company, Homer and the Gelotte brothers managed to operate for a few years, ferrying passengers, automobiles, and supplies north and south, along with a few adventurous tourists who were bused from Anchorage to Haines or Skagway, the only panhandle access points by road. Eventually, though, the cost of fuel and maintenance caught up with them, and the future of ferry travel seemed in jeopardy as the group filed for bankruptcy. By this time, however, residents of Skagway, Haines, and Juneau were becoming accustomed to this additional mode of travel, and as word spread of the demise of Chilkoot Motorship Lines, the territorial government of Alaska stepped in to save the struggling business. Having witnessed the obvious economic benefit of having a ferry system available to the southeast region of the territory, officials negotiated a purchase of Chilkoot Motorship Lines from its owners in June of 1951.

> ### PARENT PRO TIP
>
> I lived on these boats growing up, thinking it was not unusual at all to take a boat to sports competitions, music festivals, and on family trips. I have so many memories of ferry rides, and I'm glad my kids have the chance to experience it too. As an adult, though, I appreciate the scenery more than the socializing I did as a teenager on my way to a basketball game!
>
> —Jennifer, former resident of Haines and mom of three ferry-savvy children

Under the safer umbrella of governmental funding, the MV *Chilkoot* continued to sail between Haines, Skagway, and Juneau and quickly became too small to handle the increasing number of passengers and vehicles. In 1957 the MV *Chilkat* replaced the *Chilkoot*, and when Alaska joined the United States in 1959, the *Chilkat* became the first state-owned vessel in the fleet. Alaska legislators approved the Alaska Ferry Transportation Act later that year, and voters approved $18 million to expand a ferry fleet that included four new vessels and docks throughout the Southeast and Kenai Peninsula sections of the state. The Division of Marine Transportation was formally established, creating the Alaska Marine Highway System (better known as AMHS) with four ferries, aptly named MVs *Chilkat*, *Malaspina*, *Taku*, and *Matanuska* after mighty Alaska glaciers. By 1963 the newly formed AMHS delivered sixteen thousand vehicles and eighty-three thousand passengers between Haines and Ketchikan.

When the MV *Malaspina* arrived in Ketchikan on January 23, 1963, a traffic jam of interested observers and curious onlookers ensued. This is quite impressive considering the population at that time was only a few thousand people.

FERRY FACT

Southwest Alaska communities wanted in on this newfound access to the mainland, so in 1964 the *Tustemena*, or *Trusty Tusty*, came on line with a homeport in Kodiak and service to the cities of Seward, Homer, Cordova, Seldovia, and Valdez. So successful and dependable were the AMHS ferries that not even the Great Alaska Earthquake of 1964 could stop its service, despite $300 million in damage across the state and a loss of 128 lives between the quake and subsequent tsunami.

Tourism and economics both played a role in the eventual link between Alaska and the Lower 48, but it took several months for Canada and the United States to play along with the concept of a ferry that connected Alaska to Washington State. In 1968 Canadian ferries were providing transportation to and from Prince Rupert, British Columbia, then the terminus of the Marine Highway. Adding to the problem was the lack of an ocean-going vessel fit to navigate open water between Prince Rupert and Seattle, but eventually the state of Alaska purchased the *Stena Britannica* for $7 million and rechristened her the MV *Wickersham* after an Alaska

Alaska Marine Highway System crewmember James L. Smith, right, and an unidentified gentleman stand alongside the ferry *Taku*, circa 1960s. IMAGE COURTESY OF LESLIE CUMMINGS.

judge and political official. She was a big ship, solid and sturdy and able to carry 1,300 passengers and 170 vehicles—perfect for sailing the often-rough waters of the Inside Passage's southern end.

The Alaska Marine Highway quickly gained a reputation as an affordable method of getting to and from the Last Frontier without days of driving and undue wear and tear on a vehicle. When the Alyeska Pipeline was built in the 1970s and oil became a prosperous means of employment, many families moved to Alaska via the ferry, carting kids and furniture and pets via the blue canoes. Tourists, too, saw the ferry as an exciting way to see Alaska, and thanks to a fairly lax standard of sleeping arrangements back then, passengers sailing overnight pitched tents on deck or cuddled up in sleeping bags on chairs in lounge areas. That method of indie travel is now considered a signature event for many people, almost a rite of passage for teenagers and young adults who want both freedom and a chance to see the world.

In 2002 the Alaska Marine Highway received the distinction as the first and longest marine-based National Scenic Byway for its distinctive cultural, historical, and recreational attributes. In 2005 the Scenic Byway program awarded the AMHS with an added jewel of designating the highway an All-American Road, one of only 31 of 151 Scenic Byways recognized in the program. In the fifty years since the MV *Chilkoot* was first purchased from Steve Homer and Ray and Gustav Gelotte, AMHS ferries have cruised nearly 300,000 passengers and 110,000 vehicles annually up and down its thirty-five hundred miles of watery roadway. With eleven vessels and two new, larger ferries under construction, AMHS sails to thirty-five port communities between Dutch Harbor in Unalaska and Bellingham, Washington.

PLANNING AN ALASKA MARINE HIGHWAY ADVENTURE

If you've ever thought about it, stop thinking and book a trip!

—Robin C., AMHS passenger, via Facebook

1
THE JOURNEY *IS* THE DESTINATION

For my part, I travel not to go anywhere, but to go. I travel for travel's sake. The great affair is to move.

—Robert Louis Stevenson

For the uninitiated, travel in Alaska can seem overwhelming. A huge swath of real estate, almost 587,000 square miles of it, runs from Canada all the way to the Arctic Circle and beyond, so the notion of planning a vacation with kids in tow, in a place so large, can deter many. Have faith, however, because I have a plan.

In my first book, *Alaska on the Go: Exploring the 49th State with Children,* I talked a lot about focusing on one geographical area of the state to take advantage of unique opportunities for recreation, scenery, culture, and parental sanity. The Alaska Marine Highway is an excellent way to establish yourselves as Last Frontier explorers, for no other reason than the provisional floating hotel it provides without the fancy fluff of a cruise ship. Coupled with the freedom of sightseeing on your own and at your own pace, a vacation aboard AMHS ferries provides families the independence they crave with enough structure to build a workable itinerary fitting everyone's interests and ability levels.

When to Go
Since the Alaska Marine Highway serves a vital role in transportation between coastal communities, many routes operate consistently throughout

Regardless of the season, ferry travelers will be treated to coastal Alaska scenery and a relaxed, unhurried pace.

the year. Of course, water-based travel does have certain disadvantages during the winter, including wild weather and a lack of scenery due to low-hanging clouds, fog, and snow. Additionally, many of the top tourist attractions in popular cities like Ketchikan, Juneau, Skagway, and Sitka close up shop during the off-season, leaving unprepared visitors in search of their own entertainment. Here is an overview of seasonal options with respect to the ferry system.

SUMMER

As with most of Alaska tourism, summer is the prime season for access to recreational opportunities and decidedly better weather. Long days and a variety of activities mean lots of family fun with ferry itineraries running full steam ahead at ports of call. The problem is deciding how to fit it all in.

⬆ PROS

- Seasonal routes through lesser-traveled Alaska communities, like Unalaska and Dutch Harbor, are in full operation and offer adventurous travelers an itinerary full of rugged outdoor recreation and unique sights.

- Sailings to and from Bellingham, Washington, or Prince Rupert, British Columbia, are at their peak with more frequent departures and arrivals that meet high demand. Airlines also beef up routes to and from Alaska for those wanting a one-way experience, at a much more affordable price, thanks to healthy competition.
- Weather is usually warmer, with temperatures ranging from 75°F in Southeast Alaska to the high 60s in Kodiak and the Aleutian Islands during the day. Usually.
- Birds and marine mammals are very active, including humpback whales, who spend the summer months feeding on krill (plankton) and herring in preparation for their winter migration to Hawai'i. Other animals to spy include sea lions, orca whales, sea otters, seals, puffins, and bald eagles.

⇩ CONS

- Summer in Alaska, no matter where you go, is expensive. The tourism industry knows visitors will pay premium prices for those amazing experiences.
- Ferry travel during the summer is very, very crowded, necessitating reservations wherever possible. Routes may need to be adjusted depending upon availability. It is recommended that travelers make reservations as early as possible for popular routes like the Inside Passage.
- Hotels on shore are likely to be full for walk-up guests who wish to stay in a community for a few days, and prices are at their peak. Reservations are all but required.

AUTUMN

My favorite sweet spot for visiting Alaska, autumn along the Marine Highway means fewer crowds and lower prices on attractions and hotels as vendors begin wrapping up the summer season. A nice bonus is the availability of both, since most schools around the country begin toward the end of August, just when the leaves start turning color up here. Weather can be rainy and windy, or delightfully crisp and sunny; so personal comfort comes down to preparation.

⬆ PROS

- Excellent end-of-season airfares mean a significant savings for travelers, and Alaska Marine Highway deals, like the popular "Driver Goes Free" campaign, usually begin in October. Check the website for details (www.ferryalaska.com).
- Scenery becomes a textural color wheel, with the bright emerald of evergreens mixing with the yellows and reds of hardwood trees and shrubs. Early season snowfall on the highest mountain peaks just adds to the landscape's allure.
- Some attractions offer end-of-season discounts to autumn travelers, and families will certainly enjoy the uncrowded atmosphere.

⬇ CONS

- Weather can be frustrating, depending upon the location. Wild wind and driving rain can sweep into coastal areas, making ferry travel a bit uncomfortable or downright miserable.
- Some seasonal routes end after Labor Day, restricting those with adventurous appetites to the more sedate routes around Southeast Alaska and Prince William Sound.

Wildlife Safety: What We Mean by "Bear Aware"

Alaska is home to many different types of wildlife, and it is the informed visitor who is less likely to panic should a wild animal encounter occur. Animals are one of the main reasons people travel to Alaska, and yet many people still operate under the assumption that animals do not venture close to tourist attractions or visitor centers. Alaska children are taught from an early age to be stewards of their valuable land and its priceless inhabitants; they learn in school how to respect animals and behave accordingly, and your kids can, too.

The Alaska Department of Fish and Game works hard to educate all residents and visitors about the risks and benefits of recreating in Alaska alongside a few thousand wild critters. Employees visit schools and attend fairs and festivals across the state year-round with hopes of providing

- Attractions may or may not be open. Visitors should have a plan for amusing kids in port cities with little or no visitor services.

WINTER

While winter travel to Southcentral and Interior Alaska is definitely becoming more popular thanks to attractions like the aurora borealis and sled dogs, coastal communities still haven't really caught on to the idea of hanging out the welcome sign all year long. Wintertime ferry travelers, for the most part, consist of Alaskans on their way to or from important appointments, deliveries, or further travel. For those wanting to experience the real Alaska, however, this is a great way to immerse yourself in the daily life of a coastal resident.

⬆ PROS

- The port cities served by the Alaska Marine Highway tend to be a bit warmer than Interior communities. In some places snow is relatively sparse, replaced by rain that falls by the foot. Not a fan of the white stuff and don't mind the rain? This might be your trip.

useful and, in some cases, life-saving information. The comprehensive section "Living with Wildlife" on their website (www.adfg.alaska.gov) offers a wealth of practical tips for sharing the outdoors with bears, moose, and other Alaska animals.

Concerning bears, a good rule of thumb for recreating among Alaska's brown and black bears (and we have both) is to make noise, travel in groups, and carry pepper spray (available upon your arrival at most sporting goods stores and many local shops) and understand how to use it. Bears only want to eat in peace and raise their young, much like we do, so letting them know we're coming goes a long way toward wilderness harmony and safety.

- Admission to museums, cultural centers, and community events is often free or available at a very low price—a great way to meet other kids and families.
- Winter recreation is still very much available, from Eaglecrest Ski Area in Juneau to Nordic trails in Valdez. Outdoor enthusiasts can carry on gear and create a complete vacation package with the ferry as a central point for transportation.

⇩ CONS

- Winter is very dark in Alaska, even in Inside Passage communities, where clouds and rain make short days seem even shorter. For those who thrive on daylight and occasional sun breaks, winter might be a tough season in which to visit.
- Flights to and from many coastal communities slow way down in the winter, with some airlines offering only one or two flights per week to a particular destination. Thus, it is critical to plan ahead for transportation links, and flexibility is the name of the game.
- Weather can still play a major role in ferry travel, particularly when freezing spray and high winds make seas rough.

FERRY FACT

It is the rare day when a ferry cannot complete its route due to weather, and vessels have been known to arrive in port with ice coating their outer decks and railings during the winter months. That said, sailings can be cancelled due to inclement weather, and ferry staff try their best to contact ticketed passengers beforehand. Make sure to provide a contact number with your reservation!

SPRING

Springtime means worshipping the daylight hours with reckless abandon. Everybody and everything, from plants to people, pushes their faces toward ever-increasing sunlight and spends as much time as possible outdoors. By early May, tourism vendors are opening doors to visitors, making preseason deals that can't be matched during the summer months.

⬆ PROS

- This is the season to catch gray whales with calves in tow migrating from Mexico's Sea of Cortez. It's quite a sight, and one worth watching from the bow of a ferry.
- Major attractions like flightseeing or dog mushing gather steam in the springtime and offer discounts to do it.
- Daylight arrives rapidly, baby animals begin to make appearances with cautious mothers, and the green of a growing landscape becomes more obvious every day.
- Airlines begin seasonal service, but not all at once, so do your homework and find the best deal to match trip dates.

PARENT PRO TIP

It was sixteen years ago, but I traveled the Seward to Juneau run with my husband and one-year-old daughter. Mid-trip, a storm came up and the swells had to be thirty-five feet. The ferry just rode up and down and slammed into each wave. I watched my daughter's eyes roll back in her head with each sway of the ferry, and my husband was no help. He and the rest of the passengers (and many of the crew) were outside barfing off the side. All I can say is—be prepared for anything!

—Venessa, mom of very reluctant ferry passengers

⬇ CONS

- Spring has another name in Alaska, fondly (or not so much) called breakup, during which time snow melts and slushy road grit dominates the scenery. Prior to May, in fact, everything is gray or brown. Typically, May and June are considered springtime in Alaska, so plan accordingly.
- Weather in coastal Alaska can be bipolar during the spring months, with blizzards or wild windstorms meeting sunny skies and temperate days. The jet streams do the planning, not people, so a good forecast one day can suddenly turn bleak the next.

Where to Sail

The Alaska Marine Highway System is broken down into a series of routes, each with a specific timetable of arrivals and departures according to season. Thankfully, the AMHS website (www.ferryalaska.com) is quite comprehensive as a planning tool, breaking down each route by vessel and using the Google Maps function for a visual display that makes decisions easier. **Note**: Alaska is twice the size of Texas and possesses 6,640 miles of mainland coastline. Be prudent in your planning.

I'll talk more about each specific route, the interesting features, wildlife, waterways, and residents, but in the meantime, here is a quick overview.

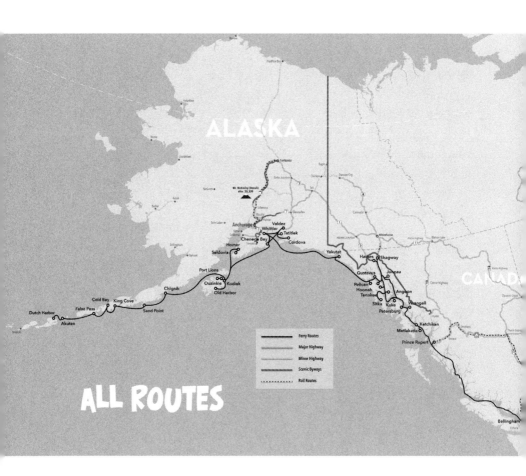

SOUTHEAST ALASKA ROUTE

The panhandle, snuggled up tight against British Columbia and the Yukon Territory of Canada, is where all northbound ferry passengers and cruise ship guests catch their first glimpse of Alaska. Towering evergreens, narrow passages, and rocky shorelines make Southeast a beautiful place to make your acquaintance, especially beautiful thanks to the enormous Tongass National Forest, the largest national forest in the United States. Southeast is a boater's paradise, and nearly every resident owns some sort of watercraft with which to fish, paddle, and explore uninhabited coves, islands, and mountains.

> **PARENT PRO TIP**
>
> You just can't beat a beautiful day on the ferry, sitting out on the back deck in the sun with your kids playing nearby.
>
> —Sarah, lifelong Southeast resident and mom of three

Southeast ferry routes take passengers between Prince Rupert, British Columbia, to the small, gold rush town of Skagway, with stops in towns like Wrangell, Petersburg, Sitka, Juneau, and Haines. The route largely follows that of the shipping lanes but also the cruise industry, whose enormous vessels disgorge up to four thousand people at a time to major Alaska port cities. Traveling by ferry, a family can escape the frenetic pace of shore excursion tours and amble the streets and visit the same attractions as cruisers but at a more sedate speed. Activities are plentiful, as are hotels and restaurants, but all can fill up quickly, making preplanning a must. Passengers can choose to begin their trip in Bellingham, Washington, or Prince Rupert, British Columbia, or in cities along the route, connecting with the ferry via Alaska Airlines (www.alaskair.com), the state's major air carrier. Another advantage of the Southeast route is access to the Alaska Highway in the communities of Skagway and Haines, making auto travel around the rest of Alaska a viable option for longer trips.

Southeast Alaska also boasts rich cultural and historical significance to the state. Sitka, on Baranof Island, is the site of the official transfer of the territory to the United States in 1867. Juneau, located along narrow Gastineau Channel, is Alaska's capital, one of two state capitals inaccessible by road (the other is Honolulu). Skagway, a former gold rush melting pot of debauchery and fortune, marks the beginning of the famous Chilkoot Trail into the Yukon, where thousands and thousands of eager gold-seekers climbed 3,501-foot Chilkoot Pass with a ton of gear on their way to dreams of striking it big. Alaska Native communities are strong in Southeast Alaska, with families of Tlingit, Haida, Eyak, and Tsimshian origin living and working a subsistence lifestyle from the sea's bounty. A deep connection to the coastal waterways of the Inside Passage drives Southeast Native culture, starting with the complex clan system of governance and tradition. Travel by ferry allows for stops in smaller communities like Wrangell and Petersburg to investigate Alaska Native

A Few Words about Customs

Due to Alaska's proximity to Canada, many ferry passengers find themselves traveling in and out of United States during their trip, most often due to a one-way drive/sail option that involves entry at one of three communities: Haines or Skagway, in Alaska, or Prince Rupert, in British Columbia.

As of June 2009, all US citizens traveling through Canada are required to show a passport at US-Canadian borders, doing away with the rule that a driver's license would suffice. There are a few categories of acceptable identification recognized by US and Canadian customs offices, including passport cards, NEXUS or FAST cards, and a regular passport. Not sure which one to select for your family? Contact the US Department of State office in your area, or visit http://travel.state.gov/content/passports/english/passports/information/card.html.

Note: Traveling aboard an Alaska Marine Highway vessel between Bellingham, Washington, and Ketchikan, Alaska, does not require you to show a passport, but the vessel does sail through Canadian waters. Provided you do not disembark the vessel if it should land on Canadian soil, no passport is necessary.

If you've chosen the drive/sail style of Alaska adventure, be aware that upon arrival at a US or Canadian border, drivers will be expected to show culture on a deeper, more personal level, and cultural tourism as an industry is very much on the mind of Alaska's government officials in this area.

CROSS GULF ROUTE

Linking the Southeast Alaska route to the rest of Alaska's coastal routes is the Cross Gulf route, snaking its way from Juneau to Yakutat and on toward Whittier in Prince William Sound, gateway to Southcentral Alaska and cities like Anchorage, Seward, and Homer.

Unlike the Southeast route, however, the Cross Gulf is more about transportation than attractions, so families with children will not find as many options for interesting things to do or places to stay. In fact, the

a vehicle registration card or proof of title and liability insurance coverage in addition to personal identification for everyone traveling with you. This includes infants! If you're traveling with pets, see your veterinarian, as proof of vaccinations, especially rabies, will need to be shown.

All adults traveling with children—either their own or those not in their full, legal custody—will be required to provide, at minimum, a copy of the child's passport or card, and a notarized letter from legal guardians authorizing the child's entry into or out of the United States or Canada. The US Department of State website has a comprehensive list of every slip of paper visitors should possess with relation to kids.

Note: Do not forget to do this! I did on a drive to Haines with a friend and her three kids. At the Canadian border, both of us were stopped for several minutes while a grumpy agent grilled my three-year-old as to where his daddy was. I was near hysteria at the thought of driving two days back to Anchorage with an already-restless toddler when the agent let us through. Lesson learned: have the paperwork.

Canada has its own rules and regulations pertaining to border regulations, so be sure to check the Canada Border Services Agency (www .cbsa-asfc.gc.ca/noncan-eng.html) for information before you travel.

trip to Whittier is roughly twenty-four hours, so most of the amusing will need to be done on board. (See part 2, Life On Board the Ferry, for ideas and options for kid-friendly fun.)

The Gulf of Alaska is full of interesting things to see, however. Look for humpback and orca whales and the never-ending stream of barges, cargo ships, and cruise ships making their way to and from Whittier or Anchorage. Alaska Native groups along this route begin to change from those found in the Southeast area to the Aleut, Alutiiq, and Athabascan groups of Southcentral and the Aleutian Islands, with traditions rooted in seafaring vessels called *qayaqs*, what we know today as kayaks.

SOUTHCENTRAL ALASKA ROUTE

Boasting Alaska's highest concentration of people, thanks to Anchorage, the state's largest city, "Southcentral," as it is known by residents, is accessible in ways that benefit visiting families. Roadways and railroads connect Whittier to Anchorage, and the Seward Highway delivers people and goods to the city of Seward and provides a link to the Kenai Peninsula, home to famous salmon fishing rivers. The Prince William Sound community of Valdez is easily reached via ferry or car, making for a wonderful round-trip vacation into the Chugach, one of the most beautiful mountain ranges in the state. Recreation rivals that of Southeast, with kayaking, fishing, day cruising, and hiking dominating the lineup. Families may choose a ferry-based road trip from Whittier, driving north toward Denali National Park or south toward areas near Homer and beautiful Kachemak Bay. Included in the Southcentral route is enormous Kodiak Island across the Gulf of Alaska from Homer, home to the equally enormous Kodiak brown bear. There's plenty to do, and the main problem may be finding enough time. This route is nearly as popular as the Southeast route, largely due to its access as a jumping-off point for other adventures, so reservations will be critical, especially if you're traveling with a vehicle.

SOUTHWEST ALASKA ROUTE

The least-familiar route to visitors, and many residents, the Southwest Alaska route travels between Kodiak and the wild, windswept islands of the Aleutian Chain, made famous in the television series *Deadliest Catch*. It can be deadly, all right, most notably during the winter months when salty, near-frozen waves reach heights of thirty feet or more. Understandably, then, the Alaska Marine Highway foregoes service along the Southwest Alaska route during the fall-through-spring months, picking back up in May when seas are decidedly calmer. The wide Alaska Peninsula and the Aleutian Islands stretch fifteen hundred miles toward Asia. The area sits atop the famous Ring of Fire, a chain of volcanoes that constantly burp and shift position, much to the consternation of residents, for this movement causes frequent earthquakes that rattle nerves and dishes with equal abandon. The Aleutian Chain is famous for wildlife refuges that shelter birds, fur seals, walrus, and orcas, and the hardy tourist is all but guaranteed a wildlife experience unmatched by anything else in Alaska. It's also a place most Americans leave out of their history studies; Dutch Harbor, for example, is home to a number of historical sites that remind us of this area's involvement in World War II.

FERRY FACTS AND NEED-TO-KNOW INFORMATION

For new passengers trying to figure out when, where, and how to best sail upon the Alaska Marine Highway can be a workout, especially when it comes to complicated fare schedules and matching up

routes to destinations. It's a complex system, but not for lack of effort by the state of Alaska and reservations agents, so take a deep breath, pull out a highlighter, and let's learn the facts.

As recommended previously, passengers should focus on routes that spark interest among all family members. The AMHS website provides a very detailed description of port communities, complete with activities and events, and experience has taught us that one or two kid-selected stops go a long way toward a successful trip with children.

Cost

Once upon a time, the Alaska Marine Highway System ferries were one of the cheapest ways to travel to or from Alaska, especially if travelers bunked on the deck in a sleeping bag. These days, with a high number of passengers and dramatic increases in fuel costs, the ferry is more expensive, especially if your family travels with a car or RV. Of course, other modes of transportation require fuel too, and the wear and tear on a vehicle driving up the Alaska Highway can be significant. Still not sure if the ferry is a financial reality? Here's a simple calculator to help you decide whether to include the ferry in your trip. All prices are based upon a **family of four traveling seven days during the** peak 2016 summer season and are meant to be used as an example only.

COMPARISON SHOPPING

- Round-trip airfare from Seattle, Washington, to Juneau, Alaska: $600/person
- Hotel: $300/night for two adults, two children at mid-range Juneau hotel
- Car rental: $600/week for midsize or compact vehicle

Total: $5,100

- One-way ferry tickets from Bellingham, Washington, to Juneau: Adult fare, $329/person (Children ages six to eleven are half price, and children under six are free.)
- Staterooms run from $88 to more than $300 for the trip, depending upon room type.
- One-way vehicle fare on the ferry: average $739

Total: $2,671

FerryAlaska.com

The Alaska Marine Highway website has page after page of helpful information that can aid in creating a workable itinerary for your family. Bolstering the website's practicality is an entire section dedicated to the ferry system's history, complete with photos, videos, and stories from former passengers and crew. It's a fun journey through time, and kids will enjoy the schematics of vessel layout and amenities and port community

- Auto travel from Seattle to Anchorage (no roads lead to Juneau): $3.35/gallon average over 2,265 miles of highway. Do the math based upon your car's fuel consumption rate and the current cost of fuel. I calculated based on a vehicle getting 20 mpg.
- Hotel: $300/night for two adults, two children between Washington and Alaska

Total: $2,455

- Cruise line travel from Seattle or Vancouver, British Columbia, to Juneau: average $700/person (does not include shore excursions, drinks, and some onboard activities)

Total: $2,800

Keeping in mind that a trip aboard an Alaska ferry is meant to be part of your family's vacation and not just the mode of transportation, it can be said that AMHS is a competitive deal. I'll get down to specifics for actual time spent on the ferry with kids later and share some money-saving tips, but for those still considering their Alaska adventure, this is a good start.

Making Reservations

With three hundred thousand passengers hopping aboard annually, Alaska Marine Highway ferries can only handle so many people per

facts. In addition, the website offers online booking for trips, which might or might not be helpful. Our last resort is usually to call reservations agents (1-800-642-0066), inform them of cities we wish to visit, and let them pull the whole thing together, especially if we're traveling over many days with multiple layovers.

The Alaska Marine Highway System ferries strive to make every trip safe, comfortable, and full of interesting sights, regardless of which route you choose.
COURTESY OF ALASKA MARINE HIGHWAY SYSTEM.

sailing, which makes reservations absolutely vital to the success of the experience. Summer routes are first to sell out, especially the Bellingham to Juneau run, so families wanting to sail the Inside Passage should begin booking no later than January for the coming year of travel.

There are generally two ways to reserve ferry tickets, and both are effective, although one requires more patience. The AMHS offers a "Plan a Trip" tab on their website that features routes, fare schedules, timelines, and port information. Based upon that information, potential passengers can then proceed to the "Reservations" tab where an itinerary will be created and tickets and staterooms (if desired) can be booked.

The other method of buying tickets is through the reservations agents at AMHS, reached by calling 1-800-642-0066. Depending upon your ease of website navigation, you may or may not find the 800-number to be more helpful.

Travel agents, if part of a company that promotes use of the Alaska Marine Highway, are able to handle booking and itinerary planning for passengers, which can be quite nice if you are unfamiliar with Alaska. One such company is **Viking Travel** (www.alaskaferry.com), located in Petersburg, Alaska. This company has been booking ferry trips and tours for years, and since they are located along the famous Inside Passage route, they know the area well.

Unaccompanied Minors

Occasionally children under the age of eighteen will travel the Alaska Marine Highway alone. Some are visiting friends or relatives in different port communities, others are part of sports teams, clubs, or youth groups. It's not uncommon for kids to have such adventures, but the Alaska Department of Transportation (under which the ferry system is owned and managed) does have some rules regarding underage youngsters traveling without an adult. As of 2016, children under the age of twelve must be accompanied by a person nineteen years of age or older.

> **PARENT PRO TIP**
>
> If it's in the budget, get one of the staterooms. Best. Sleep. Ever. I also enjoyed having our own bathroom!
>
> —Wendi, Anchorage resident and mom of two

Special Treatment for Military Families

Alaska is a state with a thriving military community, and transfers to new duty stations (known as a PCS, or Permanent Change of Station) are fairly common. This means military families who have lived the Alaska dream for two or three years must now pack up kids, pets, bicycles, and favorite toys and head to the next phase of life. AMHS tries to help mitigate this often-stressful time by offering special options for families who book through their base's Military Travel Office, generally in the form of priority for staterooms, vehicles, and gear. Families must be on official PCS orders to qualify. Contact your base travel office, or contact AMHS reservations agents at 1-800-642-0066 for more information.

If your child will be sailing aboard a ferry without you, make sure you carefully read the AMHS policies and procedures, found at ferryalaska. com or by calling 1-800-642-0066.

Bringing Pets, Bikes, or Boats

Make no mistake, AMHS crew members have seen it all. From ponies to five-person bicycles, Alaska ferries have transported quite the variety of gear and critters. Recognizing that the ferry is often the only way some of these things can safely and affordably be moved about the state, AMHS allows just about anything to be carted aboard, within reason and under strict protocols for the health and safety of said creature, passengers, and crew.

ANIMALS

Below are the basic steps for transporting animals. A complete set of regulations is available on the AMHS website under "Travel Policies" and "Animal Transport" (www.dot.state.ak.us/amhs/policies.shtml).

- If the animal is not a dog or cat, call 1-800-642-0066 for a set of special rules and allowances.
- All pets must have a current certificate of health and an up-to-date rabies vaccination, where applicable, within thirty days of travel. If your travels will take you in and out of Canada, check with US Customs Offices for further details.
- Pets must be kept in a secure kennel or vehicle on the car deck during the entire voyage. Deck calls will be offered on a regular basis during which time pet owners can take their pets for a walk around the car deck. Bring lots of bags, paper towels, and anything else you might need to clean up after your dog or cat because you'll be required to do so, although deck crew members often have some cleaning materials. Pets must be leashed at all times.
- During port calls, owners are allowed to go ashore to walk pets as well, although it is the passenger's responsibility to keep pets on a leash at all times and pay attention to all-aboard times given by stewards.

- The standard fare for transporting pets is $25 from Bellingham, and $10 from Prince Rupert, British Columbia. Travel between other ports is free.

The most exotic creature ever shipped on board an AMHS ferry was an elephant, part of a traveling circus that made its way up and around the Inside Passage in the 1970s.

FERRY FACT

BIKES

Many tourists choose to cycle their way around Alaska, particularly the Inside Passage area of Southeast, and although paved roadways are not always in great supply, there is generally enough blacktop or hard-packed trails available for a family to cruise safely around a particular town. Definitely cheaper than driving, a bike is a low-impact, low-cost way to see coastal Alaska, with the added benefit of fresh air and exercise.

- Bikes have their own fare table, ranging from an affordable $38/ bike one-way from Bellingham to Ketchikan, to $58/bike from Bellingham to Skagway. If bikes are towing trailers, however, the cost may go up, depending upon the total length, so check carefully with reservations agents before booking to make sure you've paid the correct fare. This includes the tagalong bike (attached to the frame of an adult bike) for younger riders.
- Bring a sturdy lock for each bicycle, a helmet (required in some towns, but a good idea, regardless), a bicycle tool kit, and extra inner tubes for each bicycle. Some communities are so small they do not have a bike repair shop, so cyclists must be Jacks—and Jills—of-all-trades for roadside fix-its.

KAYAKS OR INFLATABLES

With an abundance of serene saltwater upon which to float, many areas of Alaska are extremely popular with kayakers and small-boat enthusiasts. The Alaska Marine Highway can help passengers with trips to and from

Dressing kids in warm, weatherproof clothing can go a long way toward comfort and safety.

small communities with ample flat water, including those along the Inside Passage, Prince William Sound, and Kachemak Bay. Those wishing to bring a kayak or small boat, be it a stand-up paddleboard (SUP), raft, or inflatable, will pay between $60 and $80 one-way, depending upon the destination. It is helpful to have kayaks or SUPs on a small trailer or wheeled cart to make transport on and off the ferry easier on everyone, and don't forget to have your name marked clearly on the outside, and on paddles, too. Like luggage at the airport, many boats look alike!

What and How You Should Pack

Packing for an Alaska vacation typically requires more thought for gear than other family trips. The combination of variant weather patterns and a multitude of outdoor activities means parents must consider clothing, shoes, and outerwear for maximum enjoyment of Alaska. This goes double for trips aboard the Alaska Marine Highway, as coastal climates mean more rain, wind, and fog, even during the summer months.

Layering remains central for comfort and safety, even if changing weather necessitates adding or subtracting one or more layers throughout the day. These layers need not be expensive, but they should be of quality materials designed to wick moisture away from the skin and trap warmth to prevent hypothermia.

Shoes should be durable enough to survive a dunking in water (where you'll be spending a majority of your time) or a muddy stomp along a hiking trail and light enough to dry out quickly at the end of both. Casual hiking shoes or sturdy tennis shoes are fine for most activities, but in coastal areas of Alaska, the rubber boot will become your most treasured wardrobe item. With boots, kids can wade, hike, and stroll ferry decks with dry feet and solid soles. They'll look like Alaska locals, too.

LUGGAGE

Even if you're planning on driving a car aboard the ferry, you'll be required to take everything you need from your vehicle while the vessel is underway. That means lugging bags up to your stateroom or the public lounge area. There is an elevator on board each ferry, but they are small and not well equipped for the traveling family carrying several bags per person, so keep it light. We use wheeled luggage or backpacks for clothing and a wheeled cooler for food and beverages (more on that in part 2, "Life on Board the Ferry").

CLOTHING

The Alaska Marine Highway is not a fancy way to travel, so dressing kids for comfort and weather should always be your priority, and thankfully, that's pretty simple. Below is a packing list of clothing items for a typical seven-day trip to Alaska aboard a ferry.

Base

- Long underwear of polypropylene or wool, depending upon your child's tolerance (one set of pants and long-sleeved top)
- Hiking/outdoor socks (three pairs)
- Socks for day wear, casual hiking/walking (seven pairs)
- Underwear/diapers, etc.; remember that stores carrying diapers may not be within easy access of ferry docks, so bring as many as you think you might need for a few days, plus one.

Midlayer

- Pants (convertible hiking pants work well; legs zip off for shorts) (three pairs)
- Shirts, long- and short-sleeved for layering (four)
- Fleece top (one)

Top Layer/Outerwear

- Rain gear (consisting of Gore-Tex or other *waterproof* material)
- Mittens/gloves (one pair of lighter-weight wool or wool blend)
- Hat with brim to shield against the sun and a warm hat (one each)

Footwear

- Sturdy sneakers or light hiking boots
- Rubber boots (we like Bogs or XtraTuf brands)
- Indoor, slip-on shoes or well-fitting slippers with hard soles

Miscellaneous

- Sunglasses (it's bright on deck!)
- Sunscreen
- Swimsuit (many smaller communities have public indoor swimming pools, great on rainy days)
- Plastic bags for wet clothing, gear, or trash (many, in multiple sizes)
- Packable, quick-dry towels (found at any outdoor store)
- Family first-aid kit for minor ailments and injuries; don't forget regular medications, either.
- Camera, extra memory cards, charger or batteries.

- Games, books, tablets, and toys (see part 2, Life on Board the Ferry)
- Car seats for children under eighty pounds and fifty-seven inches in height. Many car rental companies now offer car seats, so ask if you need to rent a vehicle. Whether you rent a car of have your own vehicle, be sure youngsters are buckled up properly.

SLEEPING GEAR

If your family is planning to snooze in a stateroom, you won't need to bring sleeping bags or pillows. However, many families choose to roll out the bedding in public lounge areas to await their arrival at a particular destination. If you're sleeping sans stateroom, add these items to your packing list:

- Sleeping bag (rated for 25°F or lower) for every family member
- Foam pad or inflatable pad for each person
- Pillows
- Earplugs (while quiet hours are enforced on all ferries, it's still difficult for many people to sleep with ambient noise)
- Eye shades to block out the famous midnight sun
- Favorite stuffed animals (everyone rests better with a best friend nearby)

> ### PARENT PRO TIP
> In general, parents use the same bag of tricks (snacks, books, games, and toys) that they'd bring on any long flight or road trip. The big difference is that children can move around, and they are continually finding something to explore or a game to play with a new friend.
>
> —Sarah, lifelong Southeast resident and mom of three

This may sound like quite a lot of gear for one trip—and it is—but ferry crew are used to seeing families schlep several loads of stuff up and down the stairways, and nobody should bat an eye. I like to have clothing carefully parceled out by day in large zipper-type bags, and I have my son carry his own toys, games, books, and such in a personal backpack.

PLANNING AN ALASKA MARINE HIGHWAY ADVENTURE

What to Leave at Home

Alaska Marine Highway travel is reminiscent of your first college *wanderweg* to Europe with backpack and rail pass in hand. It's a fairly free-flowing atmosphere with people wandering around at all times of the day or night. While the majority of ferry passengers are honest, hardworking folks who want nothing to do with your stuff, it's always a good idea to secure valuables in a stateroom or one of the lockers on board. Leave fancy jewelry and other valuables at home, and always keep a wallet or purse on your body. I use a travel wallet for my cash, credit cards, and ID. Encourage kids to store toys, cameras, or other electronics in lockers when not in use to discourage curious fellow passengers.

PART II

LIFE ON BOARD THE FERRY

My father, Richard A. Downing, was the state's first commissioner of Public Works and instrumental in creating the Alaska Marine Highway System. One day he received a mysterious package in the mail; a former passenger had not been happy with a sandwich he purchased from the vending machine on board, so he mailed it to my father in a manila envelope with a note saying it wasn't a sandwich worth buying. Dad sent him a refund.

—Laurel Bill, author, *Aunt Phil's Trunk* series

Methods of transportation have evolved in this country over the last century, and Alaska is no exception. Whereas steamships and railroads used to provide the only means of navigating among American cities, aircraft and SUVs now ply the skies above and the roads below. In the past, travel for leisure purposes was generally reserved for those families who could afford it, and people were catered to accordingly. Today, with ever-increasing airfares and the appearance (or reality) of decreasing services, I often find myself wishing for the good old days when travelers and their luggage were treated with the utmost of care.

The Alaska Marine Highway System has retained a certain amount of this bygone era. I'm still not sure if it's the general atmosphere of chugging engines or attentive service, but each time I climb the stairs of an Alaska ferry, I'm charmed by the combination.

Many travelers use the ferry system for day trips to and from larger cities, be they visitors looking for the next leg of a vacation or Alaska residents on their way to the airport or dentist office.

Overnight passengers—or those who find themselves in the conundrum of a short journey, mileage-wise, but a late or early crossing—often reserve a stateroom. I'll address the advantages and disadvantages of choosing to sleep on a bed, or not, in private, or not. We have experienced positives and negatives of both and ultimately find that one's individual overnight style depends largely upon budget and desire for a truly authentic indie Alaska experience.

BOARDING AND SETTING UP CAMP

Let's start at the very beginning, because boarding varies depending upon mode of travel. The Alaska Marine Highway System has a carefully orchestrated process of embarkation and disembarkation that doesn't always make sense to travelers, but it is designed for both vessel balance and maximum fit.

Walk-on passengers generally board before vehicles, but this may depend upon the schedule and port crew, so arrival at the terminal at least an hour prior to departure is advisable. Ferry terminals will have a (usually covered) space for passengers to wait and tag their luggage with AMHS-provided tags, a required process before boarding. All passengers over the age of eighteen are required to possess a valid ID like a driver's license, ID card, or passport and valid tickets issued by AMHS. **Note:** Each time you leave the ferry, even if it is for only a short time, you will be required to show both the ticket and ID. Children under eighteen do not need identification but will be required to be with an adult to board the ferry unless traveling as an unaccompanied minor (see chapter 2). **Travelers with vehicles** should plan to arrive at the ferry terminal two hours before departure time. During this time, tickets may be picked up (or purchased) and a spot in line secured.

> ### PARENT PRO TIP
>
> Expect the ferry to arrive late and leave late (sometimes loading/unloading challenges occur, or weather delays force the schedule to be adjusted).
>
> —Sarah, lifelong Southeast resident and mom of two

Dogs and kids should be walked and fed, and supplies and luggage for the trip should be bundled together for easy access as soon as the car is driven on board the ferry. **Note:** There is no access to vehicles once the ferry is underway, except for periodic deck calls, when passengers can walk pets or retrieve items.

Cyclists will load either right before or right after vehicles and will secure bikes in a location designated by ferry crew. As with cars or RVs, cyclists will not have access to their bikes once the ferry is underway, so passengers should plan to bring panniers and bags with them to the upper decks. Cyclists should plan to arrive no later than one hour prior to departure.

Once on board the ferry, crew members will be available to show passengers the stairs and small elevator that reach the upper decks and lounge or stateroom areas. If you do not have a stateroom on more popular routes, the Inside Passage in particular, be prepared for a rush of people seeking out the most scenic places to sit. Ferries have multiple locations for families to spread out, but we've found the most beneficial are the table-chair configurations that allow for game-playing, movie-watching, and naps underneath.

FERRY FACT Alaska Marine Highway ferries do not provide a ship's doctor, unlike the steamships of the past and cruise lines of today. In the event of a medical emergency, ferry crew are well versed in basic first aid and will radio ahead if additional assistance is required that might necessitate evacuation of a passenger. If you require medication or have a fragile medical condition, check with your own physician prior to departure.

What to Bring on Board

As mentioned above, ferry passengers may not access vehicles or bags stored on the car deck, except during scheduled opportunities announced by the purser's office. As such, passengers should bring everything necessary for the entire trip, especially for multiday journeys.

Luggage with clothing and necessities for overnight stays on board, especially medication, diapers, baby food, and the like.

Sleeping bags and pads for those not renting a stateroom. Pillows are advisable, and if you forget to pack them, you can rent pillows—and blankets—from the purser.

Food and water for those not wishing to purchase meals in the galley or restaurant. A cooler may be brought on board. Ice is available in the galley area as well as a microwave oven and toaster. **Note:** All food must be consumed in the galley area. Eating or drinking is not allowed in the lounge or other public access areas.

> **KIDSPEAK**
>
> We brought lots and lots of pillows on board. And a suitcase full of Legos.
>
> —Elliott, age nine, Southeast Alaska route

Games, books, puzzles, laptops, smartphones, and cameras (and chargers for those items that need them). Kids may enjoy a journal, colored pencils or crayons, and a camera of their own to record their journey along the Alaska Marine Highway. Tweens and teens can do the same on smartphones, providing video and audio backup to this epic journey. **Note:** AMHS vessels provide standard 110-volt, 60-cycle AC power outlets with no surge protection.

Families in the know have brought the following items for long ferry trips:

- Blocks, small cars, construction sets.
- Games like Jenga, Uno, Scrabble, and Candyland and a deck of cards for games like Rummy, Old Maid, and Hearts. Think back to your childhood: many of those games are still winners with kids during long trips. Travel games are also well-suited for ferry journeys. Puzzles can be especially fun for the entire family as a group project.
- Books about Alaska are in ready supply at many port bookstores. We like to purchase from local booksellers, but if you prefer, you can load up a mobile device with e-books, for any age or reading stage about the forty-ninth state. **Hint:** The *Alaska on the Go* Pinterest page

has a list of kid- and adult-appropriate books: www.pinterest
.com/alaskaonthego.

- Store toys and games in a separate suitcase or plastic bin with a snap
  top. This allows kids to access them on their own and things will be
  kept tidy. Also, the bin or suitcase makes for a handy table surface on
  which to play.

Staterooms

Alaska Marine Highway stateroom options vary in layout. Some offer
four-bunk berths with a sitting area, table, chairs, and private bath; others
share a bath and shower down the hallway and have two berths. Both
budget and expeditious reservations make a difference when securing
a stateroom on board the ferry, and accessible cabins are available for
those who need them. All staterooms offer comfortable mattresses, bedding, towels, and soap. There
is no refrigeration available in
staterooms, but passengers are
welcome to eat meals in their
stateroom. Alcohol brought on
board may only be consumed in
a stateroom.

> ### KIDSPEAK
>
> I slept in the top bunk bed, and it
> was AWESOME!
>
> —Trevor, age seven,
> Southeast Alaska route

It has been my experience
that staterooms are spotlessly clean, comfortable, and a great way to sail in a private space.
Keys are picked up upon embarkation at the
purser's office, where requests can also be
made for last-minute staterooms, often with
great success. Reserve staterooms at www.fer-
ryalaska.com or by calling reservation agents
at 1-800-642-0066.

Staterooms differ between ferries, but all are well-
equipped with the basics for a comfortable sleep.
(And the bunk beds are a favorite among kids.)

Here's a helpful key to stateroom terminology that you might encounter:

Outside: A window facing the scenery and outdoors
Inside: No window
WCA: Wheelchair-accessible
2-berth: One upper and one lower bunk
3-berth: One upper and two lower bunks
4-berth: Two upper and two lower bunks
Full facilities: Bunks plus bathroom with shower, all linens (sheets and towels) provided
No facilities: Sink but no shower or toilet, all linens provided
Roomette: Most basic room with one bed, no linens provided
Sitting area: Table and two to four chairs provided

PARENT PRO TIP

Although we've been riding the ferry with children for twelve years, it wasn't until recently that we finally broke down and rented a stateroom for a particularly ugly middle-of-the-night itinerary. The comfort of the tiny room, with engines rumbling below us, was perfect. We'd never slept so well on a boat.

—Sara, Southeast resident
and mom of three

Don't Expect Room Service

Alaska Marine Highway stewards do an exceptional job of maintaining staterooms on board the ferries. That said, their service standards are not that of a hotel, so don't expect things like daily linen service, extra soaps and towels, or little bottles of lotion. Stewards will provide neatly made beds upon arrival, daily trash pickup, and extra linen if needed, for a small fee. Sheets and blankets are of industrial grade and made up so a quarter will bounce on the beds, and bathrooms are spic-and-span. That goes a long way when traveling, in my book—much farther than mouthwash or two-thousand-count Egyptian cotton sheets.

The Alaska Marine Highway website has more information that will aid in booking the most appropriate room for your family. Many large families find themselves booking one larger stateroom and one smaller, depending upon children's ages. Ask if children can camp out on the floor in a sleeping bag. This may or may not be permitted depending upon the route and number of kids.

Bunking in Common Areas

Most stories of days and nights spent aboard the Alaska Marine Highway center on lounge chairs and upper decks, for this is the way of the budget-conscious and indie traveler. Not unlike camping, sleeping on deck or in the public lounge areas is a way to truly experience the essence of Alaska's diverse demographic of residents and visitors. In the ferry's earlier days of multiday routes, passengers often flopped whenever and wherever they could find space, spreading sleeping bags, food, and beverages throughout the lounges and upper decks. Needless to say, the atmosphere was not always conducive to sleep or a scenic vacation, so AMHS promptly ramped up the rulebook and enforcement. Today, lounge or deck sleepers can rest assured they will accomplish as good a night's sleep as is possible on a noisy ferry boat.

> **PARENT PRO TIP**
>
> I need personal space, so I recommend early morning or late evening solo reflection time up on deck. I took my coffee out and just watched, and felt, and absorbed this place. It was the only time I saw orca whales.
>
> —Wendi, Anchorage resident and mom of two

Below are some guidelines and options from AMHS for those who wish to camp inside or outside on board AMHS ferries.

Camping on deck is a first-come, first-served process that often requires early arrival at the ferry terminal on the day of departure, especially in the busy ports of Bellingham, Whittier, or Juneau. Each ferry has a covered solarium area with overhead heat for chilly days and cold nights (of which there are many), and space can be at a premium during the summer months. It is my recommendation that the fastest member of the family make tracks to the solarium, dump gear on the required number of lounge chairs, and allow the rest of the family to join him or her there.

Tents are permitted on the upper decks only and within the parameters set by ferry crew. It is advisable to bring small, two- or three-person tents sturdy enough to withstand rain, almost constant wind, and other passengers' nosy tendencies. **Note:** You *must* secure your tent to the deck, and one way to accomplish this is the Alaska standby material, duct tape. Bring at least one roll, and maybe two, of the highest-quality original duct tape you can buy. Tape the corners, front, and back of the tent floor to the deck. Most ferry crew will not allow the tying of tents to other structures, but this may change depending upon the weather.

> KIDSPEAK
>
> I like sitting under the heat lamps in the solarium!
>
> —Rachel, age ten, sailing to Haines from Juneau

Camping on deck is permitted in designated areas only. Note that tents should be secured to the deck, as it often becomes very windy once underway.

Children of the ferries are adept at sleeping on any available surface—whether it's the floor, a bench, or tucked under the seats in the recliner lounge. When my children were younger, I enticed them to cuddle up with sleeping bags and pillows by coining the "nest" as a preferred sleeping spot. Even now, at twelve, ten, and eight, my children clamor to set up the nest with bedding, books, and the iPad. We can also rent blankets and pillows from the purser.

—Sara, Southeast resident
and mom of three

Recliner lounges on various decks of the ferry are excellent places to sleep if your family members are one-position sorts of snoozers. Like sleeping on a train, the recliner lounges feature large chairs that push back to about a forty-five-degree angle; this is great if you like sleeping in the dentist chair, not so much if you enjoy curling up. That said, for those who do not relish the idea of sleeping on the ground, lounges are great options. They are popular, too, so grabbing chairs sooner rather than later upon embarkation is highly advised.

Other public areas for sleeping may include the theater, observation lounges, or anyplace the crew finds to be suitable, based upon passenger count, weather, and everyone's behavior. The purser is king or queen of this multiday sleepover, and it is advisable to treat this person with every ounce of respect.

No matter where you sleep in the public domain, a few standard rules apply.

- Quiet hours begin at 10:00 p.m. and last until 8:00 a.m. Please enforce this with younger family members, no matter how excited they are.
- All bedding and related gear must be stowed away no later than 10:00 a.m. Stash bags and such under your seat, in a locker, or in your tent. If using a lounge chair, unwritten proprieties say it's yours for the duration, but gosh, if the sun is out and people need a place to sit, offer up the lounger.

- There is NO food allowed anywhere but the galley area, which we'll talk about later. Be a good neighbor.
- Passengers are responsible for their belongings. The ferry has *no* liability for lost or stolen items. Thus, keeping money, electronics, or other valuables on your person or in a locker is highly recommended. We leave jewelry at home and only bring the credit cards we know we'll use during a trip. Keep an eye on cell phones, laptops, and kids' games, too.

Items to Bring for Common Area Cohabitation

- Sleeping bag for each member of the family (rated to 25°F or lower)
- Foam pad or inflatable pad for each person
- Camping pillows that pack up into small bags
- Flashlight or headlamp for reading at night
- Backpack or bags to store items during the day
- Tent, for use on deck
- Duct tape
- Small trash bags (we like to promote a clean onboard camp)
- Reusable water bottles
- Reusable coffee mugs (preferably with lids)
- Sippy cups for smaller children
- Small storage containers with lids (a variety of uses)
- Chargers for electronics. Some ferries, like the *Malaspina* and *Columbia* do have charging stations and work and reading rooms available.
- Wipes and diapers for small children, and formula if you need it. There is none available on board any AMHS vessel.
- Earplugs and eye shades to help kids (and grownups) sleep.

All this stuff can be kept in a tidy pile near your seating area with constant supervision or placed in a coin-operated locker on the MVs *Columbia, Kennicott, Malaspina, Matanuska,* or *Taku.* Bring plenty of quarters, as the purser's desk only carries a certain amount.

Eating in the onboard dining room or cafeteria is a nice change of pace during a long trip.

EATING AND ENTERTAINMENT

Onboard Nourishment

All Alaska Marine Highway ferries have galleys that serve food and beverages, with the exception of the smaller MV *Lituya* that sails shorter segments around Southeast Alaska. These galleys are also a common area for passengers bringing their own food and beverages to picnic. The MV *Columbia* and MV *Tustemena* also offer a dining room with full meal service, and we found restaurant-style eating to be a nice change of pace after days spent building sandwiches out of ingredients found in our cooler.

AMHS crew welcome families into the galley for meals, but keep in mind that strict hours of operation are followed to allow for prep time between breakfast, lunch, and dinner. Hot coffee and water are constantly available, however, and except for the smaller, older *Tustemena*, the galley seating area on most vessels is always open.

The most popular menu items in vessel galleys are hamburgers and chicken fingers, with fish and chips not far behind.

FERRY FACT

Galleys offer hot and cold items, burgers, and cafeteria-style sandwiches, salads, and such. Beware those who do not normally allow french fries and chicken strips, or those little boxes of sugary cereal: Kids will be kids, and these are the attractive items that seem to draw their attention. That said, galley crew also make wonderful soups and grilled entrees and offer plenty of fruit and raw vegetables to sway kids away from the deep-fried goodies. Prices are comparable to restaurants, however, so the family meal budget could be smashed in short order after purchasing three meals per day for everyone. A better idea is to pack a cooler and grocery bag with some food items found at port grocery stores or brought from home.

What to Pack in Your Ferry Picnic Basket

While there is no public-use refrigeration on board the ferry, AMHS galleys do provide coin-operated ice machines, and we usually bring some foods frozen solid from home, like milk and juice. Each ferry provides passengers with a common-use microwave, toaster, and hot water dispenser. Lines can form around these areas during mealtime, so placate the kids with a snack or beverage while waiting your turn to microwave the mac and cheese or toast the English muffin.

> ### PARENT PRO TIP
> Pack snacks! The vending machines have candy and junk food. And since the cafeteria is only open during mealtimes, we like to pack a lunch or dinner and eat in a lounge.
> —Sarah, lifelong resident and mom of two

Passengers are welcome to use onboard utensils and napkins, but we usually bring along paper plates, reusable cups, bowls, and a small sponge and bottle of dish soap with which to clean up after a meal. Below is a list of suggested food items that travel well on board the ferry.

FRESH/FROZEN (store in a cooler with wheels for easier transport)
- Milk (we also like to bring shelf-stable milk in single-serving sizes)
- Juice
- Lunch meat
- String cheese, sliced cheese, or cheese sticks
- Yogurt
- Fresh fruit that transports well (apples, oranges, cut melon, and the like)
- Jam or jelly

NONPERISHABLE FOODS (keep in cloth bags or packs for easier transport)

- Bread and rolls (we like pretzel rolls from Costco, they travel well)
- Crackers like Goldfish, Wheat Thins, or other durable types
- Dry soup mixes, noodle bowls, or premade meals that are shelf-stable
- Packets of shelf-stable tuna or chicken
- Peanut butter
- Jerky
- Tortillas
- Dry cereal, oatmeal
- Dried fruit
- Pretzels, popcorn (already popped)
- Granola bars, energy bars
- Instant hot chocolate, cider, or coffee sleeves (it all costs money on board, otherwise)

> **PARENT PRO TIP**
>
> We always toss a few packets of instant hot chocolate in our packs. A hot beverage is perfect for warming up after the brisk business of sightseeing on deck.
>
> —Susan, frequent visitor of Kodiak and a mom of two

Note: The MV *Tustemena* is indeed one of the oldest in the Alaska Marine Highway fleet, and it usually sails the long, often-rough journey along the Aleutian Chain in the Southwest route. Known as the *Trusty Tusty*, she is more compact in size and available services for passengers. The dining room is open for an hour at a time during breakfast, lunch, and dinner and, unlike other AMHS vessels, is not open for free-time lounging in between those scheduled hours. Unlike the other larger vessels, it lacks a hot and cold water dispenser, accessible coffee, and a toaster, so plan ahead when packing your ferry picnic items.

Onboard Activities

Even though the Alaska Marine Highway's overseers have removed onboard US Forest Service rangers, who provided everything from maps to short presentations about the routes, I think you'll find plenty of activities to stay entertained during your journey.

Once you've booked a route, take note of the vessel (or vessels) upon which you'll be traveling, and inquire of reservations agents about amenities. In general, though, the longer the trip, the larger the ferry, and as a result, more options for keeping kids (and adults) busy and happy.

Highlights of amenities available on some Alaska Marine Highway vessels include the following:

PARENT PRO TIP

If you have a child under two, always bring a soft carrier like an Ergo or Tula. If your child is like most toddlers, he/she won't fall asleep in your lap, but there is plenty of space to walk the vessel wearing a sleeping baby.

—Sarah, lifelong resident and mom of two

Infant and toddler playrooms, usually with a mat and a few soft climbing toys for little ones. **Note:** These are not always clean, so either bring your own covering for the floor (a beach towel or blanket) or sanitize kids post-play.

Theater space, featuring a wide range of general interest films for both kids and adults

Adventure Appetites Offers Gourmet Options for Make-It-Yourself Meals

As a longtime consumer of freeze-dried camp food that looked and tasted like packing material, I was somewhat hesitant to try a similar option, especially as the parent of a picky eater. But rest assured, after trying Anchorage-based Adventure Appetites, I quickly became a believer. This is no ordinary brand of backcountry food.

Founded as a partner company to the already successful hiking and backcountry exploration company Alaska Alpine Adventures, Adventure Appetites provides premade, mixed, and measured ingredients or snacks that are perfectly portioned in either single- or two-serving sealed bags. From peanut butter bars to an enchilada soup that tingled my tongue, the menu options are diverse, affordable, and, above all, incredibly simple and healthy. Preorders can be made months in advance and either shipped to your door or picked up in Anchorage. With space at a premium, we found their vacuum-packed meals to be a lifesaver. Find them at www.adventureappetites.com.

(parents are advised to make sure they know which movies their children are watching, as the theater is not supervised). Our favorite part about the theater, however, was the interesting documentaries about Alaska and the ferry system. A schedule is posted near the purser's office, and an announcement is always made just prior to a showing.

Game arcades are present on several vessels, and while these coin-operated machines are not exactly the most current, our son found them good for a few hours of entertainment. Again, bring plenty of quarters!

Reading and card rooms can be found tucked away near common seating areas, and these can be quiet spots to read a book or nap with a small child during the day. Be aware that sleeping bags are usually not allowed in these spaces, as they are designed to be a retreat for those desiring a space to work or play a quiet game.

ALASKA MARINE HIGHWAY ROUTES AND PORTS OF CALL

As mentioned, the Alaska Marine Highway is made up of thirty-five port communities divided into regional routes. In each route chapter I'll identify ports of call, highlight attractions with appeal for families, and list a few accommodations should you decide to stay overnight on shore. As this book is meant to complement *Alaska on the Go: Exploring the 49th State with Children*, readers of both books may notice that longer reviews of attractions and lodging are more reserved here. In the case of a new destination not previously discussed in the first book (e.g., Bellingham), I've added longer explanations.

Keep in mind that routes are always subject to change due to weather or mechanical issues. This is Alaska after all, and if there exists one takeaway from any of my travel guides, it is to be prepared for delays or cancellations.

Ready? Let's sail!

ALASKA

CANADA

Barrow

Prudhoe Bay

Fairbanks

Eagle

Delta Junction

Chicken

Dawson City

Mt. McKinley (Denali)
elev. 20,320

Tok

McGrath

Talkeetna

Wasilla
Palmer

Glennallen

Carmacks

Twin Lakes

Anchorage

Valdez

Whittier

Tatitlek

Kenai
Soldotna

Seward

Cheneg Bay

Cordova

Haines Junction

Whitehorse

Alaska Highway

Watson Lake

Homer

Seldovia

Yakutat

Port Lions

Ouzinkie   Kodiak

Old Harbor

Haines   Skagway

Alaska Highway

Gustavus

Juneau

Cassiar Highway

Pelican

Dawson Creek

Hoonah

Tenakee

Angoon

Cassiar Highway

Sitka

Kake

Wrangell

Petersburg

Hyder

Ketchikan

Smithers

Prince George

Metlakatla

Prince Rupert

Terrace

Bellingham

Victoria

SOUTHEAST ALASKA ROUTE

Bellingham—Prince Rupert—Ketchikan
Wrangell—Petersburg—Kake—Sitka—Juneau
Gustavus—Skagway—Haines—Hoonah

Getting Started

Best known among visitors and most residents as the Inside Passage, the Alaska Marine Highway's Southeast route winds its way between Washington State and Southeast Alaska, home to drizzly weather and dense evergreen forests. Located in the panhandle section of Alaska, this area is hundreds of miles from the rest of the state, with 557 air miles separating the capital city of Juneau from Anchorage.

While thousands of visitors board cruise ships for the ride, staying only a few hours at the more famous Alaska port cities, many more have found the Marine Highway to be the perfect way to explore a history and culture very different from the rest of the state. Southeast Alaska is a diverse collection of communities scattered along the fringe of the panhandle. Southeast is also where you will see the signature totem pole—a tool for storytelling and oral tradition among Alaska Native groups and unique to this region.

Traveling on board a ferry offers unique vistas to small Southeast Alaska communities tucked away under canopies of cedar or spruce trees. With few traditional road systems, residents often rely upon boats to travel and transport goods around the area, and you'll be witness to fascinating examples of life in this rural, wet, and marine-rich part of the state. Try these sample routes: Juneau–Skagway–Haines–Sitka–Petersburg–Wrangell–Ketchikan (or reverse, depending upon the ferry schedules). We enjoyed multiple overnights in Juneau, Skagway, Sitka, Wrangell, and Ketchikan to maximize our adventures. We allowed two weeks for this trip. If you want to spend longer amounts of time on one ferry, travel Juneau–Sitka–Petersburg–Wrangell–Ketchikan–Prince Rupert–Bellingham (or reverse). This trip allows for one ferry and multiple short stops in various Alaska communities, taking just short of three days to reach Bellingham.

THE VESSELS

For this multiday journey, the Alaska Marine Highway relies upon its large vessels, the MVs *Columbia*, *Malaspina*, and *Kennicott*. The *Columbia* can carry 600 passengers, 134 regular cars or trucks, and 16 oversize vehicles. The *Malaspina* carries 499 passengers, 88 cars or trucks, and 14 larger vehicles; and the *Kennicott*, 499 passengers, 80 cars or trucks, and up to 20 larger vehicles. **Note**: The Alaska Marine Highway System can, and sometimes does, change up the vessels used on all routes, depending upon need.

Southeast is by far the most popular route with Alaska visitors, and reservations that can be made early, should be, especially for those passengers towing trailers or wanting staterooms. All three ferries have cafeterias, and the *Columbia* has a full-service dining room. All three ferries serve beer and wine, but children are not allowed inside the lounge areas. Movie theaters, playrooms, video arcades, and reading lounges are also found on board these vessels.

WHERE YOU'LL GO

While called the "Southeast route" in Alaska Marine Highway literature, this trip actually begins in Bellingham, Washington. Ferries join cruise ships and merchant vessels sailing through the northern reaches of Puget Sound and between British Columbia mainland coastlines and those of Vancouver and Queen Charlotte Islands.

Only one Canadian port of call, Prince Rupert, British Columbia, is offered along the Southeast route. For those wanting to experience the beautiful mountain ranges of western British Columbia and then sail through the Inside Passage, Prince Rupert provides a nice balance of driving and sailing as it is the last mainland road-access point until Skagway or Haines in Alaska.

North of Prince Rupert, ferries continue through Chatham Strait toward Ketchikan and the rest of the Inside Passage. For centuries, mariners have navigated this sheltered, calm cluster of islands as a refuge from the more violent seas of the Gulf of Alaska on the western

> **PARENT PRO TIP**
>
> Often the northern Lynn Canal communities of Haines and Skagway use the smaller ferries in the winter and are subject to high winds and freezing spray.
>
> —Sara, Alaska resident and mom of three

side. These islands, ranging from enormous to tiny, make for challenging navigation, and ferry captains must always be alert to shifting tides, weather patterns, and other vessels. It's always an adventure along this route. Some waterways are wide enough for several ships to pass through at a time, and others are so narrow only a small cabin cruiser can squeeze through the rocky, tide-driven channel.

The Inside Passage is also where the Alaska Marine Highway earns its keep. Most of this forested, rocky area is without road systems and, in some cases, airports, so travel by water is a critical element of life in the Southeast's smaller communities. I often marvel at the tenacity of residents here, making plans with so many contingencies for weather, ferry mechanics, and seasons. Sailing by, I am struck by equal amounts of envy and thankfulness.

Depending upon the vessel, Inside Passage ports of call can include smaller, more remote towns, some of which require transfers at larger port cities. But in general, traveling from Bellingham includes Ketchikan, Wrangell, Petersburg, Sitka, Skagway, Haines, and Juneau before transfers are necessary to other areas. During the summer months, the MV

SOUTHEAST

Kennicott adds to the route by sailing across the Gulf of Alaska toward Whittier, providing additional mainland access to Southcentral Alaska and road and rail transportation to Anchorage (see chapter 6, Cross Gulf Route). **Note**: If your travel plans include starting or stopping in Prince Rupert, British Columbia, remember to bring your passport.

WHAT YOU'LL SEE

For children, this route is exciting. Enormous cargo vessels, stacked high with containers or long and lean and full of oil, motor their cargos to ports like Everett, Seattle, or Tacoma. Squat tugs hauling barges that carry containers and vehicles, including household goods belonging to those moving in or out of Alaska, chug-chug their way up the Inside Passage toward Anchorage. Fishing boats, kayaks, even seaplanes—everywhere one looks, some form of transportation can be seen, and it's a fabulous way

to explain the concept of import and export to kids. For these mariners, the Alaska ferries are a common sight and a nice diversion from their usually straightforward pull north or south.

Wildlife, too, frequents this route. From gulls to humpback whales, critters big and small can be observed from the decks of an Alaska Marine Highway ferry, turning your trip into the best multiday wildlife cruise you ever saw. Ferry crew are excellent at spotting wildlife, and they don't

Looking for wildlife in the Inside Passage. Whales, eagles, otters, and other animals can frequently be spotted from the deck.

hesitate to put out an "all call" on the shipboard audio system so passengers can take advantage of the whale tail, raft of otters, or fishing bald eagle.

Look for

- Sea otters floating on their backs.
- Orca (killer) whales and their black-and-white bodies flashing in the sun.
- Humpback whales doing a lazy dive, tails high in the air.
- Dall's porpoise, a smaller, faster version of the more well-known bottlenose dolphin. These little guys hang out near the bows of ships, playing in the wake.
- Harbor seals lazing on beaches or rocks or poking their heads up from the water in calmer areas near the Inside Passage.
- Stellar sea lions, enormous, big-toothed creatures that are known to fling a salmon back and forth before devouring it in the water. Look for sea lions on navigational buoys, and listen for their grunting, barking, and belching sounds. It's quite funny.
- Bald eagles perching on treetops. Hint: look for the Ping-Pong ball in a tree, and you've spotted one!
- Hundreds and hundreds of seabirds, like cormorants, gulls, surf scoters, loons, and pigeon guillemots.

CULTURE

Southeast Alaska is a cultural tapestry of traditions, starting with Alaska Native groups whose members have resided among the coastal forests for centuries. Depending upon which section of the panhandle you decide to sail, your travels might include stops in places with Alaska Native names and established tribal traditions.

The Tlingit, Haida, Tsimshian, and Eyak live and work in Southeast Alaska and straddle the past and present through a subsistence lifestyle

SOUTHEAST

based upon the bounty from the Pacific Ocean. While different with respect to tribal philosophies, the Alaska Natives of this area rely upon a complex matriarchal clan system worth investigating.

Some Alaska Native traditions also borrow from long-ago explorers to the panhandle, some in search of industry and economic success, some for the sake of adventure. Russian fur traders and wealthy merchant mariners, who brought both progress and heartache, nearly decimated the sea otter population and incited battles for land. Eager missionaries from the United States tried to convert Alaska Native residents from their perceived "witchcraft religion" to Christianity. Whether positive or negative (and there are many negatives), traditions blending cultures somehow persisted, and the resulting combinations are fascinating. Clothing, music, religion, and food all tell a story, and the whole family will benefit from a visit to cultural centers and museums along the Southeast route.

Who Are Native Alaskans?

While traveling around Alaska as a family, visitors often ask us if we are "native Alaskans," meaning, in most cases, if we grew up here. While this innocuous query would indeed be appropriate in other places, in Alaska the terms "Alaska Native" or "Native Alaskan" are reserved for the state's indigenous people, who make up a culturally rich and diverse 18 percent of Alaska's population. Alaska Native heritage is closely guarded and intensely preserved, as you'll learn, so visitors should be prepared for gentle correction should they refer to non-Native Alaskans in this manner. Alaskans who were born and raised here refer to themselves simply as "residents" and even "homesteaders" or "sourdoughs," depending upon how far back the family tree extends.

The University of Alaska Fairbanks partners with Alaska Native communities around the state to operate the Alaska Native Knowledge Network (www.ankn.uaf.edu), an online portal accessible to anyone. Featuring resources, events, publications, and even school curriculum ideas, this is a valuable first step toward understanding the complexities of Alaska's First People.

Bellingham, Washington (BEL): The Start

Situated about ninety miles north of Seattle, Bellingham is known as a gateway city to both northern Puget Sound and British Columbia, Canada. Settled during the 1850s, the area around the current city of Bellingham was known as Whatcom and was a source for lumber during a building boom along the West Coast. The dense forests of evergreen trees were highly prized, and easy access via water could ensure construction companies had plenty of material with which to work.

Further discoveries of additional resources came shortly after. Coal mining in the nearby hills, then gold along the Fraser River, caused a true rush of newcomers to the area. In fact, the gold rush of 1858 brought nearly seventy-five thousand additional people through Whatcom, and nearby settlements quickly began a boom on their own as dwellings and stores were thrown together to accommodate high numbers of new residents.

As with many resource-dependent communities, however, Bellingham experienced booms and busts, including a mill fire in 1873 and the closing of a gold mine in 1878. But by the turn of the century, Bellingham not only had persevered, but it thrived as the center of commerce and seat of government over the smaller bayside communities. Today it boasts a vibrant cultural, historical, recreational, and educational scene that brings visitors by the thousands.

ARRIVING

By Air

Bellingham International Airport (https://www.portofbellingham.com/82/ Airport-Administration) is located approximately three miles from downtown Bellingham. Alaska Airlines, Allegiant Air, and Frontier Airlines fly into Bellingham from many US and Canadian cities. Most hotels provide transportation to and from the airport, and a taxi and public transportation system can bring ferry travelers door-to-door with relative ease.

By Rail

Amtrak (www.amtrakcascades.com, 1-800-USA-RAIL) travels between Vancouver, British Columbia, and Seattle, Washington, on a daily basis,

SOUTHEAST

with a stop in the Fairhaven neighborhood of Bellingham, within easy walking distance to the ferry terminal. The Fairhaven station is open 8:00 a.m.–9:00 p.m. daily.

By Road
Bellingham is about ninety miles north of Seattle, and about twenty miles south of the US-Canada border. Travelers should take I-5, northbound or southbound, to reach the city.

GETTING AROUND
Whatcom Transit Authority (WTA) (www.ridewta.com, 360-676-RIDE) has an extensive bus system throughout Bellingham and nearby communities. **Yellow Cab** taxi operators can be found near the airport, ferry terminal, or train station, or by calling 1-800-281-5430 or 360-734-8294. And **car rentals** are easily obtained in Bellingham, with the big names topping the list:

Avis: 4255 Mitchell Way, 360-676-8840, www.avis.com
Budget: 4255 Mitchell Way, 360-671-3800, www.budget.com
Hertz: 4255 Mitchell Way, 360-733-8336, www.hertz.com
Enterprise: 1852 N. State St., 360-733-4363, www.enterprise.com

Bellingham

Population: 82,810 (2014 Washington State Office of Financial Management)

Founded: In 1854 by mining and timber investors, however the area had been home to Lummi and Coast Salish tribes for centuries before that. Named for Sir William Bellingham, a member of the Royal Navy, in 1792 by noted explorer George Vancouver.

Known for: Port city for Alaska Marine Highway and other ocean-going vessels. Home to Western Washington University and diverse outdoor recreation options, thanks to its proximity to both the Canadian border and the North Cascades mountain range.

VISITOR INFORMATION

The **Bellingham Whatcom County Tourism Bureau** fills visitor information racks in the ferry terminal and operates a main visitor center at 904 Potter Street near I-5 (www.bellingham.org, tourism@bellingham.org, 1-800-487-2032, 360-671-3990). Here you'll find helpful staff, directions to major attractions, and lodging and transportation options.

SHOPPING/GROCERIES

Haggen Foods, Fairhaven Market
1401 12th St., Bellingham, WA 98229
Open twenty-four hours

Groceries, deli, sushi bar, cafe. Pharmacy hours vary.

Bellingham Farmers Market
1100 Railroad Ave., Bellingham, WA 98229
(360) 647-2060
www.bellinghamfarmers.org
Open Saturdays 10:00 a.m.–3:00 p.m. (April–Christmas)
Open Wednesday, on Mill Street in Fairhaven, 12:00–5:00 p.m.
(June–September)

The farmers market is the perfect place to stock up on fresh fruits and veggies before your trip. Kids and adults will love sampling the treats of

Interesting fact: Each May thousands of eager Ski to Sea participants race from the snowy flanks of Mount Baker to Bellingham Bay in a relay format. Teams must ski, run, bike, canoe, and kayak to finish a course spanning nearly ninety-five miles.

Hot tip: Bellingham's historic Fairhaven neighborhood is easily accessible from the Alaska ferry, so don't miss a day of exploration around this quaint, friendly neighborhood. Use lockers at the ferry terminal to store gear, or stay in one of the small hotels in the area.

Pacific Northwest vendors. On the last Saturday of every month, local kids are invited to set up shop themselves, and it's fun to see them sell their wares.

MEDICAL CARE

Peace Health Medical Group's St. Joseph Hospital
2901 Squalicum Pkwy., Bellingham, WA 98229
(360) 738-6792
www.peacehealth.org/st-joseph

LODGING

As a gateway city to Canada, the city of Bellingham offers a wide range of accommodations that fit many budgets. Depending upon the departure or arrival time of your ferry, it's nice to have an option for overnight lodging and exploration before heading out for other adventures.

I've classified lodging, dining, and activities with a handy pricing tool that gives a general idea of cost.

$$$ More expensive
$$ Moderate
$ Budget

Since rates do fluctuate with seasons and the economy, however, take this tool as a guide rather than law. Also, with Bellingham lodging spread out over quite a wide range of Pacific Northwest real estate, I've narrowed accommodations to those easily reached by air, sea, or major interstate, with easy access to the Alaska Marine Highway terminal.

Hotels/Motels

Best Western Plus Lakeway Inn and Conference Center $$$
714 Lakeway Dr., Bellingham, WA 98229
(360) 671-1011
www.bestwestern.com

Located very close to I-5 and a short distance from historic Fairhaven, this Best Western has undergone a facelift to update to a more modern decor. Featuring 132 spacious rooms and suites, the property also has an indoor swimming pool, spa, fitness room, Wi-Fi, library, café, and bistro and lounge. Families with small children can find rollaway beds or cribs with advance reservations. RV parking is available, and a free shuttle transports guests downtown. A shopping center is also nearby. For those needing transportation to or from Bellingham and Seattle, Best Western offers shuttle service between the hotel and Seattle-Tacoma International Airport (reservations required, visit www.seatacdirect.com for information).

Thumbs-up: Upgrades, indoor swimming pool, access to shopping and attractions, on-site dining

Fairhaven Village Inn $$$
1200 10th St., Bellingham, WA 98225
(877) 733-1100, (360) 733-1311
www.fairhavenvillageinn.com
guestservices@fairhavenvillageinn.com

Charming, historic, and within sight of the Alaska ferry terminal, this twenty-two-room inn lies at the heart of the Fairhaven District, and if you can get a reservation, it's worth the expense to lodge your family here. Owners Gene and Connie Shannon go out of their way for guests, right down to the comfortable furnishings and free Wi-Fi. Kids under twelve stay free with a parent in the same room, and cribs are available with advance notice. Some rooms have fireplaces for extra coziness, too. Access to Fairhaven's culture is right out the door, with Village Green park, walking trails, and restaurants within easy reach.

Thumbs-up: Comfort, hosts, and access to kid-friendly Fairhaven

Hampton Inn, Bellingham $$
3985 Bennett Dr., Bellingham, WA 98225
(360) 676-7700
http://hamptoninn3.hilton.com/en/index.html

For those flying in or out of Bellingham, the Hampton Inn offers convenient access. A bit dated but still clean and comfortable, this property features 132 rooms and suites, high chairs, cribs, complimentary breakfast and snacks, and transportation to the airport, train station, or ferry terminal. There is also a twenty-four-hour fitness center and a seasonal pool for the kids to enjoy on hot summer days. Free Wi-Fi and business services. While the hotel does lack the neighborhood feel of the previous two properties, it is a good value for families looking for comfortable accommodations at a reasonable price. Pet-friendly.

Thumbs-up: Complimentary transportation and breakfast, pool

Camping/RV

Bellingham RV Park $
3939 Bennett Dr., Bellingham, WA 98225
(888) 372-1224, (360) 752-1224
bellrvpark@gmail.com

If you're like many families traveling in a recreational vehicle, you know city-side accommodations can be difficult to find. Fortunately, RV travel is common in Bellingham, in part due to the ferry system. This fifty-spot park is perfect for those wanting a quick overnight before or after their ferry trip. A clean, comfortable clubhouse has coffee and snacks, showers, laundry, free Wi-Fi, and television. Kids are more than welcome, and the hosts are very willing to share their experience with those less versed in RV travel. Pet-friendly. Keep an eye on smaller children, though, as the small roadways are often busy with enormous RVs that can't see kids.

Thumbs-up: Kid-friendly, accessible to I-5 and downtown

Larrabee State Park $
245 Chuckanut Dr., Bellingham, WA 98229
(360) 902-8844, (888) 226-7688
www.parks.wa.gov/536/Larrabee

This 2,683-acre park sits on the saltwater shoreline of Samish Bay, not far from the Fairhaven District. A scenic route north or south bypassing busy I-5, Chuckanut Drive is frequently the winner of Pacific Northwest most scenic drive polls, and it's easy to see why. Towering trees, scenic ocean vistas, and a plethora of seabirds and marine mammals to watch: that's the benefit of camping here. With fifty-one tent sites, twenty-six utility sites, and eight primitive sites, the campground is busy during the summer, so reservations are a must, especially between May and October. Both tents and RVs are welcome here, but those with vehicles over forty feet should check with park staff to make sure they'll fit. Firewood is available from park hosts. Showers on-site May–October. Hiking trails and a small playground are a short walk away. **Note:** Working train tracks run through the park west of the campground, so be aware of occasional noise and vibration (although what kids don't love a train?).

Thumbs-up: Hiking trails, views, true camping experience

FEEDING THE FAMILY

Bellingham is a trendy town. From hipster brewpubs to small, cozy bakeries, families should have no trouble finding something that appeals to everyone. Here are a few favorites among our family members. (All establishments take major credit cards unless otherwise noted.)

Boundary Bay Brewery and Bistro $$–$$$
1107 Railroad Ave., Bellingham, WA 98225
(360) 647-5593
www.bbaybrewery.com
Open daily 11:00 a.m.–11:00 p.m., reservations available Sunday–Thursday

This downtown restaurant is busy busy on weekend evenings, but it is well worth the wait for the craft brews, live music, and good food. **Hint:** Make reservations if you can; the wait will be almost nonexistent. If you do have to wait, enjoy the live music and people-watching. The menu for kids is fabulous and affordable, with homemade mac and cheese, pasta and fresh marinara sauce, drool-worthy burgers, and sides of grapes, carrot sticks, and potato chips.

Skylark's Hidden Cafe $$–$$$
Historic Fairhaven District
1308 11th St., Bellingham, WA 98225
(360) 715-3642
www.skylarkshiddencafe.com
Open daily 8:00 a.m.–midnight

I wasn't too sure about the kid-friendliness of Skylark's at first. Then we entered the beautiful restaurant for lunch and found kind staff willing to adjust our son's burger to his liking as well as delicious, hearty food. Big breakfasts, lunches, and dinners featuring old favorites for meat and potato lovers. We also enjoyed browsing their late-night menu for snacks should we be out exploring and return looking for a bite before bedtime.

Colophon Cafe $$
Historic Fairhaven District
1208 11th St., Bellingham, WA 98225
(360) 647-0092
www.colophoncafe.com
Open Sunday 10:00 a.m.–8:00 p.m., Monday–Thursday 9:00 a.m.–8:00 p.m., and Friday–Saturday 9:00 a.m.–9:00 p.m.

Located on the popular Fairhaven Village Green, the Colophon is a delightful place to eat with children. Featuring items like soup, grilled cheese, bagels, ice cream, and the Maia Plate with hummus, pita bread, veggies, and fruit, this is a health-conscious parent's dream.

Fat Pie Pizza $$–$$$
Historic Fairhaven District
1015 Harris Ave., Bellingham, WA 98225
(360) 366-8090
www.fatpiepizza.com
Open daily 11:00 a.m.–10:00 p.m.

Need a pie of the Italian kind? Swing into Fat Pie Pizza for Chicago- or Detroit-style pizzas. Thick, flaky, or crispy, these pizzas will fill up even the most ravenous teenager while appealing to younger family members, too. A bonus is the 15 percent discount with your Fat Pie receipt at Rocket Donuts next door.

Fairhaven Fish and Chips $$
Historic Fairhaven District
1020 Harris Ave., Bellingham, WA 98225
(360) 733-5021
Hours vary, call ahead

A converted double-decker bus is home to this fish and chip shop, serving up flaky, moist fish with traditional UK flair. Seating is sparse and outside, so this is a great take-away option on nasty weather days or an eat-in-the-park option on sunny afternoons when the world appears just about perfect.

FAMILY FUN IN BELLINGHAM
Whether you have a few hours or a few days, Bellingham should not be overlooked during your Alaska Marine Highway journey. With high value placed on kids, families, and the outdoors, Bellingham has plenty of

places and spaces to keep you hopping. It's a vibrant, fun college town that thrives on activity, be it biking a waterfront path or attending an outdoor concert. Take advantage of Bellingham's culture—you'll be glad you did.

Museums and Cultural Experiences

Bellingham Railway Museum $
1320 Commercial St., Bellingham, WA 98225
(360) 393-7540
www.bellinghamrailwaymuseum.org
Open Tuesday–Saturday 12:00–5:00 p.m.

The railroad played such an important part in Bellingham's history that it would be a shame to miss this little museum. From the intricate models to displays depicting life aboard a passenger train, the museum is a nice size—not too large, not too small—for families. Great for older kids who have a good grasp of history and can read the interpretive signs. It's still fun for non-readers, but toddlers may be frustrated by things they cannot touch.

Spark Museum of Electrical Invention $-$$
1312 Bay St., Bellingham, WA 98225
(360) 738-3886
www.sparkmuseum.org
Open Wednesday–Sunday 11:00 a.m.–5:00 p.m.

For all that electricity has done for humankind, it's a wonder more of us, myself included, are not curious about its origins and inventions.

Need Coffee?

If you're like my husband and me, the day just isn't right without a shot or two of dark espresso to jolt us into an adventurous mind-set. Fortunately, **Tony's Coffee** in Historic Fairhaven can help (1101 Harris Ave., Bellingham, WA 98225 (360) 738-4710, www.tonyscoffee.com). Also serving baked goods and kid-friendly treats along with that caffeine, Tony's is a nice walk from the ferry terminal and an easy stroll from Fairhaven hotels. We like to sit outside and watch people, for Tony's attracts plenty of local residents who often bring their pooches and sit outside with us.

The Spark Museum is an eclectic, electric experience that takes kids into the science of it all, with room after room of history to back it all up. Interactive and creative with helpful volunteers (many of whom are or were teachers) to lead the way, this is an amazing place for kids ages five and up. Electricity changed us, and the museum is full of examples of how and why. For older kids, try the MegaZapper Show, an incredibly loud but wildly addicting experience.

Warning: Small kids could be scared by the harmless but startling "BANG" of an electrical charge during the show.

Western Washington University Campus
516 High St., Bellingham, WA 98225
(360) 650-3000
www.wwu.edu
Various campus stores and buildings open daily, call ahead or visit website for details

I am an advocate of visiting college campuses while vacationing. Full of history, culture, art, and outdoor places to wander, usually for free, a college like WWU has all that and more. The school has trails to hike, interesting buildings and sculptures to see, and lots and lots of trees everywhere. While parking can be a hassle on school days, it is fun for older kids to feel part of the college scene. Weekends, of course, are decidedly less crowded and thus, easier parking.

Outdoor Recreation
Taking advantage of mild temperatures and scenic topography, Bellingham is a doorway to the outdoors. From hiking to boating, this area is rich with opportunities to capture a little fresh air on your way to other adventures.

Boulevard Park–South Bay Trail FREE
This two-mile trail winds between the Historic Fairhaven District and downtown Bellingham, with views of the waterfront, ships, and equally historic homes. Mostly level, the trail also features a long section of boardwalk with interpretive signs that explain the history of town, the bay, and Whatcom County. Find the trail in Fairhaven along Tenth and Mill Streets. Excellent for all ages, and great for biking.

Whatcom Falls Park FREE

With 5.5 miles of trails, Whatcom Falls is a favorite park among Bellingham locals any time of year. To get there, take exit 253 off I-5 and drive two miles east on Lakeway Drive to the park entrance. Look for the signature waterfall and a historic bridge that will pique the interest of curious kids. Stroller-friendly and level with some up-and-down areas.

Stimpson Family Nature Reserve FREE

Take exit 253 off I-5, travel Lakeway Drive east, taking a right turn at all forks. When you reach Lake Louise and Austin Road, you'll see the reserve is on the left side of Austin Road. Park in the small lot. From there follow a three-mile loop trail that is perfect for introducing kids to the enormous trees that put Bellingham on the map. From Douglas fir to western red cedar, the trees are tall, straight, and hang gracefully along the trail edges. Hike the entire loop and see a beaver pond, tiny frogs, and perhaps a spotted owl, as we did during our visit. The trails do have some ups and downs and become narrow, so packs for tiny children are recommended. Dress kids in sturdy shoes for optimum fun, and be prepared for weather changes.

Biking

While we found plenty of bike shops in Bellingham (the city is, after all, flush with trails of all kinds), we were unable to locate one that rented bikes or trailers for kids. So if you've brought along bikes for your Alaska Marine Highway adventure, you're in luck. If you have tall teenagers who fit an adult bike, try these places for bike rentals.

Jack's Bicycle Center $$
1907 Iowa St., Bellingham, WA 98225
(360) 733-1955
www.jacksbicyclecenter.net

Mountain and road bikes available for rent, near downtown Bellingham.

Fairhaven Bicycle $$
1108 11th St., Bellingham, WA 98225
(360) 733-4433
www.fairhavenbike.com

Road and mountain bikes, both clipless and standard

Bellingham's Bicycle Routes map is a downloadable PDF of all the bicycle-accessible trails in the greater Bellingham area. It's great to have along while exploring. Find it at https://www.cob.org/documents/gis/maps/COB_Bikemap.pdf.

Prince Rupert, British Columbia (YPR): Connecting with Canada

The only Canadian stop along the Alaska Marine Highway, Prince Rupert is important due to its road systems connecting Alaska, British Columbia, and Washington State. A small port city, Prince Rupert is a popular embarkation or disembarkation port for those travelers wishing

The Bellingham Cruise Terminal is easily reached via train, car, or airplane and is located in the core of the Historic Fairhaven District.

to sightsee along beautiful roadways of the United States and Canada. Located on Kaien Island, Prince Rupert is a hub for British Columbia's North Coast and an important port of call for shipping of goods both north and south.

Incorporated in 1910, Prince Rupert was in a prime position for the fishing and timber industry, but it wasn't until World War II that its value was truly realized. Recognized as a valuable asset for Allied troops moving toward the Aleutian Islands and Pacific Ocean, US soldiers helped complete a road connecting the mainland to Prince Rupert and constructed several forts to protect the city.

Once the war was over and life returned to the new normal, industries like fishing and forestry became major sources of income for Prince Rupert

Prince Rupert

Population: 15,000 (2014 data from British Columbia Tourism)

Incorporated: March 10, 1910, and named for Prince Rupert of the Rhine, who was first governor of the Hudson's Bay Company, as a result of a competition to name the city. The prize was $250.

Known for: Passenger rail service through VIA Rail Canada to connect ferry passengers with transportation options to Vancouver and the United States. Timber, salmon and halibut fishing, and tourism remain the top industries.

Interesting fact: In 1949 the Queen Charlotte earthquake shook buildings, broke windows, and reached 8.1 on the Richter scale.

Hot tip: Catching the ferry here or getting off and driving south are excellent options for families wanting a sail/drive experience. Not only will you capture the essence of this beautiful section of North America, but you'll couple that with time as a family on board the ferry, void of typical road trip angst that plagues many parents. For reference, Prince Rupert is located 480 miles north of Vancouver, more than a day's drive.

residents. However, as is true with many instances of border management, sometimes the relationship between Canada and the United States would grow testy, occasionally rearing up as one side or the other declared rights to everything from salmon fishing to the type of steel used to construct a new ferry dock. All things being equal, though, Prince Rupert and the Alaska Marine Highway remain important partners in the Southeast route's success.

Quiet, beautiful, and welcoming, Prince Rupert charms most visitors, especially those who hail from busier areas of the world. It's refreshing to slow down and enjoy the salty air and relaxed pace of life.

ARRIVING

Note: *Do not forget* passports (and notarized documentation for children not accompanied by both parents) to secure entry into or out of Canada.

By Air

Air Canada (www.aircanada.com) has regular service to the Prince Rupert airport from Vancouver. The flight is approximately two hours, and while it may save time, it could also prove more cumbersome and costly once you add taxis, tickets, and other expenses.

By Rail

VIA Rail Canada (www.viarail.ca, 1-888-842-7245) provides service between Vancouver and Prince Rupert on a regular basis through the Skeena route. From Vancouver, passengers can also make arrangements for rail service to Bellingham or Seattle, Washington (or reverse). The train travels through beautiful sections of British Columbia, including Jasper and Prince George—a two-day trip but worth the extra time.

By Road

Highway 97 winds north from Vancouver to Prince George and then intersects with Highway 16 west to Prince Rupert. Travelers should heed all road trip tips mentioned in *Alaska on the Go: Exploring the 49th State with Children*, including an emergency kit, food, water, shelter, and cash.

GETTING AROUND

The **Prince Rupert Transit System** (www.bctransit.com/prince-ruper:), operated by BC Transit, offers several routes around the community. Adult fare is $1.75 CDN, kids K–12 $1.50 CDN. A day pass can be purchased as well. **Skeena Taxi** (250-624-2185) provides service from the ferry dock and beyond. **Rental car** options are available as well.

> **Hertz:** 207 3rd Ave. E., (250) 624-2151, www.hertz.com
> **National:** 106-815 1st Ave. W., (250) 624-5318, www.nationalcar.com

VISITOR INFORMATION

Tourism Prince Rupert operates a visitor center located at 215 Cow Bay Road (www.visitprincerupert.com, 250-624-8687), not far from the historic Cow Bay area. Quite familiar with ferry passengers, information center staff and volunteers will be able to help your family find activities, dining, and the nearest washroom.

SHOPPING/GROCERIES

Overwaitea
841 3rd Ave. W., Prince Rupert, BC V8J 1A2
(250) 624-9032

A regional chain of stores with a wide variety of grocery items and a pharmacy.

MEDICAL CARE

Prince Rupert Regional Hospital
1305 Summit Ave., Prince Rupert, BC V8J 1A2
(250) 624-2171
www.northernhealth.ca

Serving the greater community, this facility has an emergency room, pharmacy, and nonurgent health hotline (just dial 8-1-1 from anywhere in British Columbia) for questions.

LODGING

Prince Rupert is a great place to stay overnight on your way to or from the Alaska ferry dock. It's not a large town, however, so reservations should be made well in advance if you decide to stop longer than a day. Keep in mind that all rates are listed in the Canadian dollar.

Hotels/Motels

Aleeda Motel $$
900 3rd Ave. W., Prince Rupert, BC V8J 1A2
(888) 460-2023
www.aleedamotel.com

Located near the ferry terminal, the Aleeda offers thirty-one units with kitchenettes and is pet-friendly. Free coffee for grown-ups and free Wi-Fi for all. **Note:** Ask for a nonsmoking room, as this property still accepts smoking guests.

Thumbs-up: Budget-friendly lodging, access to ferry dock

Prince Rupert Hotel $$–$$$
118 6th St., Prince Rupert, BC V8J 1A2
(855) 737-8774
www.princeruperthotel.com

A historic hotel in the heart of Prince Rupert, this property has undergone a renovation in hopes of retaining the charm of its early days while upgrading to a more modern feel. A free breakfast is included in all stays, and an on-site sports pub is a bustling place in the evening. Free Wi-Fi access in all areas of this eighty-eight-room, six-story hotel. Cribs available on request.

Thumbs-up: Style, downtown location, waffle bar at breakfast

Anchor Inn $$–$$$
1600 Park Ave., Prince Rupert, BC V8J 1A2
(888) 627-8522
www.anchor-inn.com

The closest property to Alaska Marine Highway ferries, the VIA Rail, and other transportation options, Anchor Inn prides itself on friendly service and access. Breakfast is included, but recent renovations have added kitchenettes in some rooms. Rollaway beds can be arranged in advance. Pet-friendly. Free Wi-Fi throughout the building.

Thumbs-up: Friendly service, plenty of kid-friendly space, breakfast, and assistance in arranging activities

Camping/RV

Kinnikinnick Campground and RV Park $-$$$
333 Skeena Dr., Port Edward, BC V0V 1G0
(866) 628-9449
www.kinnikcamp.com

Heck, just saying "kinnikinnick" makes me want to stay here! Located about ten minutes from Prince Rupert in nearby Port Edward, this is an option for those wanting a more rustic experience. With RV and tent sites and a comfortable cabin that sleeps six, Kinnikinnick also features showers, electricity, and water and an on-site manager to greet you, even if your ferry is late.

Thumbs-up: Camping and wilderness experience, cabin option, trails, and on-site manager

FEEDING THE FAMILY
With a waterside location, Prince Rupert is flush with options for seafood, including kid-pleasing fish and chips. For such a small town, Prince Rupert also has quite a variety of restaurants, ranging from fast food to Asian, and many are within walking distance of the downtown core and ferry terminal.

Stiles Place Seafood and Grill $$-$$$
346 Stiles Pl., Prince Rupert, BC V8J 1A2
(250) 627-7433
Open Tuesday–Sunday 11:30 a.m.–2:30 p.m., and for dinner 4:30–9:30 p.m.

Traditional favorites reign here, and kids will enjoy their own menu. Look for steaks, chops, burgers, and a nice gluten-free menu.

Javadotcup $-$$
516 3rd Ave. W., Prince Rupert, BC V8J 1A2
(250) 622-2822
javadotcup@citytel.net
Open daily at 7:00 a.m.

Need a place to relax, sip coffee, and browse the Internet? Javadotcup is a comfortable spot for the whole family to enjoy a light meal and coffee or hot chocolate. Great on a rainy day. Friendly service and good food.

La Gondola Cafe $$-$$$
710 1st Ave. W., Prince Rupert, BC V8J 1A2
(250) 624-2621 (dining room), (250) 624-3359 (drive-in or take-out)
info@lagondolacafe.com, www.lagondolacafe.com
Dining room open daily 4:30–9:00 p.m., drive-in open 10:30 a.m.–9:30 p.m.

Fill up the kids with traditional Italian and "Canadian" cuisine. Pasta, bread, burgers, milkshakes, seafood—you name it, La Gondola's got it. Plus, they are a reliable take-away restaurant and drive-in, too. Why not?

FAMILY FUN IN PRINCE RUPERT
Surrounded by forests and saltwater, Prince Rupert is a cultural and recreational bonanza for visitors. Whether you're staying for a day while waiting for a ferry, or several days after disembarking, this community is warm and welcoming and full of fun.

Museums and Cultural Experiences

Museum of Northern BC $-$$
100 1st Ave. W., Prince Rupert, BC V8J 1A2
(250) 624-3207
www.museumofnorthernbc.com
Open daily 9:00 a.m.–5:00 p.m. (June–September); Tuesday–Saturday 9:00 a.m.–5:00 p.m. (October–May)
$6/adults, $3/teens ages 13–19, $2/kids 6–12, $1/kids 5 and under, free for members

If this is your first experience learning about Pacific Coast Native people, or First Nations as they are called in Canada, be sure to visit this beautiful facility. An excellent way to gear up for Alaska Native cultural centers, this museum is a walk through history. Don't miss the main gallery, where the area's economic, industrial, and ceremonial ties are linked together. The museum also manages the smaller Kwinitsa Railway Museum a few blocks away, where kids will enjoy the old depot and exhibits from Prince Rupert's past. Best for school-aged kids.

North Pacific Cannery National Historical Site $$-$$$
1889 Skeena Dr., Port Edward, BC V0V 1G0
(250) 628-3538
www.northpacificcannery.ca
10:00 a.m.–5:00 p.m. May 1–September 27; open daily in July and August, open Tuesday–Sunday in May, June, and September
$12/adults, $10/seniors, $8/youth, free for kids 5 and under; $10/person for groups of ten or more

Without canneries, the fishing industry would never have succeeded. Thus, the North Pacific Cannery experience offers kids a chance to see how much fishermen relied upon the hard-working men and women of canneries, even 125 years ago. Choose either a guided tour or walk through the sites on your own. Dine at the Mess House, see a movie, and experience some of the arts and crafts made by this multicultural workforce. Dress for outdoor weather conditions. All ages will enjoy this activity.

First Nations Carving Shed FREE

Located next to the Museum of the North on First Avenue in downtown Prince Rupert, this free attraction is a wonderful place to introduce children to the art of wood carving, a staple for life as a Pacific Coast Haida member. Watch current projects, see samples of past work, and witness ongoing efforts to preserve a valuable skill passed down over many generations.

Outdoor Recreation

With lush, green forests and waterfront scenery, Prince Rupert is a nice place to stretch your legs before or after a long ferry trip.

Cow Bay and **Pacific Mariners Park** are a short stroll from the ferry dock (take a left upon disembarking) and a great place to allow kids the opportunity to run off some energy. Mariners Park is about halfway between the ferry dock and Cow Bay, and it offers tired little legs a bench or two for resting and great views of the waterfront. Cow Bay is a fishing-centric village within Prince Rupert city limits and is where the bulk of tourists head upon arrival. It's fun to look at the historic buildings and watch fishing boats arriving and departing.

McClymont Park sits beyond Cow Bay and adds another dimension to your family stroll. Spend some time here watching cyclists, Rollerbladers, and families enjoying the paved pathway.

Service Park is a great place to count totem poles and catch a view of the city. Located in the center of Prince Rupert's commercial district, the park is elevated enough to provide a bit of challenge for younger kids but is very accessible nonetheless. Beautiful flower beds line much of the walkway, and the views warrant binoculars and a camera.

Sunken Gardens Park is the result of a makeover from what was to be a city courthouse in the 1920s. Plans changed, the courthouse was built nearby, but the hole in the ground stayed. Filled with gravel walkways, tunnels, and gorgeous flower gardens, this is a fun and colorful family stop.

Butze Rapids Park and Trail provides families with a bit more hiking and an interesting wonder of nature. The five-kilometer trail leads to a phenomenon known as "reverse rapids" of the area tides, with swirling and whirling water at the tip of the park's shoreline. The trail itself features interpretive signs, benches, and boardwalks that can be slippery. Jogging strollers or backpacks for babies are recommended. Take your time and any age can complete this hike. Find the park about five miles outside Prince Rupert, along Highway 16, the main entrance to the city.

Ketchikan (KTN): Alaska's First City

Hello, Alaska! As your ferry travels northward through the famed Inside Passage, Ketchikan is the first port of call in the forty-ninth state, which is how it earned the title "First City." Located on enormous Revillagigedo Island, Ketchikan is a fishing and forestry town perhaps best known for its weather. Rain, and lots of it, falls in this community of nearly fourteen thousand people, and rarely do visitors escape the sound of dripping liquid sunshine as they slosh their way to activities and attractions.

Ketchikan is a hub for the Alaska cruise industry, and rare is the day when no behemoth vessels are docked in the middle of downtown's port. The waterfront area is packed with people on these days, making the ferry an excellent choice for those who wish to explore this culturally rich and historic community. With no roads connecting the city to other places in Alaska or Canada, Ketchikan is also wonderfully remote, as are many of the communities you will visit on the Alaska Marine Highway. Truly, your family will experience the importance of ferry service to these seaside towns.

Officially incorporated in 1900 but founded nearly a decade earlier, Ketchikan's roots lie in natural resources, most notably salmon. Fishermen could easily catch the nutritious delicacy but often had no way of preserving it before shipping to markets. A man named Snow initially built a saltery in 1883, and shortly after, a cannery was built by business partners Mike Martin and George Clark. When Ketchikan was incorporated in 1900, its population was around eight hundred, with stores, a school, and too many bars and bordellos.

It is those bordellos that capture the interest of tourists today, most notably along Creek Street, where red-light-district customers visited debauched drinking establishments in between working on the docks. At one time, up to thirty bordellos were built along Ketchikan Creek, earning the city a somewhat dubious reputation.

As the community grew, so did industry, with gold mining and forestry adding income to Ketchikan's economy. Mining didn't last long, but the old-growth forests on both Revillagigedo Island and surrounding islands provided a seemingly endless supply of logs to be shipped and milled from the port. As the years went by, however, and the timber industry underwent greater restrictions on just where and what could be cut, including governmental laws relating to wildlife, the timber industry all but died in Ketchikan and the surrounding area. Today only a few operations are allowed to log in Southeast Alaska's forests, and all activity is highly regulated.

The Tongass National Forest takes up much of this forested land. At 17 million acres, the Tongass is the largest reserve of coastal rainforest in the world, and you'll see why once you sail past its mossy, spruce-laden islands and hidden coves. Misty Fjords National Park also lies within reach of Ketchikan and is accessible only by floatplane, making it a truly remote Alaska adventure for those with the time and budget. It's worth both, however, to see bears fish for salmon, clouds hover over mountaintops like curtains, and marine mammals like otters and seals appear as furry dots on the gentle swells of seawater.

Culturally, Ketchikan is home to both Tlingit and Haida Alaska Native groups, which make up a broader group of Pacific Coast Native tribes. Centered on traditions related to coastal life, folklore and artwork tell stories about ravens, whales, eagles, and wolves. Both are matrilineal societies, meaning children inherit rights from the maternal side of the family. The Tlingit tribe also uses a complex moiety (half) that divides families into Eagle, Wolf, and Raven clans. Rules about whom may marry who and when and how drive the tribal structure, and great emphasis is placed on family units with respect to raising children. Visitors to Ketchikan's many Native cultural centers will hear tales about this familial tree that are so different from the traditional parent-sister-brother nuclear family system many of us are familiar with.

ARRIVING

The **AMHS ferry dock** is located just beyond the downtown core of Ketchikan at 3501 Tongass Avenue. Some small cruise ship lines dock near here as do many private boat owners. The terminal is almost three miles from downtown, so taxis will prove helpful if you are traveling without a car.

If you won't be arriving on the ferry or a cruise ship, the **Ketchikan International Airport** (www.borough.ketchikan.ak.us/130/Airport) is your only other option. The airport is actually located on its own island, Gravina, and is accessible only by a small commuter ferry. **Alaska Airlines**

Ketchikan

Population: 13,938 (entire Ketchikan Gateway borough, 2010 US Census)

Founded: In 1900, as a salmon cannery and saltery

Known for: Salmon fishing and totem poles. In fact, Ketchikan is known as the salmon capital of the world and has the highest number of standing totem poles anywhere.

Interesting fact: Ketchikan receives up to two hundred inches of rain per year!

Hot tip: Make use of dockside walkways to explore the city on foot. When dressed appropriately (i.e., prepared for rain), walking this town is much easier than driving, even with kids.

SOUTHEAST

(www.alaskaair.com, 1-800-252-7522) is the major air carrier, with daily flights to and from Seattle. **Note:** Carry cash—$6/adults, $3/kids—for the airport ferry ride. Ticket booths do not accept credit cards.

GETTING AROUND

Municipal bus service operates daily all around the Revillagigedo Island road system, with slightly reduced schedules on Sundays. Fares are around one dollar, allowing an affordable way to see Ketchikan's major attractions. Find schedules and routes at www.kgbak.us/bus/info. A free downtown shuttle operates May through September on a ten- to twenty-minute circuit from berth 4 (at the cruise ship terminal) around downtown attractions.

Ketchikan Taxi Cab Tours also offer a means of sightseeing with the luxury of your own personal driver. Reach them at www.ketchikan taxicabtours.com/taxis.php or (907) 254-7286.

The Alaska Marine Highway administration and operations offices are located in Ketchikan.

FERRY FACT

VISITOR INFORMATION

The **Ketchikan Visitors Bureau** (www.visit-ketchikan.com, 1-800-770-3300) has two locations in the greater downtown area: a satellite office at cruise ship berth 3 and a main office at 131 Front Street. Both offer friendly service along with restrooms, Wi-Fi access, an ATM, and recommendations for attractions and activities.

SHOPPING/GROCERIES

Safeway
2417 Tongass Ave., Ketchikan, AK 99901
(907) 228-1900
Open daily 5:00 a.m.–midnight

Groceries, deli, pharmacy, bakery, fuel station.

MEDICAL CARE

PeaceHealth Ketchikan Medical Center
3100 Tongass Ave., Ketchikan, AK 99901
(907) 228-8300
www.peacehealth.org

LODGING

If you plan to spend a few days in Ketchikan, be sure to make reservations early. This is a busy place during the summer months, and rooms are hard to find for spur-of-the-moment needs.

Hotels/Motels

Cape Fox Lodge $$$
800 Venetia Way, Ketchikan, AK 99901
(866) 225-8001, (907) 225-8001
www.capefoxlodge.com

Tribal-owned facility with seventy-two rooms. Located on a bluff overlooking the city with a funicular tram taking guests up and down town. Kids under twelve stay free with a paying adult. Shuttle to ferry dock or airport.

Thumbs-up: Views, Alaska Native art and decor, pedestrian friendliness

Best Western Plus Landing Hotel $$-$$$
3434 Tongass Ave., Ketchikan, AK 99901
(800) 428-8304, (907) 225-5166
www.landinghotel.com

Closest accommodations to ferry terminal, with 107 rooms, some configured as family-friendly suites. Complimentary shuttle service, on-property restaurant. Children under twelve stay free with paying adult.

Thumbs-up: Proximity to ferry and airport, on-site restaurant

Super 8 $$
2151 Sea Level Dr., Ketchikan, AK 99901
(907) 225-9088
www.super8.com

A waterfront location with access to Ketchikan's only mall for shopping needs, Super 8 is a good choice for families. Free breakfast and free Wi-Fi, great water views, close to ferry dock. Ask about large family suites. Kids seventeen and under stay free with paying adult.

Thumbs-up: Breakfast, complimentary shuttle to ferry, location

Camping

You will need a car to camp in the greater Ketchikan area and among the towering trees of the Tongass National Forest. Be prepared for rain. **Last Chance Campground** (1-877-844-6777) is located ten miles out of town on Revilla Road. Campsites are $10/night, some available by reservation. **Signal Creek Campground** (1-877-844-6677) is in the Ward Lake area of the Tongass, about seven miles from downtown Ketchikan and four miles from the ferry terminal (take North Tongass Highway to the junction with Revilla Road). Rates are $10/night with twenty-four sites available, some by reservation. And **Settlers Cove State Recreation Site** (www .dnr.alaska.gov/parks/aspunits/southeast/settlerscvsrs.htm) is a state-run area at Milepost 18 on North Tongass Road. It offers fourteen tent/RV sites for $10/night and is popular with local residents. Reservations are not accepted.

FEEDING THE FAMILY

It's all seafood, all the time in this self-proclaimed Salmon Capital of the World, so if you have time to stop in town for a few days, try these kid-friendly choices.

Alaska Fish House $$–$$$
3 Salmon Landing (next to the Lumberjack Show venue), Ketchikan, AK 99901
(907) 247-4055
www.alaskafishhouse.com
Open daily 6:00 a.m.–7:00 p.m. (April–October)

Advertising fish but cooking up all manner of burgers and fries, too, the Fish House is a nice choice on a rainy, windy Alaska day. Try the smoked salmon cornbread and hand-battered fish and chips. Yum. **Note:** This place can be very, very crowded when cruise ships are in town, so plan to stand around, or get there early!

O'Brien's Pub and Eatery $$
211 Steadman St., Ketchikan, AK 99901
(907) 247-2326
obrienspubandeatery@gmail.com
Open daily 11:00 a.m.–11:00 p.m.

Located near the entrance to famous Creek Street, O'Brien's is a favorite for a casual atmosphere, good beer, and kid-friendly pretzels with homemade soup. Deep-fried salmon fritters are the size of golf balls and very tasty.

Heen Kahidi Restaurant and Lounge $$–$$$
Cape Fox Lodge
800 Venetia Way, Ketchikan, AK 99901
(866) 225-8001, (907) 225-8001
www.capefoxlodge.com/dining.html
Open daily at 7:00 a.m.

What could be more fun than taking a funicular up the hill for a meal and then walking down afterward? Kid-friendly menu featuring chicken fingers, burgers, pancakes, and other treats. Nice view of downtown Ketchikan and beautiful artwork throughout the lodge.

FAMILY FUN IN KETCHIKAN
The ferry typically does not stay in Ketchikan for long, usually about an hour or so, but those who choose to begin or end a journey here can find plenty of fun. Make sure you have the rain gear handy at all times, and pack extra clothing while you explore this culturally vibrant city.

Museums and Cultural Experiences

Southeast Alaska Discovery Center $
50 Main St., Ketchikan, AK 99901
(907) 228-6220
www.alaskacenters.gov/ketchikan.cfm
Open Monday–Friday 8:00 a.m.–5:00 p.m., Saturday–Sunday 8:00 a.m.–4:00 p.m.
(May–September); Thursday–Saturday 10:00 a.m.–4:00 p.m. (October–April)
$5/adults, free for kids 15 and under; $15 season pass

The center is a great way to become acquainted with Southeast Alaska's history, industry, and lifestyle. Interactive exhibits, scavenger hunts, and helpful rangers all make this a worthwhile stop for the whole family. Free films and a Junior Ranger program.

Exploring totems in Ketchikan.

Potlach Totem Park FREE
9809 Totem Bight Rd., Ketchikan, AK 99901
www.potlachpark.com
potlachpark@yahoo.com

This park is an excellent choice for those relying on public transportation. Southeast Alaska's Native culture comes alive here, with tribal houses, intricately carved totem poles, and kid-pleasing dioramas of ancient villages. Wander the short trail system and take time to see blooming fireweed and salmonberry bushes. An exhibit of antique cars and firearms completes this experience for kids preschool and older. Take your time in this beautiful place.

Saxman Native Village $$
Tongass Highway, in Saxman village, 2.5 miles south of Ketchikan
Tours arranged by Cape Fox Tours
(907) 225-4846
www.capefoxtours.com
Open May–September
Guided tours available for $20–$30/person, depending upon age, or take a self-guided tour for around $3/person

Definitely catering to the cruise ship crowd, Saxman is nonetheless a good option for those with less time and more money. If you don't want to go along with the crowd for a tour, take the self-guided option and see the carving shed and towering totems and meet residents of this small Alaska Native community. When we were there last, local kids were selling fry bread to support the school, and we had a chance to chat with them about life in Southeast Alaska.

Great Alaskan Lumberjack Show $$
420 Spruce Mill Way, Ketchikan, AK 99901
(907) 225-9050
www.lumberjacksports.com
Open May–September, with three to five shows daily
$37/adults, $18.50/kids 3–12, free for kids 2 and under

Ketchikan's love of trees used to translate into big money for the hundreds of lumber companies making their living from enormous old-growth timber stands. Those days are gone now, but the lumberjack persona remains strong at this raucous show that children love. Lots of good-looking "bulls of the woods" climb poles, spin logs in water, and yell a lot to prove that lumberjacking is only for the strong of body and voice. Great for kids age two and up. Sit near the front if you can for best sound effects and audience participation opportunities. Consider combining this with the Saxman Native Village tour.

Ketchikan Walking Tour FREE
Starts on the cruise ship dock at the Ketchikan Visitor Center (131 Front St.)
www.visit-ketchikan.com

Let your kids be guides while you explore this funky seaside town. Grab a free map at the visitor center and hoof it around downtown. With plenty of directional signs and interpretive information, it's a great way to spend a few hours. Check out Creek Street, the salmon hatchery, totems, and even the local school.

Outdoor Recreation

Alaska Rainforest Sanctuary $$–$$$
116 Wood Rd., Ketchikan, AK 99901
(877) 947-7557, (907) 225-5503
www.alaskarainforest.com
Open May–September
Tours average $85/person, depending upon length of tour and age of guest

Weigh at least ninety pounds? Reached the tween years (ten or older)? Good news! You can zipline through the tippy top of a rainforest canopy. Adrenaline junkies, get ready for a beautiful zip, a suspension bridge walk, and even a few bears wandering below. A forest walk is available for those too young or unable to spend a few hours connected to trees by a cable.

Alaska Sea Cycle Tours $$-$$$
802 Monroe St., Ketchikan, AK 99901
(907) 821-2728
www.alaskaseacycletours.com
Open May–September
Tours begin at $155/adults, $85/kids, for a three-hour trip

Haven't had enough of the water? Try these boat-kayak-bicycle machines and explore on your own near placid Ward Cove. Great for kids of practically any age. Guides provide PFDs, gear, snacks, and drinks for everyone. Kids twelve and younger need an adult in their party. Pick-up available from many downtown locations.

Settlers Cove State Recreation Site FREE
Mile 18, N. Tongass Hwy., Ketchikan, AK 99901
www.dnr.alaska.gov/parks/aspunits/southeast/settlerscvsrs.htm

Settlers Cove has a lovely system of family-friendly trails. Try the Hollow Cedar Beach Trail for an accessible hike to a beach picnic shelter. A longer hike takes you to Lunch Creek Falls Loop, where you connect to Lunch Creek Trail and a view of the waterfalls. Bring a pack for tiny children. Watch for slippery spots, and always be bear aware.

Perseverance Trail, Tongass National Forest FREE
Directions at www.fs.fed/us/r10/tongass/recreation/rec_facilities/ktnrec.html

Catch this trail for a short stroll to Lake Perseverance and the summer blueberry patches, or go fishing in the lake. The trail is gravel and board-walk, so most kids can manage without trouble. Strollers may struggle on the boardwalk in the rain, but overall, a nice hike. Be bear aware. Look and listen for birds in the trees!

Wrangell (WRG): A Gem of Southeast Alaska
Wrangell is only ninety miles north of Ketchikan but feels a world away, and for all purposes, it is. Accessible via boat or aircraft, Wrangell is a

unique example of small-town life, and once you arrive here, you're likely to realize this is the Alaska you had been hoping for. Located near the top of beautiful Clarence Strait and at the mouth of the mighty Stikine River, Wrangell is also one of the most diverse little towns you'll find in the entire state, thanks to a number of historic events and interesting individuals.

Situated on Wrangell Island and sandwiched between the mainland and Etolin Island, Wrangell has seen a surprising number of residents and visitors over the last hundred years or so. Explorers, fur hunters, and on-the-way gold seekers found the town to be quite to their liking from a navigational perspective and in the value of wildlife, like sea otters that could be killed for their fur. While Russian fur traders were the first non-Natives to claim Wrangell for preservation of their interests by building a fort in 1833, George Vancouver was actually the first white man to set foot upon Wrangell's soil during a quick survey visit in 1793. It must have been superficial, however, because Vancouver missed finding the Stikine River that leads into what is now Canada and the Coast Mountain Range.

Wrangell

Population: 2,448 (2010 US Census)

Founded: In 1867 as Fort Wrangel after Alaska became a territory. First settled in 1834 as a Russian outpost and was known before that as one of the most powerful Stikine Tlingit settlements.

Known for: An interesting governance, flying flags of the Tlingit Nation, Russia, Great Britain, and the United States.

Interesting fact: Wrangell is one of the oldest non-Native settlements in Alaska.

Hot tip: Take time for a charter tour of the Stikine River and surrounding areas. The geology, anthropology, and cultural history are fascinating.

At any rate, when the Russians built Fort Redoubt Saint Dionysus, as Wrangell was first called, the local Tlingits relocated to the center of the new town on a small plot of land, now called Shakes Island (named after then chief Shakes V). Here the Tlingit helped manage fur trading with their own shrewd abilities, which in turn led the fur industry toward a resurgence in value.

Shortly after the fort was completed, however, the famous Hudson's Bay Company showed up, wanting a piece of the action and intending to build their own post on the Stikine River. When the Hudson's Bay ship arrived in the community, Russian commanders refused them entry, saying the British had no right to the land. The Tlingit people joined the fray, claiming their right to the furs (and thus the ongoing trade influence), so the Hudson's Bay sailors returned to the city of Vancouver to ponder their options.

Eventually the British, Russians, and Tlingits reached a land-lease agreement in 1840 at the cost of two thousand otter skins to the Russians and delivery of food to Russian colonies on the west coast. The British saw the potential of Wrangell's resources and took the deal.

When Alaska was purchased from Russia in the famous Seward's Folly bargain in 1867, one more flag was due to fly from the post of Wrangell, so named for Baron von Wrangel of the Russian-American Company who originally founded the area. Once the Americans had established a military presence in the town, a flag of the United States of America flew high and proud, making a total of four to be hoisted up the flagpole over the previous forty years.

When the Alaska purchase was completed, the town settled, and a leadership who's who established, Wrangell really began booming, with fishing, mining, and timber taking center stage. The Stikine River held gold, and by the 1898 rush, Marshall Wyatt Earp arrived to spend a short stint of ten days as head of law enforcement. He couldn't stay, however, since he and his wife were on the way to find fortune (and make history) farther north.

Aside from Wyatt Earp, perhaps the most colorful individual to explore the land around Wrangell was naturalist John Muir, whose writings managed to stir a sense of adventure in travelers—and still do today. Muir came to Wrangell Island for the first time in 1879 and wasn't too impressed by the wet forests, boggy shorelines, and lack of public facilities. Nonetheless, he stuck around and met up with missionaries like Sheldon Jackson and Samuel Hall Young and made his way up and down the wilderness of the island and adjoining waterways. It was Young who joined Muir on many of his earliest exploits, journeying by steamship up the Stikine River and ogling over craggy mountains and miles of glacial ice. The Stikine made an impression on both men, and Muir called Big Stikine Glacier a "broad, white flood," unlike anything he'd ever seen before. Today, Big Stikine Glacier is separated from the river by a large moraine (mounds of boulders left from glacial retreat) and a glacial lake, but lucky visitors can still witness the awe-inspiring size of this enormous icy behemoth. There is no doubt that Muir's observations of and writings about nature have inspired a legion of intrepid Alaska adventure-seekers, and Wrangell is as good a place as any to begin.

ARRIVING

If you'd like to begin or end your ferry journey in Wrangell, there is one airport with daily service from Seattle or Anchorage via **Alaska Airlines** (www.alaskaair.com, 1-800-252-7522). Alaska Marine Highway service can arrive or depart at random times, depending upon the vessel, time of year, and schedule. Check with AMHS reservations agents to be sure you have a schedule that fits with your airline arrival or departure.

If Wrangell is a ferry pass-through on your way elsewhere, be aware that time in town can be very limited—less than an hour, which is hardly enough minutes to do more than grab a latte at the nearby restaurant. Those wanting to explore this charming community should make plans to stay a few days, or until the next ferry arrives.

GETTING AROUND

Most of Wrangell can be explored **on foot**, thanks to a network of streets, trails, helpful tour operators, and a small taxi service. **Northern Lights Taxi**

(907-874-4646) operates all day and most of the night, seven days a week, and they accept credit cards or cash.

VISITOR INFORMATION

Wrangell Convention and Visitor Bureau/James and Elsie Nolan Center
296 Campbell Dr., Wrangell, AK 99929
(907) 874-3699
www.wrangellalaska.org

Walking tour maps, a museum, list of hikes and cultural sites, and free movies about Wrangell and Southeast Alaska.

SHOPPING/GROCERIES

City Market Inc.
423 Front St., Wrangell, AK 99929
(907) 874-3333

Full grocery store with some not too bad deals on produce, considering how long it took to get it to Wrangell. Fax and copy center and postal center. **Bonus:** Free deliveries to the ferry if you call ahead.

Bob's IGA
223 Breuger St., Wrangell, AK 99929
(907) 874-2341

Strictly the basics, but with a deli and bakery, too. Closed on Sundays.

MEDICAL CARE

Wrangell Medical Center
310 Bennett St., Wrangell, AK 99929
(907) 874-7000
www.wrangellmedicalcenter.com

Emergency room, lab, radiology services.

LODGING
If you choose to stay and explore Wrangell, make plans with the cooperation of Alaska Marine Highway scheduling experts. Depending upon the ferry and your desired destination, arrivals or departures from Wrangell can be within one to three days.

Hotels/Motels

Alaskan Sourdough Lodge $$
1104 Peninsula St., Wrangell, AK 99929
(800) 874-3613, (907) 874-3613
www.akgetaway.com

Owned and operated by a former mayor of Wrangell, this property is comfortable and affordable. Free continental breakfast, extra option for sack lunches or dinner. With only sixteen rooms, guests mingle and families should be at ease. A shuttle is available for ferry or airport transportation. No cribs available. Tours can also be arranged via the hosts.

Thumbs-up: Lots of space for families, including the Family Room with four twin beds or one king and two twins

Stikine Inn $$-$$$
107 Stikine Ave., Wrangell, AK 99929
(888) 874-3388, (907) 874-3388
http://www.stikineinn.com

Located near the City Dock and Front Street, this property is great for those who want to see and do everything near the downtown area and surrounding waterways. On-site restaurant and a courtesy shuttle. Within easy walking distance of the ferry dock.

Thumbs-up: Access, nice views

Bed and Breakfasts

Fennimore's Bed and Breakfast $-$$
312 Stikine Ave., Wrangell, AK 99929
(907) 874-3012
www.fennimoresbbb.com

An excellent option for ferry travelers, Fennimore's is mere steps away from the ferry dock. Great food, bikes to borrow, and accommodating hosts make this a favorite. Try the kitchenette rooms for more meal flexibility.

Thumbs-up: Accessibility, family-friendly hosts

Grand View Bed and Breakfast $$
P.O. Box 927, Wrangell, AK 99929
(907) 874-3225
www.grandviewbandb.com

I recently stayed at Grand View for the first time and found hospitality positively radiating from every corner. Three rooms, one accommodating a single bed and a queen bed, are comfortable and decorated in Alaska-themed motifs. A full kitchen and enormous living room with sweeping views make this a win for families. Hosts Leslie and Alan Cummings do everything they can to make your visit a meaningful Wrangell experience. They also offer a small charter company for those wanting to fish or sightsee.

Thumbs-up: Enormous common areas, full kitchen, kid-friendly access to beach and nearby park

Camping

City of Wrangell RV Park at Shoemaker Bay $
Mile 5, Zimovia Highway (about five miles from the center of town)
(907) 874-2444
parksrec@ak.net

This city-run campground has twenty-five spaces for RVs, with prices ranging from $15 to $25/night. A nearby recreation center is great for showers, a swimming pool, and weight room at no extra charge.

Thumbs-up: A pool!

The **Tongass National Forest** website (www.fs.usda.gov/tongass) has a comprehensive listing of all the campgrounds in the Wrangell Ranger District (under "Recreation" and "Camping & Cabins"). Some are very remote and with limited space, so plan carefully.

FEEDING THE FAMILY
Eating in Wrangell is quite simple, and kids will enjoy the lack of fuss with food preparation.

Stikine Restaurant and Café $$
107 Stikine Ave., Wrangell, AK 99929
(888) 874-3388, (907) 874-3388
Café open daily 6:30 a.m. to 6:00 p.m.; restaurant open daily 6:30 a.m. to 9:00 p.m.

Located in the Stikine Inn, near Front Street and the City Dock, fresh local favorites like clam chowder and fish and chips headline here, but steaks, burgers, and fry bread (a Native staple) pizza are also big sellers. Craft beer and berry lemonade, too. Just passing through Wrangell? This is a quick jaunt from the ferry for some take-out goodies.

Diamond C Cafe $-$$
223 Front St., Wrangell, AK 99929
(907) 874-3322

Lots of local atmosphere is found here, with breakfast and lunch available daily. Soups, burgers, and espresso. We like this place for the unpretentious and friendly atmosphere.

FAMILY FUN IN WRANGELL
Wrangell's value lies in its unhurried pace and valuable place in Alaska's history. A great way to experience the town is through a self-guided walking tour that begins at the James and Elsie Nolan Center and museum on Campbell Drive. Take about an hour to explore the museum with its important exhibits that tell Wrangell's story, then grab a map before hitting the streets of town. Below are some interesting spots to stop along the way.

Wrangell's Children Corner the Gemstone Market
No lemonade stands here—Wrangell kids are too busy selling garnets. The beautiful burgundy-colored gems are sold all around town by local children in an impressive business venture that dates back to the late 1800s. The Wrangell garnet ledge was originally founded in 1881 by a group of men who soon discovered garnet mining was more difficult than the gold most prospectors sought, and ultimately the ledge (located five miles north of Wrangell Island, on the mainland) was mined by a group of women from Minnesota. Tough, press-savvy, and pretty successful at their toils, the mining mamas, teachers, and businesswomen eventually drifted away, and individual garnet seekers began to step forward.

In 1962 Fred G. Hanford acquired the ledge with the intention of donating the entire site to the Boy Scouts of America, stipulating that "for only so

Museums and Cultural Experiences

Chief Shakes Tribal House $
(907) 874-4303
wcatribe@gmail.com

Located on tiny Shakes Island in the middle of Inner Harbor is a replica of a nineteenth-century tribal house. Built in 1940, the house underwent extensive renovation in 2013, and visitors can feel the beat of Alaska Native culture while attending daily performances. Pay careful attention to the totems standing outside and see if your kids can decipher the stories behind characters' appearances. The grave of Chief Shakes himself sits at the top of a little hill just off Case Avenue. Look for the site's distinctive orca totems marking the area. To reach the house on your own, take Front Street to Shakes Street, then turn left to Shakes Island. Often brilliant red flags mark the dock walkway, and performers will greet guests during scheduled performances. Call ahead for times and days.

Totem Park is on Front Street, just past the City Market. Stop by and view the Kahlteen totem at the front and wander the gravel pathways

long as the said grantee . . . shall use the land for Scouting purposes shall permit the children of Wrangell to take garnets from there in reasonable quantities." Today, kids from Wrangell make an annual pilgrimage to the garnet ledge, located at the mouth of the Stikine River, to try their hand at prying loose the rough, dirty-looking gemstones. No power tools are allowed, and only children under eighteen and their parents can mine.

How much cash do these enterprising youngsters glean from their efforts? Some kids have paid for college educations. Children set up tables along City Dock and sell their shiny stones to passengers disembarking the Alaska ferry, sometimes making up to $2,000 each summer.

around the back. You can feel the effort it took to create such wooden wonders, and it's well worth the time to visit.

Farther out of town along Evergreen Avenue (a twenty-minute walk along a local road) sits the famous **Petroglyph Beach**, a State Historic Site and a fascinating mystery of Southeast Alaska. Read the interpretive signs at the accessible platform before hopping down onto the rocky beach and searching for petroglyphs. Nobody really knows who carved these forms into the smooth, large rocks sitting shoreside, or why, and the closest guess of when places the carvings at a thousand years old, or more. A fun activity is to create rubbings of the mock petroglyphs at the platform and take some of that mystery home with you. **Note:** Do not allow kids to climb on the actual petroglyph rocks—history needs our tender loving care, you know. Also remember that all beach rocks are slippery with an abundance of rain and sea kelp.

Outdoor Recreation

Wrangell is an outdoor paradise for active families. Everything centers on nature's bounty, and that includes recreation. From kayaking to hiking

Don't forget to explore Petroglyph Beach in Wrangell for a glimpse into ancient Alaska Native history.

to jet boat tours, the greater Wrangell area offers a wide variety of kid-friendly fun.

HIKING

Search the **Southeast Alaska Trail System** website (www.seatrails.org) for a complete listing of the area's hikes, broken down by day, overnight, accessible, etc.

If you have a car, **Nemo Point Saltwater Trail** is a scenic one-mile round-trip hike along a forested boardwalk. Children of all ages will enjoy walking through the cedar, spruce, and hemlock forest to the beach at trail's end. Drive 13.4 miles from town to Nemo Loop Road (also known as Forest Road 6267) and follow it another 5.2 miles to the trailhead. Allow one to two hours, plus time at the beach. Bring rain gear and sturdy shoes or boots that accommodate slippery surfaces. Suitable for all ages. Jogging strollers are appropriate, but carriers may be best.

Mount Dewey Trail is an in-town treasure. It's short—only a quarter mile one-way—but the views are super, and during the summer, the blueberry picking is divine. Head up Third Street from downtown, go behind the high school, and follow the stairs leading up to Reid Street. Then bear left and follow the residential street to a sign marking the trailhead. Bring a camera, a bag or bucket for berries July through August, and water for thirsty kids. No strollers here as the trail is steep and often consists of boardwalk. Watch for slippery steps on wet days. **Note:** This is a great before-bed hike.

KAYAKING

The calm waters of Zimovia Strait and surrounding coves make for wonderful kayaking adventures. Heck, the downtown area alone is an interesting historical adventure via watercraft.

Breakaway Adventures $$
P.O. Box 2107, Wrangell, AK 99929
(888) 385-2488, (907) 874-2488
www.breakawayadventures.com
Kayak and canoe rentals, prices range from $60 per day

WILDLIFE

Kayaking can be a prime way to experience Alaska wildlife out on the ocean. If that's not your bag, though, try these other options instead.

Anan Wildlife Observatory $$-$$$

Tongass National Forest
(907) 874-2323
www.fs.fed.us/r10/tongass/recreation/wildlife_viewing/ananobservatory

Managed by the Tongass National Forest, Anan Wildlife Observatory is tightly controlled by rangers May through September and access is limited to those with prearranged free permits, which are issued on a first-come-first-serve basis. Located deep in the Tongass National Forest, accessible only by floatplane or boat, the observatory can be experienced along the banks of Anan Creek, site of an ancient Tlingit fishing area. Boasting the largest pink salmon run in Southeast Alaska, Anan attracts black and brown bears each summer, and this is the only place you'll find both together. A half-mile trail leads from the estuary near Anan Creek to the observation decks, and every step of the way visitors are able to witness the daily life of the area's bears since they also use the trail for their own travels to and from fishing areas. This trip is best suited for kids age seven and up. While the space is patrolled by rangers and guides, the experience does come with stressful moments of very close bear encounters.

You can visit Anan without a guide, but given the somewhat unpredictable nature of both bears and children, my recommendation is to travel under the supervision of a charter outfit. Trips last around five hours and include lunch, guide services, and plenty of time boating to and from the site. Plan on spending a few hundred dollars per person for this daylong excursion, but the cost is well worth this incredible experience. **Note**: Anan Wildlife Observatory is thirty miles from Wrangell, so plan accordingly for weather, mealtimes, and bathroom protocol. Boats are noisy and small but fun. Ask about PFDs for children.

Alaska Waters $$-$$$

City Dock at 107 Stikine Ave., Wrangell, AK 99929
(800) 347-4462
www.alaskawaters.com, info@alaskawaters.com
Open May–September

Alaska Waters provides guided trips into the Stikine Wilderness and Anan Wildlife Observatory. They also add an element of Alaska Native culture to every tour, thanks to a knowledgeable crew with lifelong ties to Wrangell and Southeast Alaska. Tours begin at $85 and range from short culture-based tours of Wrangell by water, or longer trips up the Stikine River and to LeConte Glacier.

Petersburg (PSG): Alaska's Little Norway

Norwegian entrepreneur Peter Buschmann saw more than pretty colors when he looked at the blue ice of LeConte Glacier. He saw money. Ice was critical to the fish business, and Buschmann found the abundance of it to be a perfect reason to build a cannery, Icy Straits Packing Co., in the late 1800s. In 1910 the city of Petersburg was incorporated and began to thrive as its residents, many of them directly from Norway, enjoyed mountains, cold water, and deep fjords. Today Petersburg is a delightful stop along the Alaska Marine Highway's Southeast route, and the city's Norwegian culture remains strong in both heritage and architecture.

For families, time spent in Petersburg means low-key fun found in the form of fishing, kayaking, hiking, and cultural connections with local residents. The town itself is located at the northern tip of Mitkof Island, a twenty-three-mile-long stretch of musky bog and forested hillsides, where the Wrangell Narrows meets Frederick Sound. It is a fishing village full of dramatic sea tales and fascinating people with a strong Alaska Native history.

Petersburg is located where humpback whales often spend days feeding on the rich krill and herring. Towering mountains, including the elusive Devils Thumb, can be spotted from the deck of a ferry, and LeConte Glacier often shows off its bluish hues to marine travelers as they go around the corner toward or from Petersburg.

The Wrangell Narrows is equally impressive. Providing a skinny passage between Mitkof Island and around Zarembo Island on the way to Wrangell, the Narrows is a navigational challenge for mariners. Commonly known among Alaskans as Christmas Tree Alley for the red-and-green navigational markers, a trip through the Narrows is an opportunity not to be missed. Watch for sea lions, eagles, Sitka black-tailed deer, black bears, and other vessels both small and large.

As is true with most Southeast Alaska towns, Petersburg relies heavily on the Alaska Marine Highway as an option for transportation, even though there is also an airport serving Seattle, Anchorage, and a few points in between. And most residents, in typical Alaska fashion, adapt to this lifestyle and wouldn't have it any other way, raising children, working, and playing near the sea that has provided so much over the years.

ARRIVING

The Alaska Marine Highway stops in Petersburg a few times a week, traveling both north and south. If you decide to spend a day or two in this charming village, consult AMHS reservations agents ahead of time to be sure they have a sailing calendar that matches your family's schedule. Often the ferry will dock for up to an hour in Petersburg (no guarantees, however), and passengers may disembark for a short stroll to town and back before the ferry commences travel. If you'd like to end or begin your

Petersburg

Population: 3,937 (2010 US Census)

Founded: In 1897 as a fish processing and packing site by young Peter Buschmann of Norway.

Known for: Close ties to Norway and its culture, with Christmas being a highlight.

Interesting fact: Much of downtown Petersburg has retained the charm of Norwegian culture. Homes and businesses are designed to model those of far-off Norway.

Hot tip: After arriving in Petersburg via the ferry, take time to wander the boat docks of this fishing-centric harbor. Look for giant sea lions who often swim between, under, and around vessels in search of a wayward fish.

journey in Petersburg, **Alaska Airlines** (www.alaskaair.com, 1-800-252-7522) provides twice-daily jet service to and from Seattle or Anchorage.

GETTING AROUND

Walking or biking is the best way to see Petersburg. With a series of in-town trails and a low traffic count, Petersburg is the perfect place for strolling or pedaling with kids. If you do need a ride, **Viking Cab** (907-518-9191) will transport you and your luggage just about anywhere, including the Petersburg Airport. **Life Cyclery** (907-650-7387) offers bicycle rentals, including trailers for kids and gear for around $30/day for the first bike and $10/day for additional bikes.

VISITOR INFORMATION

Located on the corner of First and Fram Streets, the Petersburg Chamber of Commerce and Visitor Center (www.petersburg.org, visitorinfo@alaska.com, 907-772-3646) is an easy walk from the ferry dock. Find information about lodging, food, and recreation, plus free fun stuff for kids.

SHOPPING/GROCERIES

Hammer & Wikan Inc.
218 N. Nordic Street, Petersburg, AK 99833
(907) 772-4246
www.hammerandwikan.com
Open Monday–Saturday 7:00 a.m.–8:00 p.m., Sunday 8:00 a.m.–7:00 p.m. (May–September)

Groceries, deli, produce, and organic choices in one locally owned spot. Also owners of the True Value convenience store on Main Street, where lattes and snacks can be purchased. Free dockside delivery, too.

MEDICAL CARE

Petersburg Medical Center
103 Fram St., Petersburg, AK 99833
(907) 772-4291
www.pmc-health.com

A thirteen-bed hospital with emergency services.

Petersburg Rexall Drug Inc.
215 Nordic Dr., Petersburg, AK 99833
(907) 772-3265
www.petersburgrexall.com
Open daily, but hours vary. Call for seasonal hours.

Medical equipment, supplies, and prescriptions.

LODGING
Petersburg welcomes children with open arms since families who visit during a vacation are often of the most adventurous sort.

Hotels/Motels

Scandia House $$
110 Nordic Dr., Petersburg, AK 99833
(800) 722-5006, (907) 722-4281
www.scandiahousehotel.com, info@scandiahousehotel.com

With thirty-three rooms right in the heart of downtown, Scandia House is just a short walk from the ferry dock. Private kitchen, free continental breakfast, and kids under twelve stay free. Rent a small skiff to explore the shorelines, if you wish, or toss a line in the water. Smoking and nonsmoking rooms available, so be specific when making reservations. Courtesy van available for hiking or airport shuttle.

Thumbs-up: Norwegian atmosphere, hosts, location, and access to kitchen

The Tides Inn $$
307 N. 1st St., Petersburg, AK 99833
(800) 665-8433, (907) 772-4288
www.TidesInnAlaska.com, tidesinn@alaska.com

Also located downtown, the Tides Inn offers affordable lodging with forty-five rooms, a free continental breakfast. Children eleven and under stay free. Access to Avis car rental services is also an option. All rooms have Wi-Fi, and some have kitchenettes. Walk to local restaurants, the museum, and ferry dock. This is a smoking and nonsmoking establishment.

Thumbs-up: Affordability, access to downtown and activities

Vacation Rental

Broom Hus Vacation Rental $$-$$$
411 S. Nordic Dr., Petersburg, AK 99833
(907) 722-3459
Broomhus.com, broomhus@aptalaska.net

Charming, spacious, and close to activities, this home sleeps up to six people with a kitchen, baths, and free continental breakfast provided. Located approximately five minutes from harbor and ferry dock. Transportation is available.

Thumbs-up: Old-town Petersburg charm, full kitchen, independence for families

Camping/RV

Ohmer Creek Campground
Mile 22 Mitkof Highway, Petersburg, AK 99833
(907) 772-3871
www.fs.fed.us/r10/tongass/recreation/rec_facilities/psgerc.htm
Fee structure changes each year, so see website for current information and rates

A ten-site RV/tent campground operated by the Tongass National Forest, this area offers no power or water for RVs. Potable water and pit toilets are available. Hike the short Ohmer Creek trail (0.25 mile) through a temperate rain forest.

Thumbs-up: Nature trail and quiet, USFS-maintained sites

FEEDING THE FAMILY
Petersburg has a nice lineup of kid-friendly eating establishments ranging from traditional fish and chips to chowder houses and good old french fries.

Coastal Cold Storage $-$$
306 N. Nordic Dr., Petersburg, AK 99833
(877) 257-4746, (907) 772-4177
Open Monday–Saturday 6:00 a.m.–7:00 p.m., Sunday 7:00 a.m.–2:00 p.m. (summer); Monday–Saturday 7:00 a.m.–2:00 p.m. (fall and winter)

Grab-and-go fish and chips, shrimp, clams, and sometimes oysters. Free Wi-Fi stop for those who need to check in with the rest of the world. Also the place to ship seafood back home. No spring hours because they're all out fishing. **Note:** Not a lot of indoor seating, so take-away dining is often the best option.

Inga's Galley $$
104 Nordic Dr., Petersburg, AK 99833
(907) 772-2090
ingasgalley@gmail.com
Open Monday–Friday 11:00 a.m.–8:00 p.m., Saturday 11:00 a.m.–7:00 p.m.

Located in a tiny shack without much in the way of outdoor seating, Inga's doesn't look like it would serve gourmet seafood, but that it does. Rockfish and chips, excellent burgers, and smoked salmon chowder. Some kids may not appreciate the extent of Inga's menu, but our son did okay with what was listed, mostly the fries.

Helse Restaurant $-$$
13 Sing Lee Alley, Petersburg, AK 99833
(907) 772-3444
Open Monday–Friday 8:00 a.m.–5:00 p.m., Saturday 10:00 a.m.–3:00 p.m.

Helse's is the locals' hangout. Open all year, it features homemade bread, soups, sandwiches, and ice cream, in addition to espresso and coffee.

FAMILY FUN IN PETERSBURG
Even if you only step off the ferry temporarily, Petersburg is worth a walk-through. Its charm and low-key atmosphere may be just what your family needs.

Museums and Cultural Experiences

Clausen Memorial Museum $$
203 Fram St., Petersburg, AK 99833
(907) 772-3598
www.clausenmuseum.org
Open Monday–Saturday (May–September), hours vary, so call ahead
$3/person, free for kids 12 and under

A nice little museum for kids in elementary school on up, it offers an informative layout of Alaska Native cultural history and a background into Petersburg's rich fishing industry. A few blocks uphill from the ferry dock, it's also an excellent way to stretch legs before reboarding the boat.

Sandy Beach Petroglyphs and Prehistoric Fish Traps

If you have time, make the hike from downtown to Sandy Beach (located at Sandy Beach Road and Haugen Drive) and witness two ancient symbols of life so long ago. Managed by the US Forest Service, both the fish traps and petroglyphs are amazing reminders of Alaska's history. It's difficult to see the fish traps, so go at low tide and bring along the informational flyer and map provided by the USFS office downtown (12 N. Nordic Dr.). Remind all in your party to tread lightly to avoid damaging the wood pieces of the traps.

Outdoor Recreation

WALKING AND HIKING

Short on time? Take a quick **walking tour** of downtown Petersburg that starts at the ferry terminal. Stop by the **Sons of Norway Hall** and see the beautiful rosemaling designs (flowery decoration on shutters), view the cool Viking ship next door, and see **Hammer Slough**, full of squawking gulls and the occasional sea lion near the boat docks. Allow about an hour.

A longer walk takes visitors up Excel Street, past the old Lutheran Church, and to the community ball fields and skate park. Here two options are available: One takes a right onto a **short nature trail** and boardwalk that winds through a wetland for about three-quarters of a mile. Watch for Sitka black-tailed deer here. The other option is to head left at the ball fields and walk the **Hungry Point Trail** through a muskeg meadow filled with skunk cabbage, wildflowers, and the occasional blueberry patch. Look for nice views of the mountains, too. Great for jogging strollers or new walkers, and even big kids will appreciate the sights. The hike is about forty minutes one way, so either arrange for pick up by taxi at the end, or take a left at Sandy Beach, arriving downtown along the waterfront sidewalks.

Be sure to stop by **Outlook Park**, located along Sandy Beach Road, about halfway between Hungry Point and Sandy Beach Park. Take a picnic lunch to the timber-frame shelter, built to model a Norwegian stave church, and peer through telescopes to spy whales, icebergs, and busy sea lions. Also see if Devils Thumb is sticking up from the Coast Mountains. It's not always visible due to cloud cover.

FISHING

The easiest way for kids to experience fishing in Petersburg is to drop their own line in the calm waters off the **harbor docks**. Besides the obvious affordability of such a venture, it's also a great way to look for sea lions, jellyfish, anemones, and other marine life that floats and swims these parts. Pick up gear at Hammer & Wikan True Value store or the Trading Union on Nordic Drive. No license is required for kids under fourteen. **Note:** South Harbor is a fun place to fish. Boats are lined up in a cornucopia of colors, and old-timers love to talk with youngsters.

Kake (KAE): Cultural Traditions

On the north end of Kupreanof Island, just around the corner from Frederick Sound's whale-rich waters, sits the little village of Kake, Alaska. Only thirty-eight miles from Petersburg as the raven flies, Kake is home to around 650 residents, mostly Alaska Native Tlingit members of the Kake tribe. As with many of the smaller ports along the Alaska Marine Highway, Kake's size and location rely upon the ferry system for transportation, delivery of goods, and now, tourism.

Living a subsistence lifestyle bolstered by logging and fishing, Kake residents have a pretty quiet existence, but it wasn't always this way. The Kake have always been fiercely protective of their home and the surrounding waterway of Keku Strait, a major trade route for the tribe and others in the area. When, in 1869, a band of early explorers scuffled with a member of the tribe and killed him, the resulting chaos caused a US Navy vessel, the USS *Saginaw*, to sail in and regain control of trade routes. A cannery was built in Kake around 1912, and it operated through 1977, exhausting its workers by pushing them to process tons and tons of salmon without much regard for safety or working conditions. In decrepit condition now, the cannery remains a staple of Kake's history, and there is a movement to preserve the eighteen buildings on the cannery site.

Today residents of Kake are still protective of their homeland, relying upon the sea and each other to provide sustenance while opening their

Sitka (SIT): Culture, History, and Commerce

Located on the western coast of Baranof Island, Sitka represents the best of a community full of opportunities for learning about Alaska's cultural history. The Tlingit people have thrived on Baranof Island for more than ten thousand years, finding the temperate rain forest ideal for living off the land and sea. When Vitus Bering arrived with his expedition team in 1741, he quickly saw the value of the sheltered bays and abundant game and planted the Russian flag. A fort quickly followed and so did the ire of the local Tlingits, who destroyed the New Archangel settlement in a bitter battle, which in turn led to back-and-forth fighting until 1808.

village to visitors who wish to know more about the Tlingit culture and Alaska. The ferry stops in Kake twice a week headed north- and southbound, often long enough for passengers to disembark for a bit of exploration in the town.

One thing ferry passengers are sure to see is an enormous totem pole standing on the crest of a hill just above the town. At 132 feet in height, it is the tallest totem pole in the world and was constructed by the tribe in 1967.

Kake is an independent traveler's dream, with excellent kayaking, fishing, and hiking opportunities close to town and within the Tebenkof Bay Wilderness. Big John Bay Trail and Goose Lake are popular hikes, and the Dog Salmon Festival is a local staple event celebrating the return of the dog, or chum, salmon

Wildlife abounds in and around Kake, with humpback whales frequenting the area as they feed on rich krill, and bears wandering the length and width of Kupreanof Island's mountains and beaches. Stop by Gunnuck Creek Fish Hatchery, in fact, to see black bears watching for salmon spawning in the chilly waters.

Those wishing to spend the night in Kake have one option in the form of **Keex Kwaan Lodge**, a small property featuring Wi-Fi, a breakfast buffet, and access to fishing charters (www.kakealaska.com, 907-723-8386).

Sitka then became the capital of Russian America, a swath of land that extended from Fort Ross, California, all the way to the far northern reaches of Alaska.

The Alaska Marine Highway stops in Sitka seven days a week during the summer months, reinforcing its value as a port community for both visitors and residents. Of all the Southeast Alaska communities our family has visited, Sitka somehow manages to charm us every time we set foot upon its damp and spongy soil. Whether hiking through forests hiding stately totem poles or watching a dance troupe perform rousing Russian numbers, it's pretty much guaranteed that everyone will find something to do, no matter their age.

ARRIVING

Yep, you guessed it: Sitka is accessible only by boat or airplane. **Alaska Airlines** (www.alaskaair.com, 1-800-252-7522) has daily service from either Seattle or Anchorage. If you decide to begin or end your Alaska Marine Highway trip in Sitka, the convenience of daily service means more flexibility in an itinerary. The ferry dock, like so many others in Alaska, is located several miles out of town, and ferries often arrive or depart late at night. Below are a few options for navigating the transportation system and private carriers who know Sitka's ferry schedules like clockwork.

GETTING AROUND

For a smallish town, Sitka has some great transportation options, mostly due to the arrival of a few large cruise ships each summer. Escape the crowds and find solitude by renting a car. Sitka has one and only car rental option with **North Star Rent-a-Car**, located at Rocky Gutierrez Airport at 600 C Airport Road (1-800-722-6927, 907-966-2552, www.northstar rentacar.com, nstar@alaska.net). North Star prides itself on a 100 percent smoke-free car rental experience.

Moore Taxi and Tours (907-738-3210, moorebusi@gci.net) operates from 4:00 a.m. to 11:30 p.m., providing taxi service to and from many Sitka destinations. They also provide a nice option for getting out of town and seeing sights without a formal tour company. Rates vary, so call ahead for pickup at the airport or ferry dock.

The **Visitor Transit Bus "UnTour"** (907-747-7290) operates only when the big cruise ships (i.e., those with a thousand or more passengers) are in port. A free service to move people smoothly around town, this is a great way to see the city upon arrival and to plan ahead for further adventures. Kids will enjoy stops at local attractions, too. The bus is available near the cruise ship tender docks (downtown waterfront, near the bridge) and operates until the final tenders arrive or depart each day. Call for the most current schedule, but buses generally rotate through the downtown area every twenty-five minutes or so. Look for the bright-yellow bus stop signs.

Community Ride (907-747-7103, publictransit.sitkatribe.org), Sitka's public bus system, operates Monday through Friday, 6:30 a.m.–6:30 p.m. The hourly routes cover most of the commerce areas of town, including

Walk the small boat harbor and watch fishing boats readying for their next trip. The marina is located within walking distance of downtown and is always bustling with activity.

the ferry terminal. Visit the bus system's website for the latest schedule. All buses are accessible for wheelchairs/strollers.

VISITOR INFORMATION

Harrigan Centennial Hall (330 Harbor Dr., www.cityofsitka.com/government/departments/centennial, 907-747-3225) is the epicenter of Sitka's visitor information. Located on the harbor, within full view of the beautiful scenery, this is where to find brochures, make tour arrangements, and pick up transportation for many land and sea tours. It's also close to the city's library, a great spot to relax and read for a bit of downtime.

The **Sitka Convention and Visitors Bureau** maintains the information within Centennial Hall and on a fabulous website (www.sitka.org), which has information on everything from planning a trip to finding a restaurant, not to mention some awesome pictures of Sitka from its annual photography contest.

Sitka

Population: 9,084 (2010 US Census)

Founded: In 1867 as capital of the new US territory of Alaska, but Russian traders jumped on land in 1741, and Tlingit Indians inhabited the prosperous land for more than ten thousand years prior.

Known for: Incredibly rich Alaska Native cultural history, with twenty-four local attractions listed on the National Register of Historic Places.

Interesting fact: Sitka was known as the Paris of the Pacific during the 1800s for its charming architecture and interesting allure of adventure for wealthy travelers.

Hot tip: The Alaska ferries stop here on a daily basis, so if you want to stay over a few days, this is the place.

SHOPPING/GROCERIES

Market Center
210 Baranof St., Sitka, AK 99835
(907) 747-6686

A full-service grocery and convenience store, this is a good spot to stock up on kid-friendly snacks and drinks. They also have sandwiches, salads, and a coffee shop.

MEDICAL CARE

Sitka Community Hospital
209 Moller Ave., Sitka, AK 99835
(907) 747-3241
www.sitkahospital.org

Acute, outpatient, and emergency care

Harry Race Pharmacy
106 Lincoln St., Sitka, AK 99835
(907) 747-8006
www.whitesalaska.com, whites.inc@acsalaska.net

Medical supplies, medications, and personal items

LODGING

Plenty of downtown lodging options are available for visiting families. If you're using the Alaska Marine Highway ferry, ask your hosts if they provide transportation to or from the ferry terminal. Arrival and departure times can be in the middle of the night, and it's best to know ahead of time for other arrangements if necessary.

Hotels/Motels

Sitka Hotel $$
118 Lincoln St., Sitka, AK 99835
(888) 757-3288
www.sitkahotel.net, stay@sitkahotel.net

With fifty rooms within walking distance of most of Sitka's attractions, the Sitka Hotel is clean and bright. Victoria's Restaurant is also on site, and kids under twelve stay free. Laundry, free Wi-Fi, and twenty-four-hour desk service. Front desk will assist with taxi and shuttle arrangements to airport or ferry.

Thumbs-up: Location and affordability, restaurant is a nice addition for families

Shee Atika' Totem Square Inn $$-$$$
201 Katlian St., Sitka, AK 99835
(866) 300-1353, (907) 747-3693
www.sheeatika.com, totemsquare@sheeatika.com

This Native-owned hotel and conference center is large and usually busy, so make reservations well in advance. The sixty-eight-room property is located right on the waterfront, near a large patch of grassy parkland. Shee Atika' has sixteen suites and provides Wi-Fi, an on-site restaurant called the Dock Shack, a snack center, and shuttle service to many local attractions. This is a nonsmoking hotel. The hotel can arrange fishing charters and other tours.

Thumbs-up: Proximity to Sitka attractions, full-service atmosphere, and transportation

Super 8 Sitka $$
404 Sawmill Creek Rd., Sitka, AK 99835
(907) 747-8804
www.super8.com

This thirty-five-room hotel, located a short walk from downtown, offers clean rooms with typical budget-hotel style. Kids seventeen and under stay free. Free Wi-Fi and continental breakfast, coin-op laundry facilities, and hot tub. Transportation must be arranged by you, however, so keep this in mind should you require a ride to or from attractions, ferry terminal, or airport.

Thumbs-up: Affordability and a quiet location

Bed and Breakfasts
The Sitka Bed and Breakfast Association offers a listing of B&Bs (www.accommodations-alaska.com), as does the Sitka Visitors Bureau.

Inn at Raven's Peek Bed and Breakfast $$-$$$
4260 Halibut Point Rd., Sitka, AK 99835
(907) 738-0140
www.ravenspeekbandb.com

Located five miles from downtown, this quiet and beautiful complex features one- and two-bedroom suites and a hearty Alaska breakfast served each morning. In addition, guests have the option of renting the Raven's Reveal Treehouse, nestled in a grove of spruce trees and featuring a true tree house in which to "roost" for the night. **Note:** You will need to arrange for your own transportation to and from the B&B.

Thumbs-up: The tree house, for sure. And the food, that is a close second.

Alaska Ocean View Bed and Breakfast Inn $$–$$$
1101 Edgecumbe Dr., Sitka, AK 99835
(888) 811-6870, (907) 747-8310
www.sitka-alaska-lodging.com, alaskaoceanview@gci.net

This one-suite property offers great views, a quiet atmosphere, and a nonsmoking environment. It's a bit out of town, so you'll need transportation to get here. Full breakfast; dietary needs accommodated.

Thumbs-up: Quiet location, excellent views

Vacation Rentals/Cottages

Fairweather Vacation Homes $$$
308 Monastery St., Sitka, AK 99835
(907) 747-8601
www.fairweatherdreams.com, fairweather308@gci.net

Actually two vacation rental properties near the downtown area, these are great options for families. Kitchens, living space, and easy access to all the fun stuff in Sitka make either the Fairweather or Dreaming Bear suites good choices. If you're catching a plane or ferry, you can store gear on-site.

Thumbs-up: Location, ample space, kitchens, and deck at each property

Camping/RV

Sitka Sportsman's Association RV Park $
5211 Halibut Point Rd., Sitka, AK 99835
(800) 750-4712
www.rvsitka.com

A nifty RV and tent park located next door to the Alaska Marine Highway ferry terminal and seven miles from town. Sixteen RV sites and a grassy area for tents are available at a nightly rate of $25/RV and

$19/tent. Sewer hookups, bathrooms and showers, and Wi-Fi (most of the time). Families will enjoy access to a rocky beach and kayak put-in area.

Thumbs-up: Great access to the ferry dock and waterfront, plus hot showers

Starrigavan Campground $
Tongass National Forest, Sitka Ranger District
(877) 444-6777
www.recreation.gov

Flush with opportunities to get completely away from town, Starrigavan features three loops of camping areas. Of the three loops, only eighteen spaces are available for RVs, so reserve early. Fees range from $12 to $16/night, with a fourteen-day limit. Lots of hiking nearby and a beautiful bird-viewing shelter. Also inquire about US Forest Service cabins for rent. These bare-bones cabins are available for a nominal overnight fee to save sleeping in a fabric tent, if you so desire. They go fast, though. Practice your bear-aware techniques and secure all trash and smelly items.

Thumbs-up: Scenery, remote location, and access to great hiking

FEEDING THE FAMILY
We love eating in Sitka, that's all there is to it. Children are welcome in just about every establishment. Below are a few favorites among the home team.

The Bayview Restaurant and Pub $$–$$$
407 Lincoln St., Sitka, AK 99835
(907) 747-5300
www.sitkabayviewpub.com
Open Monday–Friday 11:00 a.m.–late, Saturday–Sunday 8:00 a.m.–late

Yes, it's a sports bar, but this is no ordinary pub-and-grub. Located near the harbor, with views, great food, and very kind staff, Bayview is a winning choice for lunch or dinner any day. Breakfast is added on the weekends, with waffles, egg dishes, and kid-pleasing french toast on the menu. Speaking of kids, they have their own lineup of dishes like mac and cheese, chicken tenders, and fish and chips. Bayview also has stacks and stacks of coloring books and piles of board games and puzzles to keep young people happily occupied.

Larkspur Cafe $-$$
2 Lincoln St., Ste. 1A, Sitka, AK 99835
(907) 966-2326
www.larkspurcafe.blogspot.com
Open Monday–Tuesday 11:00 a.m.–3:00 p.m., Wednesday–Sunday 11:00 a.m.–10:00 p.m.

Occupying a restored cable house, with creaky floors and a large back porch, the Larkspur offers fresh food with a view. In the same building as locally produced Raven Radio, the funky dining room often has small concerts, so some kids might not like the loud atmosphere. But the music is fun, the food is excellent, and it's always worth a visit. We love the halibut tacos (spicy and crunchy), and the staff will adapt many items for kids, so don't be afraid to ask. My son loves to drink their fresh lemonade from a mason jar.

Pizza Express $-$$
1321 Sawmill Creek Rd., Sitka, AK 99835
(907) 966-2428
Open Monday–Saturday 11:00 a.m.–9:00 p.m., Sunday 12:00–9:00 p.m.

Eating out with kids can be tough when on vacation, but we ultimately found this restaurant to be perfect for our picky eater. Pizza Express is located in the Sawmill Creek Plaza, by the way, so look for a long strip mall. Bonus: They deliver Monday through Saturday until 10:00 p.m.

Dock Shack Café $$-$$$
201 Katlian St., Sitka, AK 99835
(907) 747-2755
www.dockshack.com
Open daily 6:00 a.m.–8:00 p.m.

Part of the Shee Atika' Totem Square Inn complex, the Dock Shack Café sells comfort food for a family. Offering a Little Bear Bites menu for kids, both portions and prices are reasonable for breakfast, lunch, and dinner. The corn dog nuggets are always a hit, as is the Little Bear Breakfast of eggs, bacon, sausages, and hash browns. Parents will also like their menu, with calamari, halibut bites, and some excellent salads.

FAMILY FUN IN SITKA

The charm of Sitka is evident. From the distant mountains to up-close Russian influences, Sitka's natural and man-made sights are quite wonderful. Stroll the neighborhoods and paved pathways around town; it's here you'll discover the essence of kid-friendliness and hospitality. Take advantage of local playgrounds and fishing holes, too, and discover why so many families consider Sitka to be just about perfect.

Museums and Cultural Experiences

Sitka Historical Society and Museum $
330 Harbor Dr., Sitka, AK 99835
(907) 747-6455
www.sitkahistory.org
Open Monday–Friday 9:00 a.m.–5:00 p.m., Saturday 10:00 a.m.–4:00 p.m.
(May–September)
$2/person

Located along the harbor front inside Centennial Hall (where you'll also find visitor information), the Sitka Historical Museum covers information and culture dating back to the community's Tlingit, Russian, and American past. A nice first stop, the museum doesn't have tons of exhibits that appeal to the under-ten crowd, but our son enjoyed the dioramas and US Navy information regarding World War II, when a small air station was built on nearby Japonski Island as protection. Suitable for kids age eight and older. **Note:** The nearby harbor, park, walking paths, and public library might be a good divide-and-conquer activity for little ones and a parent while olders get their museum fix.

Sitka National Historical Park and Sitka Cultural Center $
103 Monastery St., Sitka, AK 99835
(907) 747-0110
www.nps.gov/sitk/
Open daily 8:00 a.m.–5:00 p.m. (May–September); open daily 9:00 a.m.–3:00 p.m.
(October–April)
$4/person ages 16 and older, free October–April

The site of a bloody battle between invading Russian traders and the indigenous Tlingit Indians, the Sitka National Historical Park is a landmark place and one appealing to a wide spectrum of visitors. Walk the 110-acre property and look for towering totems that appear to be rising straight from the earth. Explore the beach and imagine yourself immersed in a fight with strangers from so far way. Step inside the cultural center and get a Junior Ranger activity booklet that helps explain the reasons behind the battle and why this site is so sacred to Sitka. Local carvers and silversmiths are often on hand to share their skills with visitors.

Note: The trails on the property are fantastic for kids and parents. Jogging strollers will be fine here. Be bear aware. Allow at least two hours for indoor and outdoor exploration, so pack snacks and drinks. The beach is awesome for looking under rocks.

Sheldon Jackson Museum $
104 College Dr., Sitka, AK 99835
(907) 747-3004
www.museums.state.ak.us/sheldon_jackson
Open daily 9:00 a.m.–5:00 p.m. (mid-May–mid-September); Tuesday–Saturday
10:00 a.m.–4:00 p.m. (mid-September–mid-May)
$5/adults, $4/seniors 65 and older; $3/adults and seniors in winter; free for kids 18 and under year-round

Part of the state of Alaska's museum system, Sheldon Jackson Museum presents a collection of items from the Reverend Jackson, a missionary who explored Alaska from the top down and eventually settled in Sitka to establish a now-closed college. The oldest museum in Alaska, the building alone is worth a visit. A round, rotunda sort of structure, kids will enjoy peering up into its rooftop. Drawer after drawer of artifacts and specimens are available to gaze upon, and children can try their hand at mat weaving, writing, and wayfinding at various stations set up around the building. This museum is suitable for kids of school age since many exhibits are fragile and/or involve reading. But it's like a big treasure box.

Castle Hill, located downtown at 100 Lincoln Street, is not a museum but rather the site of an early stronghold of the Tlingit tribe until it was taken over by the Russians and a series of structures were built upon the knob of a hill. The last, called Baranof's Castle, was the site of the transfer of Alaska to the United States in 1867, a date Sitka celebrates each year at Castle Hill. Climb the stairs or walk the graduated pathway, but however you get up there, stop for the view and to see the old cannons. Suitable for all ages.

Outdoor Recreation

Like most Southeast Alaska communities, Sitka receives a lot of rain but many sunny days, too. If you're expecting to hoof it around town, consider footwear that transitions from rocky beach to pavement to wooded trail and back again, in any sort of weather.

We like to take a break at the **community park** along the waterfront, near the corner of Davis and Lincoln Streets. Across the street is the **Sheldon Jackson Museum** and campus. Restrooms, playground equipment, and a long grassy area are at your disposal.

Whale Park is located six miles south of town, along Sawmill Creek Road. Built in 1995, the park provides an opportunity to spy humpback whales in the late fall and early spring as they migrate north or south. The park features a boardwalk, small picnic shelter, and free viewing scopes. A nice bonus is the hydrophone to listen to whales "singing" with one another.

Kayaking is fabulous in Sitka. With tons of marine wildlife, kayakers can explore a variety of sheltered areas with a guide or on their own (if experienced). Try **Sitka Sound Ocean Adventures** (www.kayaksitka .com) for a 2.5-hour paddle around the harbor and nearby islands with a guide. Recommended for kids ages six and up. The company has lots of other trips, too, so look for their signature blue bus just outside Crescent Harbor, on the dock.

Alaska Fact

In 1867 Secretary of State William H. Seward offered Russia a paltry two cents per acre for the land that eventually would be Alaska—a sum total of $7.2 million. This chunk of land was originally thought of as Seward's Folly, but thank goodness Russia said yes!

HIKING, WALKING, AND PARKS

Sitka is blessed with a wealth of trails, most of which are easily found within the city limits. Below are a few favorites. **Note:** Parents should remember their bear-aware techniques when hiking around Sitka.

Sitka National Historical Park (see above, "Museums and Cultural Experiences") features a three-quarter-mile loop trail through a spruce and hemlock forest, showcasing the many totems brought here over the years. Begin at the National Park Service building and follow the Indian River, looping back to the parking lot. The area also extends across the Indian River and around to the other side, where a picnic shelter and more trails (totaling about 1.5 miles of walking) offer great views of spawning salmon toward July and August.

Sitka's Cross Trail can be accessed either at Keet Goosh Elementary School, near Edgecumbe Street, or at Sitka High School, near Monastery Street. This refurbished trail is wide with a gravel surface that accommodates jogging strollers and new walkers nicely. It's also a great trail for mountain bikes. Spanning seven miles across the outskirts of town, this is a good choice for those who are seeking refuge from downtown and want to get in some serious miles. The trail ends at Indian River Road (another access point). For more information, visit the Sitka Trail Works website at www.sitkatrailworks.org.

Beaver Lake Trail is a wonderful first hilly hike for youngsters who have expressed interest in something other than walks along even terrain. Beaver Lake is located at the end of Sawmill Creek Road, where Blue Lake Road veers off to the left. Find this wonderfully maintained trail at the end, near Sawmill Creek itself. The first mile of this 2.9-mile round-trip hike is pretty easy but transitions into switchbacks, rocks to climb over and around, and some interesting formations created by volunteers from Sitka Trail Works. Psst—offer a treat to the one who spots the waterfall first. Suitable for kids ages five and up. This is not a trail for wheels; infants and toddlers should be in packs. **Note:** Watch smaller children as you near the lake—there is little shoreline to speak of and banks toward the water can be steep.

The Sitka black-tailed deer is one of the noisiest animals found in Alaska! These social animals sometimes sound like sheep, bleating and baaaa-hing their way through the dense coastal rain forests of Southeast Alaska.

Alaska Fact

GUIDED TOURS

While a family can easily explore Sitka on their own, if time is a factor or you'd like an interpretive approach to explore the community, we recommend **Sitka Tribal Tours** (www.sitkatours.com, 888-270-8687), who can arrange fast visits to such attractions as the Tlingit Clan House, the Alaska Raptor Center, Totem National Historical Park, and other stops of interest. Tours usually last three hours and come with narration by local Native residents. **Note:** With its on-off fast pace and typical touristy feel, this tour is best for kids old enough to handle the crowded, busy atmosphere. Strollers are allowed, but front- or backpacks would work best for infants.

OTHER ADVENTURES

Sitka Sound Science Center $
834 Lincoln St., Sitka, AK 99835
(907) 747-8878
www.sitkasoundsciencecenter.org
Open daily 9:00 a.m.–4:00 p.m. during the summer
$5/person

The Sitka Sound Science Center is located in a recently renovated concrete building along Lincoln Street, across from the Sheldon Jackson Museum, and is in the process of building itself into a top-notch facility for marine learning and research. The organization has outside tanks for young salmon and indoor touch tanks for closer exploration of the rich variety of marine creatures that call the Sitka Sound home. Young volunteers are on hand to help, making this a truly community-supported place. Great for all ages. Allow about an hour to touch and see all the fun stuff indoors and out. **Hint:** This makes a great stop on the way to or from Sitka National Historical Park.

New Archangel Dancers $
208 Smith St., Sitka, AK 99835
(907) 747-5516
www.newarchangeldancers.com
Ticket prices and show times vary; inquire via phone

Promoting Sitka's strong Russian influence, the New Archangel Dancers are a fun, colorful, always-moving part of the community's history. This all-woman troupe is famous for their handmade costumes and difficult dance moves, and I was impressed by our son's interest. Perhaps it was the whirling spins or the "Hey!" that accompanied many of the leaps and jumps. Whatever the reason, this is one hour of compelling activity. Encourage kids to ask questions at the end of the show. Many of these ladies are moms too and understand the need to inquire about why a girl is wearing boy clothes (the answer is fascinating, by the way).

Fortress of the Bear $
4639 Sawmill Creek Rd., Sitka, AK 99835
(907) 747-3032
www.fortressofthebear.org
Open daily 9:00 a.m.–5:00 p.m. (April–September)
Donations accepted

Housing rescued brown bears that as cubs found themselves alone and too small to survive, the Fortress of the Bear facility is located outside of town. On a two-acre patch of land where bears frolic below and guests stand on a platform above, the facility is working to improve the area as the bears grow and require more space. If you're going to see bears at other Southeast Alaska destinations or elsewhere in the state, I'd skip this, frankly. But if seeing brown bears up close is a must-do for your family, then stop. The bears are acclimated to their human family and can be quite funny when asking for a fish snack, much to the delight of youngsters in the crowd.

Alaska Raptor Center $$
1000 Raptor Way, Sitka, AK 99835
(800) 643-9425, (907) 747-8662
www.alaskaraptor.org
Open daily 8:00 a.m.–4:00 p.m. (May–September)
$12/adults, $6/kids 12 and under

Southeast Alaska's only rehabilitation center specifically for raptors, the Alaska Raptor Center houses eagles, hawks, owls, and other birds at its forested property outside of town. A popular stop on the cruise ship excursion route, the Raptor Center is best visited around the arrival of the motorcoach crowd (call ahead). A short introductory tour is required before you enter the rehabilitation area, where a large indoor flight center reintroduces birds to the concept of flying after illness or injury. If you join a formal tour group, staff will bring out a bird to view up close. Walk around the outside area and wander a short trail to the creek; it's worth navigating and gets you away from the crowd.

Juneau (JNU): A Capital Place to Visit

A visit to Juneau is a must for families touring Southeast, if for no other reason than to see one of two capitals in the United States inaccessible except by boat or plane. That's right, no roads lead to Juneau, which makes for interesting governing processes, and it's easy to see just how important to daily life the Alaska Marine Highway truly is. Located on the shores of Gastineau Channel in the northcentral area of the Alaska panhandle, Juneau is surrounded by high mountains, deep water, and a resourceful resident population who love their city and its quirky leadership of the rest of the state.

Juneau got an auspicious start as a gold mining camp. Two miners, Joe Juneau and Richard Harris, were sent by a Sitka mining mogul to explore the area and report back on the prospects, which were unusually good thanks to a local Tlingit chief by the name of Kowee. The Tlingit, Haida, and Tsimshian people had lived along the channel and surrounding forests for thousands of years and were generally peaceful with the newcomers. Today the Tlingit people are most numerous in the greater Juneau area. In 1880 the original town site was laid for a community by the name of Harrisburg, until Mr. Harris ticked off the local businessmen and Joe Juneau's name prevailed.

When Sitka lost clout in the early 1900s due to a decline in the fur and whaling industries, Juneau became the next in line as a territorial capital. A formal brick-and-mortar building was completed in 1929, and as Alaska grew, first as a territory and then as a state, discussion began about the overall benefit of having a capital city so far from the major centers of Alaska commerce. With Anchorage as the state's largest city, these days many government officials split time between offices in both cities, and transportation costs soar ever higher each year. Yet Juneau remains Alaska's capital city, and families who live and work there are deeply involved in their community and its rich historical significance to Alaska as a whole.

While riding the ferry to or from Juneau, take a few minutes to stand outside and think about the logistics of a state capital with only boats and one smallish airport providing transportation to the legions of politicians, lobbyists, constituents, and civil servants who spend legislative sessions in the city. Juneau is one busy place then, with people crossing streets clad in business suits and rubber boots, huddling under rain jackets or umbrellas as they rush about their day. During the summer, cruise ships dominate the landscape, sometimes with an extra ten thousand people filling those same streets looking for souvenirs, taking photos, and partaking in Alaska seafood meals while floatplanes buzz about the channel like enormous mosquitos.

I like Juneau. It's where decisions are made (or at least argued about) and the independent spirit that formed our state resides. It's also where we usually decide to begin a ferry trip, since most Southeast connections pass through the city, and access from the Lower 48 and Anchorage is easy. The city even has its own suburb in the form of Douglas Island, where a community ski area, hiking trails, beach access, and a great local pub make it definitely worth crossing the enormous concrete bridge spanning Gastineau Channel for a visit.

ARRIVING

The Alaska Marine Highway ferries arrive and depart not from downtown Juneau, actually, but from Auke Bay, a small community located about fourteen miles from the city center. It's a popular ferry dock, and transportation options are plentiful to get to Juneau proper with taxis, the local bus service, and myriad shuttles picking up and dropping off passengers from area hotels. It's a good idea to make plans in advance for your transportation, since everyone else will be doing the same thing upon arrival.

If you need to fly to Juneau to start your ferry adventure, **Alaska Airlines** (www.alaskaair.com, 1-800-252-7522) offers daily service to and from Anchorage and Seattle. The gate area of **Juneau International Airport** (www.juneau.lib.ak.us/airport) provides a small play table and a few toys for kids under five if you find yourself with extra time. Otherwise, as is

SOUTHEAST

standard at AMHS terminals, plan on arriving at the docks two hours before departure if you have a vehicle and at least one hour prior to arrival if walking aboard.

GETTING AROUND

Since Juneau has only forty-five miles of major roadway along its mountainous coastline, it's pretty easy to navigate the city and outlying areas. A great way to explore Juneau's outskirts is via rental car, offering both flexibility and opportunity to see the forests and beaches up close. Most of the rental agencies are located near the baggage claim of the Juneau airport.

Avis: 1873 Shell Simmons Drive, (907) 789-9450, www.avis.com
Budget: 1873 Shell Simmons Drive, (907) 789-4111, www.locations.budget .com/ak/juneau
Hertz: 1873 Shell Simmons Drive, (907) 789-9494, www.hertz.com

A **public bus system** is widely available throughout the borough of Juneau and into the bedroom community of Douglas, across the Gastineau Channel on Douglas Island. **Capital Transit** (www.juneau.org/capitaltransit, 907-789-6901) costs $2/adults, $1/kids ages six to eighteen, with free transfers. **Note:** Passengers must board with exact change, so carry some

Juneau

Population: 32,832 (Juneau city and borough, 2010 US Census)

Founded: In 1880, originally as Harrisburg

Known for: Alaska's capital city, accessible only by air or water

Interesting fact: The Juneau borough is larger than the state of Delaware.

Hot tip: Visit during Fourth of July celebrations, which actually begin July 3 in the nearby community of Douglas. A parade, sandcastle-building contest, and fireworks make this a true family event (www.traveljuneau .com/events).

cash if you want to take the bus. Buses are equipped with bike racks for those wanting to supplement their two-wheel tours with four on occasion.

Taxi service is available through a three-companies-in-one service. **EverGreen Taxi, Capital Cab**, and **Taku Taxi** offer one convenient number for three separate services (www.evergreentaxi.com, 907-586-2121). Call twenty-four hours a day for a traditional sedan or vans to maximize passenger and gear transportation.

VISITOR INFORMATION

Juneau Convention and Visitors Bureau operates a kiosk at Marine Park, the cruise ship terminal downtown (www.traveljuneau.com). Hours of operation are 8:00 a.m.–5:00 p.m., May–September. Information can also be found at the Juneau airport near the baggage claim area. The visitors bureau tries to keep a volunteer at the desk here to answer any questions as passengers arrive in Juneau.

SHOPPING/GROCERIES

Foodland IGA
615 W. Willoughby Ave., Juneau, AK 99801
(907) 586-3101

Formerly Alaskan and Proud Grocery, this new store offers expanded produce, meat, and deli departments to meet the needs of busy downtown shoppers. Within walking distance from most major hotels.

Safeway
3033 Vintage Blvd., Juneau, AK 99801
(907) 523-2000
local.safeway.com/ak/juneau-1820

Located along the Glacier Highway, near the Juneau airport. Offering full-service deli, coffee shop, bakery, and groceries. On the bus line as well.

MEDICAL CARE

Bartlett Regional Hospital
3260 Hospital Dr., Juneau, AK 99801
(907) 796-8900
www.bartletthospital.org

Emergency services, radiology, pharmacy, and medical supplies

LODGING

Lodging in Juneau means either staying in the middle of downtown, convenient to many local attractions, or staying on the outskirts of town, where trails, scenic vistas, and access to air transportation are available. Both areas boast a fine assortment of options, and the decision rests largely upon your schedule of activities, duration of stay, and ferry itinerary.

Downtown Juneau Hotels

Driftwood Lodge $-$$
435 Willoughby Ave., Juneau, AK 99801
(907) 586-228
www.driftwoodalaska.com, driftwood@gci.net

The Driftwood is located next door to the Alaska State Museum and within walking distance of downtown attractions. Despite a dated appearance, the property's sixty-three units are a clean and affordable option for families who want some space. We usually stay in a kitchen suite with dishes, sink and stove, and sitting room. The bedrooms are spacious and the bathrooms are clean. While nonsmoking rooms are available, there are indeed many smokers who frequent the Driftwood Lodge. Baggage storage and courtesy transportation to and from the airport or ferry are available. In-room coffee, television, and Wi-Fi (although Internet is slow, slow).

Thumbs-up: Affordability and location, open year-round

Prospector Hotel $$
375 Whittier St., Juneau, AK 99801
(907) 586-3737
www.prospectorhotel.com

Recent upgrades inside the Prospector bear mention. Located on a corner of land near Whittier Street, the Prospector offers affordable and spacious rooms with tons of convenience. A restaurant is on-site, rooms are huge, and staff is welcoming. The property is also next door to the Alaska State Museum and close to other downtown attractions. Refrigerators, microwaves, and Wi-Fi available in all sixty-two rooms.

Cribs upon request. No transportation but it's on the local bus route, and taxi service is available.

Thumbs-up: Attractive renovations, location, affordability, and space

Goldbelt Hotel Juneau $$-$$$
51 Egan Dr., Juneau, AK 99801
(888) 478-6909, (907) 586-6909
www.goldbelthotel.com

Goldbelt Hotel, with 106 rooms featuring standard and junior suites, is located near the waterfront, local transit station, small cruise ship dock, and attractions. An on-site restaurant, Zen, is a sort of Asian-fusion dining experience that my son loves. Complimentary transportation to and from the airport is available, as is in-room coffee, Wi-Fi, and, in the junior suites, a microwave and fridge. Cribs available upon request. The hotel also underwent a major renovation recently, with many upgrades to room decor and furnishings, providing a more modern appearance that was sorely needed.

Thumbs-up: Location, transportation, and a nice on-site dining option

Mendenhall Valley Hotels

Best Western Country Lane Inn $$-$$$
9300 Glacier Hwy., Juneau, AK 99801
(888) 781-5005, (907) 789-5005
www.countrylaneinn.com

Located eight miles from downtown Juneau and a short drive from the airport, the Country Lane Inn offers sixty-five nonsmoking rooms and suites to accommodate just about any family. The property is well decorated, with excellent service, a free hot breakfast, and complimentary shuttle service to airport or ferry terminals and downtown. Cribs are available, as is a microwave, coffee maker, and high-speed Internet. We appreciated the kitchenette suites, where a simple meal could be made. A great choice for families with transportation or those who want to explore the valley area. Mileage rewards available for some airlines; check with your air travel company.

Thumbs-up: Great service, free breakfast, and many amenities for guests

Vacation Homes and B&Bs

A great listing of Juneau B&Bs can be found at www.southeastalaskabnbs
.com/juneau.html, but below are two of our favorites.

Silverbow Inn $$–$$$
120 2nd St., Juneau, AK 99801
(800) 586-4146, (907) 586-4146
www.silverbowinn.com

In the heart of downtown Juneau, the Silverbow Inn has location going
for it. It's in a prime spot for exploring the city, with museums, restaurants,
and the waterfront close by. The Silverbow is also a hot tapas and wine
bar. Guests in the eleven rooms receive an evening wine and cheese social
hour every day. Wi-Fi, a rooftop garden, and Jacuzzi/sauna complete the
package. No transportation provided, but the inn is on the bus line and
taxis are very familiar with the location. **Note:** Ask about parking options
if you bring a rental car.

Thumbs-up: Location, atmosphere, great food

Alaska Cabin and Beach House $$$
3184 Indian Cove Dr., Juneau, AK 99801
(907) 523-1963
www.alaskabeachcabin.com, lodging@alaskabeachcabin.com

A more intimate option for families who want to be away from town,
this cabin–beach house combination is located in Indian Cove, near the
Alaska Marine Highway terminal. With an unobstructed view of a rocky
beach and the water beyond, this is a peaceful location. Visit the local
beach park or take the kids fishing. The house comes with a full kitchen,
pots and pans, linens, private baths, and a host of other personal touches,
which is why it's at the top end of our price range. However, for what
you'll receive in hospitality, it's worth a second glance, especially if you'll
be in Juneau more than just a few days. No transportation. Wi-Fi available. Crib upon request, well in advance. **Note:** Parents of toddlers, the
backyard area can be tricky with little ones due to a lack of fencing and
free-flowing tides coming in and going out.

Thumbs-up: Remote, quiet location; outdoor recreation; full kitchen
facilities

Camping/RV

Due to Juneau's small downtown area, campgrounds are generally located toward the Mendenhall Valley area, where the landscape is decidedly more spread out with a lot more parks and trails.

Mendenhall Lake Campground $

8510 Mendenhall Loop Rd., Juneau, AK 99801
(907) 586-5255
www.fs.fed.us/r10/tongass/recreation/rec_facilities/jnurec

Secluded and beautiful, this Tongass National Forest campground is located on Mendenhall Lake, a thirteen-mile drive from downtown Juneau. The sixty-nine-site property has a wide range of available areas, from walk-in tent sites to full-service RV slots. Each site has a fire grill, picnic table, dump site, and tent pad, with potable water and pit toilets nearby (no showers). Plan to purchase or bring your own firewood since nothing can be removed from the forest. Open May–September. From $28/night for RVs to $10/night for tent sites.

Thumbs-up: Lakeside location, variety of campsites, a lot to see nearby

Spruce Meadow RV Park $

10200 Mendenhall Loop Rd., Juneau, AK 99801
www.juneaurv.com

Spruce Meadow is near Mendenhall Glacier, just four miles away from the park. While it's outside the main downtown area, the city bus stops right outside the property, and park hosts will assist you with schedules. The park has forty-seven sites in a forested location, and it's not uncommon to see local wildlife. Kids will enjoy the chance to play on the lawn and meet other young travelers, and grown-ups will like the Wi-Fi, laundry, and free showers. I personally love this place's connection with their community: guests who donate to a local charity receive two dollars off their stay. Open all year. From $37/night for big rig spaces to $21/night for (limited) tent spaces.

Thumbs-up: Clean facilities, excellent staff, access to downtown and to Mendenhall Glacier via the bus

FEEDING THE FAMILY

Since many visitors use Juneau as either a jumping-on or jumping-off point, showing up means a desire for fresh seafood. We understand. We also understand that many kids (mine included) do not appreciate the finer points of dining on salmon or halibut, so we've offered up some variety in our Juneau restaurant section.

The Hangar $$-$$$

2 Marine Way, Ste. 106 (Merchants' Wharf Mall), Juneau, AK 99801
(907) 586-5018
www.hangaronthewharf.com, info@hangaronthewharf.com
Open Sunday–Friday 11:00 a.m.–1:00 a.m., Saturday 11:00 a.m.–3:00 a.m.

The Hangar's bar and grill is a popular hangout for hordes of visitors who, upon seeing the establishment's sign hanging waterside, run as fast as they can in the hopes of noshing on some fish and chips. They're right, for the seafood here is tasty, the atmosphere slightly nutty, and the variety just superb. Our son appreciates the simple handmade cheeseburgers, my husband likes the spicy halibut tacos, and I have a thing for the salmon burger. **Note:** For the best seating (on the window side), call ahead to make reservations. This place gets crowded when ships are in port or when it's raining—pretty much all the time in the summer.

Sandpiper Cafe $$-$$$

429 Willoughby St., Juneau, AK 99801
(907) 586-3150
Hours vary, but generally Monday–Saturday 6:00 a.m.–3:00 p.m., Sunday 6:00 a.m.–4:00 p.m.

This restaurant, while operating under odd hours and having occasional long waits, is still a favorite. Fresh ingredients and a creative menu mean a good start to your day of sightseeing, so give it a chance. A nice menu for kids features items like french toast and pancakes. Be patient and try for a table during nonpeak hours. It's worth it.

Gold Creek Salmon Bake $$$

1061 Salmon Creek Ln., Juneau, AK 99801
(800) 791-2673, (907) 789-0052
www.bestofalaskatravel.com, info@bestofalaskatravel.com
Tickets for dinner and show $42/adults, $28/kids 12 and under

Think Hawaiian luau but in a Last Frontier setting, with musicians belting out songs about Alaska's history, and you've got the gist of the Salmon Bake. Geared to the cruise ship crowd but lots of fun for kids, the bake is full of silly antics, food, and lots of forty-ninth-state kitsch. The meal features all-you-can-eat salmon, chicken, pasta, and sides plus entertainment. After dinner, wander to the campfire and roast marsh-mallows or try your hand at gold panning and give a pat on the head to the company's mascot, Mac, an enormous malamute who loves kids. Transportation provided from most downtown locations.

FAMILY FUN IN JUNEAU

As an Alaskan, I love Juneau because of its unique ability to serve as the seat of our state's government despite being located a good distance from the rest of the state. As a visitor, I love Juneau for its high-quality muse-ums, walkability, and fascinating landscape. I even love the weather. Most cruise ships spend only a few hours or, at the most, a day in Alaska's capi-tal city. Buck the trend if you can, stay for a few days, and get to know this community. The good news about traveling via the Alaska ferry system is the access you'll have to local experiences other tourists might miss. And with a daily ferry departure to so many other Alaska destinations, it's easy to schedule a little extra time without feeling stranded.

Museums and Cultural Experiences

History comes alive in Juneau, and hundreds of Alaska schoolkids make the pilgrimage here every year to see, in person, how their state was born through the efforts of a few dedicated individuals. I've listed the three best museums to visit with kids, offering a nice glimpse into the past lives of those who made the area home and those who came to find their fortune and glory.

Alaska State Museum $$
395 Whittier St., Juneau, AK 99801
(907) 465-2901
www.museums.state.ak.us
Open daily 8:30 a.m.–5:00 p.m. (May–September)
$7/adults, $6/seniors 65 and older, free for kids 18 and under

Located a short walk from the cruise ship terminal and waterfront area of downtown, this state-run museum is crammed with interesting artifacts and exhibits about Alaska's diverse past. Coming off a complete remodel (actually, more of a demolition-then-rebuild effort) that took two years, the museum has undergone a transformation. Everything is designed to be applicable to Alaska history, culture, or industry, and it even features a new and improved kids' space. This is a do-not-miss Juneau attraction, if for nothing else than to witness the newness and pride this facility affords.

Juneau-Douglas City Museum $
114 W. 4th St., Juneau, AK 99801
www.juneau.org/parkrec/museum
Open Monday–Friday 9:00 a.m.–6:00 p.m., Saturday 10:00 a.m.–5:00 p.m. (May–September)
$6/adults, $5/seniors 65 and older, free for kids 12 and under

I like this museum. It's small, cozy, and easy to navigate with kids. We usually take about a half hour to explore the space, which is nice for younger children. For school-agers, ask for a copy of the activity page upon arrival; it's full of word searches, scrambles, and other fun stuff. While the old-time photos and information about the evolution of the city of Juneau and nearby Douglas is indeed interesting, it's the mining exhibit we like best. Hands-on, noisy, and completely kid-friendly—that's what draws us here. Great for kids preschool on up.

Last Chance Mining Museum $$
1001 Basin Rd., Juneau, AK 99801
(907) 586-5338
Open daily 9:30 a.m.–12:30 p.m. and 3:30–6:30 p.m.
$4/person

Visitors, check fancy-excursion expectations at the door. Last Chance is run by a former Juneau schoolteacher on a shoestring budget because she believes everyone should know about mining in Alaska. The place is dusty and old but is the real deal as far as history is concerned. Let kids check out the tools and machinery that once supported the efforts of the world's largest hard-rock gold mine. Pan for gold along the creek and take the short hike to the actual mine sites.

Note: The museum is reached via a forty-five-minute schlep from downtown via foot (about ten minutes by car) up Gold Street and through the mountain valley to Basin Road. Plan on a lot of walking, so bring the jogging stroller or pack for little ones. Watch youngsters on the trails and near the old mine buildings.

Outdoor Recreation

Juneau has a wonderful community playground on the outskirts of town along the **Twin Lakes** park area (www.juneau.org/parkrec), just off Glacier Highway. Head toward the airport from downtown and the park will be on the right. A nice bike trail continues along the lakes and a local fishing hole is often popular with local kids. Other outdoor recreation options abound, including ziplining, kayaking, biking, boat charters, and flightseeing.

ZIPLINING

Alaska Zipline Adventures $$-$$$
110 N. Franklin St., Juneau, AK 99801
(907) 321-0947
www.alaskazip.com
Open May–September
$150/adults, $99/kids 8–12, more if jeep tour or glacier hikes are added

Located near the community of Douglas, across Gastineau Channel from Juneau, Alaska Zipline Adventures offers an exceptional canopy tour on the property of Eaglecrest Ski Area. Alaska Zipline is one of the few zipline companies allowing kids under ten or seventy pounds to participate, and we love their accessibility and attention to families. Try the Original Zipline Tour, lasting four hours and sending guests through Alaska-themed platforms. Teens will love this experience, and parents can be secure in the knowledge base of staff, who strive to make every zip safe and enjoyable.

KAYAKING

Alaska Boat and Kayak $$-$$$
P.O. Box 211202, Auke Bay, AK 99821
(907) 789-6886
www.juneaukayak.com, info@juneaukayak.com
Open May–September
$110/person, with no discounts for kids

Offering kayaking adventures around the greater Juneau area, Alaska Boat and Kayak's most family-friendly adventure is its Mendenhall Lake paddle, a self-guided tour of the glacially fed lake. This four-hour trip includes transportation from downtown Juneau, all gear, a snack, and a map of the area. For a family who enjoys kayaking on their own, this is a great way to explore a glacier up close. **Note:** If you love kayaking, this is a super trip. Children should be familiar with kayaks and proper safety techniques. The company also offers guided trips for those who'd like someone to lead the way. Check the website for a list of current tours.

BIKE RENTALS

Cycle Alaska $$
1107 W. 8th St., Juneau, AK 99801
(907) 780-2253
Open Sunday–Friday 10:00 a.m.–6:00 p.m., Saturday 9:00 a.m.–5:00 p.m.
Prices vary according to bike and duration of rental. Tours begin at $119/adults, $89/kids ages 10–12 for 4.5 hours of guided biking and sightseeing. Helmets, gloves, rain gear, and water included in rental price.

Juneau has a super bike trail system just waiting for your bigger kids to explore. Even though Cycle Alaska doesn't offer trailers or tagalongs, kids from age ten and up will enjoy a bike ride with Mom or Dad, either on a self-guided adventure or via one of their tours. If you're heading out on your own, ride along the waterfront of Franklin Street or head out on twelve miles of paved pathway along Glacier Highway. Whatever direction you choose, it's great.

GLACIER AND WILDLIFE CRUISES

There is no doubt that people come to Juneau to find whales, and even if you're traveling on the ferry, it's sometimes nice to go with the experts.

Dolphin Jet Boat Tours $$–$$$
9571 Meadow Ln., Juneau, AK 99801
(800) 719-3422, (907) 463-3422
www.dolphintours.com
Five tours per day starting at $110/adults, $85/kids, free for kids 2 and under

At three hours, these tours are great for families with wiggly kids who may not be able to handle a full- or even half-day trip on the water. A great value as well, Dolphin Tours will find the whales with their jet boats and hydrophones or you get some cash back to pocket. An onboard naturalist will keep kids and adults engaged with stories and interesting whale facts. Restrooms, heated indoor space, and binoculars available. Recommended for kids four and up.

Allen Marine Tours $$-$$$
13391 Glacier Hwy., Juneau, AK 99801
(888) 289-0081, (907) 789-0081
www.allenmarinetours.com, juneauinfo@allenmarine.com
Rates depend upon itinerary but average around $120/adults, slightly less for kiddos, call for current pricing

Just in case you haven't seen enough of the glacial beauty that defines much of Alaska, Allen Marine will take you there. Their five-hour Tracy Arm Fjord and Glacier Explorer tour is just right for families with kids. On board the company's high-speed, comfortable catamarans, everyone can relax inside if it's rainy or head up to the top decks to look at scenery unfolding off the bow. We love Allen Marine's attention to kids, with complimentary snacks and drinks, an onboard naturalist who knows how to engage youngsters, and lots of stops for photo ops. Watch for whales, seals, eagles, otters, and those beautiful blue icebergs. Suitable for all ages, do watch nonwalkers and crawlers.

FLIGHTSEEING

Era Helicopters LLC $$$
6910 N. Douglas Hwy., Juneau, AK 99801
(800) 843-1947, (907) 586-2030
www.eraflightseeing.com
From $286/person to almost $500/person for dogsled tours, call for current pricing

Era Helicopters offers families many options for cozying up to a glacier, along with plenty of exciting activities. Choose from a glacier landing expedition or a dogsled tour and really give the kids something to talk about once they return home. I'd recommend this tour for kids four and up, depending upon the child. The Glacier Adventure Tour is two hours,

SOUTHEAST

and the Dog Sled Tour is approximately three hours, which includes about thirty minutes of actual on-sled time with the dogs.

Temsco Helicopters Inc. $$$
1650 Maplesden Way, Juneau, AK 99801
(877) 789-9501, (907) 789-9501
www.temscoair.com
Call for current pricing

In 1983 Temsco was the first helicopter tour company to figure out that folks might actually enjoy a trip to gaze at a huge hunk of ice. All grown up now, Temsco offers three tours out of Juneau with views of glaciers and the Inside Passage as well as optional adventures with Alaska's beloved sled dogs. A great family tour is the fast but worthwhile Mendenhall Glacier Tour, at just under an hour. Guests will revel in the opportunity to actually stand atop the Juneau Icefield at Mendenhall Glacier and see, feel, and hear the wondrous world of ice. Dog Sled Tours consist of the same fabulous flight plus a bit more time on Mendenhall Glacier for a pooch lovefest, a total of 1.5 hours. Glacier boots are provided. Kids over four will probably do well on either of these trips.

FERRY FACT

Students from high schools within five hours of Juneau regularly take the ferry to sports and academic events. It's not uncommon to see an entire track or softball team lounging in sleeping bags on the upper decks, waiting for their arrival in Juneau for a meet or game.

Hiking, Walking, and Parks

Downtown Juneau is a fun place to explore. From steep streets crammed with vintage homes to the bustling cruise ship area, there's a lot to see on foot. Stop by the visitor kiosk at the cruise ship terminal and pick up a downtown Juneau map, which lists points of interest. Hot spots for kids include the governor's house, Alaska State Capitol, and a number of bronze statues depicting the rich history of the city and state. Some areas are reached by steep stairways, but if you have little ones in a stroller, a nice access point to upper Juneau is near the bus depot at Main Street.

Mount Roberts Tramway and Trail System $$-$$$
409 S. Franklin St., Juneau, AK 99801
(888) 820-2628, (907) 463-3412
www.goldbelttours.com
Open Monday 12:00–9:00 p.m., Tuesday–Sunday 8:00 a.m.–9:00 p.m.
(May–September)
$29/adults, $14.50/kids 6–12, free for kids 5 and under

These bright-red, totem-marked trams whisk passengers to the top of beautiful Mount Roberts for a signature Alaska experience. Located along Franklin Street at the end of the cruise ship dock, the tram is always busy and especially so when ships are in port. Our advice? Head up later in the evening or first thing in the morning to escape the crowds, and pay heed to the number of ships tied up at the dock. Once up top, hike the beautiful trails, enjoying Alaska Native carvings, wildflowers, and an incredible view. The visitor center also offers films, a gift shop, and restaurant. Many trails are accessible, so do bring the jogging stroller for shorter hikes. But if you want to go up higher, plan on a pack for infants. Our son first hiked this trail at age five and did fine.

Mendenhall Glacier Visitor Center and Trails $
8510 Mendenhall Loop Rd., Juneau, AK 99801
(907) 789-0097
www.fs.fed.us/r10/tongass/districts/mendenhall
Open Monday 11:30 a.m.–7:30 p.m., Tuesday–Sunday 8:00 a.m.–7:30 p.m. (May–September); Thursday–Sunday 10:00 a.m.–4:00 p.m. (October–April)
$3/person to enter the visitor center May–September, free entry during the off season; all outside activities are free

Mendenhall Glacier is often the first glacial view for Alaska visitors, and fortunately it's a great show-off. This towering wall of ice is fronted by a lake with bobbing blue icebergs and brave kayakers bundled against a chilly breeze. The US Forest Service has done a super job of fixing up the trails around the property, most especially the Trail of Time, where a wide, completely accessible path is full of interpretive signs to show how the glacier has retreated over time. The visitor center staff can also provide a list of other, more challenging hikes in the area, worth it if you have the time. Be sure to visit the creek too, and watch for black bears fishing along the banks. Be bear aware at all times! Everyone can enjoy this area. **Note:**

The Glacier Express shuttle runs from downtown Juneau. Check at the visitor center kiosk for current running times and prices.

Gustavus (GUS): Gateway to Glacier Bay

Just a hop by airplane across Icy Strait from Juneau (a mere fifty miles) sits the small community of Gustavus, gateway to Glacier Bay National Park. Built on the site of glacial outwash and a prime fishing and gathering ground for ancient Tlingit Indians, Gustavus offers visitors a chance to see remote Alaska, whether for a few days or just a few hours. While many cruise ship visitors and others do a quick in-and-out tour of the area, mostly to explore the national park, others wisely decide to spend a few nights, and with Alaska Marine Highway access, why not? Since only about four hundred year-round residents call Gustavus home, it's easy to capture a bit of Alaska's wonderful hospitality in this friendly community.

ARRIVING

The **Alaska Marine Highway** makes twice-weekly stops in Gustavus. The smaller MV *LeConte* travels directly to Gustavus from Juneau, and the *Kennicott* stops by the community every other week on the Cross Gulf route. If you plan to stay, however, the direct method is best, so consult AMHS reservations agents for assistance on connecting the route dots.

Alaska Airlines (www.alaskaair.com, 1-800-252-7522) flies jet service from Juneau, a flight so short you'll barely have time to hand out snacks to the kids. **Air Excursions** (www.airexcursions.com, 1-800-354-2479, 907-789-5591), a small company with service to Juneau, Gustavus, Haines, and other Southeast Alaska communities, will transport kit and caboodle multiple times a day. They also offer flightseeing, by the way.

VISITOR INFORMATION

The **Gustavus Visitor Association** (www.gustavusak.com, 907-697-2454) can provide plenty of information about lodging, transportation, and nearby activities, both in town and around Glacier Bay National Park.

LODGING

Gustavus has a number of suitable accommodations for families or groups.

Gustavus Inn $$-$$$
1270 Gustavus Rd., Gustavus, AK 99826
(800) 649-5220
www.gustavusinn.com

This is a truly Alaskan homestead experience. The hosts also own Glacier Bay Tours and Charters (see website) and can assist with arranging tours of the area, fishing trips, and kayak adventures. Borrow a bike and explore the countryside nearby or inspect the beautiful vegetable garden and flower beds. Transportation to and from the airport and ferry dock are complimentary.

Blue Heron B&B $$
1 State Dock Rd., Gustavus, AK 99826
(907) 697-2337
www.blueheronbnb.net, deb@blueheronbnb.net

Blue Heron has two cabins that lend themselves well to a family vacation. Both the Fireweed and Lupine Cabins have kitchenettes that include a microwave, toaster oven, and fridge for easier overnights with kids. Guests also have the option of showing up for a full breakfast in the main house, featuring many Alaska favorites. Bikes are available to borrow. Transportation provided to and from the airport and ferry dock.

Wild Alaska Inn $$-$$$
23 Mountain View Rd., Gustavus, AK 99826
(800) 225-0748, (907) 697-2704
www.glacierbay.biz, mail@glacier-bay.com

Inn owners will meet you at the ferry dock, spin you around the water for a whale-watching trip, and share their extensive knowledge of the area. Breakfast is included in the price, and dinner can be arranged in advance if you'd like to stay in for an evening. Take advantage of the bikes available for guests or the ten-minute drive from the national park headquarters.

Glacier Bay Lodge $$$
179 Bartlett Cove Rd., Gustavus, AK 99826
(888) 229-8687, (907) 697-4000
www.visitglacierbay.com

If you'd like to stay in the national park, this is your only hotel option. It is managed by Aramark, concessionaire of most Alaska national parks, and offers basic hotel rooms, a restaurant, gift shop, lovely lobby area with a rocky fireplace, and access to the park's activities. A park-operated day cruise also departs from this hotel, so a stay here can be worthwhile if exploring Glacier Bay National Park tops your list of must-dos. **Note**: The national park is ten miles from town, out Park Road. Transportation can be arranged at the Gustavus Airport or by calling **TLC Taxi** (907-697-2239).

FEEDING THE FAMILY
Feed the kids sandwiches, fruit, chips, and a variety of other good stuff at the **Bear Track Mercantile and Deli** (907-697-2358), located on Dock Road downtown. The **Homeshore Café** (907-697-2822), located at the Four Corners area of downtown, has awesome pizza to fill up even the heartiest eater. Or try Glacier Bay Lodge's restaurant, the **Fairweather Dining Room**, the national park's only restaurant (1-800-451-5952).

FAMILY FUN IN GUSTAVUS
Gustavus delivers casual, family-friendly activities that can be as calm or wild as you desire. Kayaking is always popular here, so try **Glacier Bay Tours and Charters** (www.gustavusinn.com, 1-800-649-5220) or **Glacier Bay Sea Kayaks** (www.glacierbayseakayaks.com, info@glacierbaysea kayaks.com, 907-697-2257). Plan on spending around $100/adult and about half that for kids for a half day of guided paddling. Bartlett Cove is a nice area for the less kayak savvy. Marine and land mammals frequent the area and the water is usually pretty calm, especially in the late afternoon hours.

Beachcombing and tidepooling can be fabulous here, so dress the kids in their wet-weather gear (even if it's sunny) and have at it, remembering, of course, to handle living things with the utmost care. See any litter? Pick it up and pack it out, preserving the beach for future visitors. Start near the Gustavus Dock and wander from there.

Go hiking along the **Nagoonberry Loop Trail**, a 2.2-mile loop trail just off of Glen's Ditch Road, close to the airport. Scenic overlooks, a gravel tread, and the Gustavus Beach are wonderful motivators for kids of all ages. Make some noise while hiking so bears and moose know you're coming.

Glacier Bay National Park (www.nps.gov/glba, 907-697-2230) is huge, bordering Canada on its northeastern side and boasting an impressive landscape of 3.3 million acres. Also one of the reasons people cruise to Alaska, Glacier Bay National Park is home to no fewer than eleven named tidewater glaciers within the park boundary, and thus the park brings thousands of visitors to their icy flanks each year.

Don't forget to explore the park from the ground, too, beginning at the visitor center, located in the Glacier Bay Lodge. Here kids can get their Junior Ranger activity book, take a guided nature walk, or investigate the interesting exhibits. Parents can receive assistance with planning their park adventure, find out about cruises, or relax in the restaurant. Local Alaska Native groups also perform on a regular basis; check at the front desk upon arrival.

A great walk or bike ride with kids is the (mostly) flat **Bartlett Lake Trail**, opened to bicycles in 2012. Follow all signage and stay on the old roadbed if you bike. If hiking, continue a loop to the Towers Trail and make a round trip. Check at the Glacier Bay National Park Visitor Center for a map. Be bear aware.

Skagway (SGY): A Gold Rush Reborn

The northernmost point of the Inside Passage is where visitors will find the small town of Skagway. Living up to its Tlingit name, which means "windy place with white caps on the water," Skagway is on the itinerary for many cruise lines and road-trippers who venture south from Anchorage or north from Canada. In fact, Skagway is one of the only Southeast Alaska cities to which one can drive (the other being nearby Haines), making the community accessible from all angles.

It's a frontier town redux, with false-front buildings, a narrow-gauge railroad, and lots of wild behavior. The famous Wyatt Earp showed up to be sheriff for a time, only to say a fast "no way" to the lawlessness of would-be gold seekers and merchants who were out to make a fast buck. Skagway swelled to almost ten thousand people in 1898, and I often wonder what the local Tlingit people, who had lived in this windy corner of the world for thousands of years, thought of all this craziness. Skagway is full of stories and interesting historical attractions that capture the active imagination of children, with enough adventure to keep them busy dawn to dark.

Ferries provide daily service to Juneau and nearby Haines, making Skagway a doable (albeit long) day trip for some and a stop along the way for most as they continue on to other adventures. At nearly five hours from Juneau, the trip is beautiful and offers plenty of opportunities for whale watching and relaxing. After arriving, we spent three days exploring Skagway and found the frontier attitude and outdoor recreation to be spectacular. Since the town is a major cruise ship port of call and is also accessible by road, accommodation and dining options are many, which makes travel with kids all that much easier.

FERRY FACT

In 2014 the Skagway ferry dock sank and service was suspended for several months while crews scrambled to rebuild.

ARRIVING

The **Alaska Marine Highway** ferry terminal is located right downtown and within walking distance of many hotels.

Driving to Skagway involves a pretty extensive itinerary, but the basic directions involve taking the Alaska Highway (Highway 1) to Whitehorse, where you'll pick up the Klondike Highway and drive 112 miles to Skagway. *The Milepost* (www.milepost.com) is an indispensable guide with information on road conditions and more. Be aware that you'll be crossing the US-Canadian border, so make sure you heed all regulations pertaining to identification and such (see chapter 1, "A Few Words about Customs"). Watch for wildlife, tour buses, bikes, and roadwork.

Skagway also has a small international airport for those who endeavor to arrive or depart via airplane. Located on Alaska Street near downtown and the ferry dock, it can be accessed easily. For flight information, contact Fjord Flying Service in Juneau (http://www.fjordflying.com).

GETTING AROUND

Skagway can be easily visited without a car. It's a small community and so many tour operators provide transportation that a vehicle is not necessary. Rent bikes from **Sockeye Cycle Company** (www.cyclealaska.com, 907-983-2851) on Fifth Street. Our family was pleased to find bikes for bigger kids, tagalongs for little ones, and helmets, gloves, and water bottles for extended rides. Biking is a great way to see the community, and Sockeye Cycle will also take guests on a guided tour as part of their package trips.

A second bike company, **Alcan Outfitters** (www.alcanoutfitters.com, 907-642-0745), rents fat-tire bikes for adults and bigger kids. These chunky bikes are popular among the mountain biking community and can provide some serious fun for teens. Located in downtown Skagway.

The headquarters for Klondike Gold Rush National Historical Park is located in downtown Skagway.

VISITOR INFORMATION

Skagway Convention and Visitors Bureau
Second and Broadway St., P.O. Box 1029, Skagway, AK 99840
(907) 983-2854
www.skagway.com, skagwayinfo@gmail.com
Open daily 8:00 a.m.–5:00 p.m. during the summer months, generally
May–September

Visit with local volunteers and pick up information and walking tour maps. The visitors bureau is located downtown in an interesting building covered with varnished tree branches, a conversation piece for sure.

SHOPPING/GROCERIES

Fairway Market IGA
Fourth and State St., Skagway, AK 99840
(907) 983-2220
www.fairwaymarket.iga.com

The usual grocery items, produce, baby products, and a bakery/deli.

MEDICAL CARE

Rasmuson Community Health Center
350 14th Ave., Skagway, AK 99840
(907) 983-2255
Open 8:00 a.m.–5:00 p.m. for basic health care needs

LODGING
Just about every overnight establishment features some of the historical aspects of Skagway's charm, but some are more appropriate for kids than others. Below are a few options, both in the downtown district and on the fringe of activities, shops, and restaurants.

Hotels/Motels

Historic Skagway Inn $$–$$$
Seventh and Broadway, P.O. Box 500, Skagway, AK 99840
(888) 752-4929, (907) 983-2289
www.skagwayinn.com, stay@skagwayinn.com

This historic retreat features a downtown location, old-world charm, and a family-run atmosphere. Guests can choose a room with a private bath (most expensive) or a shared bath. Beautiful gardens outside are steps away from shops and activities. Complimentary transportation is available, and kids twelve and under stay free. Portable crib and rollaway available and a small DVD player for children to borrow. Near the local park, too. Full hot breakfast included, and Olivia's Restaurant is on-site.

Thumbs-up: Location, historic furnishings, attention to kids

Chilkoot Trail Outpost $$$
Mile 7 Dyea Rd. along the Chilkoot Trail, P.O. Box 286, Skagway, AK 99840
(907) 983-3799
www.chilkoottrailoutpost.com, info@chilkoottrailoutpost.com

Stay in cabins or suites nestled within forested land near the Chilkoot Trail, the famous route to the goldfields during the Klondike Gold Rush of 1878. Located seven miles from downtown Skagway, this outpost boasts views of Long Bay and the beautiful Lynn Canal. Bikes are available and hitching a ride into town is easy. Check out the campfire pit with s'mores-making every night, or take a hike on the Chilkoot. A great option for those looking for seclusion and outdoor recreation, and it's worth every penny. Breakfast included.

Thumbs-up: Fabulous wooded location, access to outdoor recreation, plenty of space indoors and out

Skagway
Population: 961 (year-round residents, 2010 US Census)

Founded: In 1897 when a steamship arrived from Seattle full of gold seekers ready to find their fortunes in the mountains.

Known for: Unscrupulous activities by Randolph "Soapy" Smith, who tried to outwit local business owners and swindle them out of hard-earned money through gambling schemes, prostitution rings, and other debauchery.

Interesting fact: Skagway has one K–12 school with about 125 students.

Hot tip: Make time to travel to the former settlement of Dyea, approximately nine miles from town, for hiking, mountain biking, and a history lesson.

Sgt. Preston's Lodge $$-$$$

Sixth and State St., P.O. Box 538, Skagway, AK 99840
(866) 983-2521, (907) 983-2521
www.sgtprestonslodge.com

Sgt. Preston's is an affordable downtown lodging option. Just a block off the main downtown area, the property offers forty rooms, some larger than others but all featuring private baths. Complimentary transportation to the ferry is available, and kids twelve and under stay free. **Note:** This is a popular place for travelers with pets, so if you or your kids have animal allergies, ask about cleaning procedures.

Thumbs-up: Location, shuttle to ferry dock, kids stay free

Camping

The **Dyea Campground** (pronounced "Die-ee") is a National Park Service site and is open all year. With twenty-two lovely sand, gravel, and small-treed sites that are only $10/night Memorial Day to Labor Day (free the rest of the year), this is a fun campground with lots of free roaming areas for kids (www.nps.gov/klgo/planyourvisit/campgrounds, 907-983-9200). No hookups, but pit toilets, picnic tables, and fire rings are provided—and don't forget the bug spray. The campground is located nine miles from downtown Skagway along the Dyea Road. Be on your best bear-aware behavior.

FEEDING THE FAMILY

Most visitors are part of an organized tour from cruise ships, but if you're dining on your own, Skagway delivers some delightful restaurants.

Sugar Mamas $-$$

382 5th Ave., Skagway, AK 99840
(907) 983-2288
Open daily from 11:00 a.m.

Specializing in cupcakes, but serving other kid-pleasers too, Sugar Mamas lives up to its name. The best cupcakes in Southeast, as far as we're concerned. Try the hot dogs, burgers, and tacos, and then swing back for dessert.

Starfire $$
Fourth Ave., between Broadway and Spring St., Skagway, AK 99840
(907) 983-3663
Open Monday–Friday 11:00 a.m.–10:00 p.m., Saturday–Sunday 4:00–10:00 p.m.
(summer months, generally May–September)

After a busy day of biking, hiking, and sightseeing, our family fell into chairs at Starfire, hoping for something offering a little pep. This small restaurant may not look like much, but the perfectly seasoned Thai food turned us into believers. Patio seating in nice weather. Great service and portions are nicely presented for kids.

The Stowaway Cafe $$–$$$
205 Congress Way, Skagway, AK 99840
www.stowawaycafe.com
Open daily 10:00 a.m.–9:00 p.m.

Set in a little green house on the waterfront, the Stowaway serves diners fresh food, professional service, and hip ambiance. Our son loved the busy but happy atmosphere, and I loved the halibut bacon wrap.

Skagway Brewing Company $$
Seventh and Broadway St., Skagway, AK 99840
(907) 983-2739
www.skagwaybrewing.com
Open daily from 11:00 a.m.

Locally brewed beer, pasta, burgers, fish and chips, tater tots, and more. Also offering a great gluten-free menu. Noisy, sometimes chaotic, but oh so fun.

FAMILY FUN IN SKAGWAY
There's a lot of action in Skagway, most of it naturally centered on the gold rush. As a major cruise ship port, activities are definitely geared toward the city's younger visitors.

Museums and Cultural Experiences

Klondike Gold Rush National Historical Park
(inside the White Pass Yukon Railroad Depot)
P.O. Box 517, Skagway, AK 99840
(907) 983-2921
www.nps.gov/klgo
Open daily 8:30 a.m.–5:00 p.m. (May–September)

The National Park Service has its brand upon many a historic building in Skagway and Dyea and with positive results for visiting families. Four buildings—the White Pass Yukon Railroad Depot, Mascot Saloon Exhibit, Moore House, and Chilkoot Trail Center—are all open to the public and showcase life back in the crazy 1890s, when gold was all anybody thought about. Check out an adventure backpack filled with interesting activities that take your family all around the community on a walking tour–scavenger hunt. Kids will love the Junior Ranger Activity Center on Fourth and Broadway (open Monday–Friday 10:00 a.m.–12:00 p.m. and 1:00–3:00 p.m.). An interpretive ranger staffs the center, and kids can play games from the late 1800s, try on clothes, feel a real fur pelt, and work on that cool Junior Ranger badge.

FERRY FACT

Before the Alaska Marine Highway ferries arrived, people in Skagway wishing to visit friends or family in Haines had to drive up and over Chilkoot Pass, through Haines Junction, and down the highway, a distance of more than a hundred slow, uphill miles that took at least two extra hours, depending upon weather. The ferry cut that time down to under an hour.

White Pass Yukon Route $$–$$$
231 2nd Ave., Skagway, AK 99840
(907) 983-2734
www.wpyr.com, info@wpyr.com
Open May–September
Tickets for the three-hour round-trip journey to White Pass are $119/adults, $59.50/kids

One of the marvels of modern engineering, the White Pass Yukon Route is an authentic narrow-gauge railroad that climbs three thousand feet in a mere twenty miles. It steams through canyons, over bridges, and through tunnels to the summit of White Pass on the US-Canada border, where some excursions turn around and others continue on to Carcross, British Columbia, and the Yukon Territory community of Whitehorse (don't forget passports). Most families choose the three-hour tour to the summit and back, since there's plenty to experience. Are your kids train crazy? They'll love the chance to sit on authentic train benches or stand on the outdoor platform, smelling the coal-fired steam engine and feeling the rock and roll of the cars.

Note: This could be a tough trip for kids under three due to the lack of services and the swaying, noisy cars. Ask when cruise ships come in and choose a trip at a quiet time. Two trips per day for the three-hour White Pass trip, 8:15 a.m. and 12:45 p.m.

> **PARENT PRO TIP**
>
> If you take the White Pass Yukon Route railroad, take advantage of the opportunity to stand outside on the car's platform. The combination of chugging and puffing noise from the engine and the creaking of the car takes you back in history.
>
> —James, Anchorage resident and dad of two

Outdoor Recreation

Chilkoot Horseback Adventure $$–$$$
P.O. Box 440, Skagway, AK 99840
(907) 983-4444
www.alaskaexcursions.com
Open May–September
Around $160/person for horseback tour and transportation

Saddle up, tween and teen buckaroos, for a 3.5-hour adventure along the historic trails of yesteryear. Operated by tour company Alaska Excursions at a little ranch in the town site of Dyea, riders are transported from downtown Skagway to the corrals and spend almost two hours riding their own horses through Klondike Gold Rush National Historical Park. Your own horse? Yep. (I can almost hear the screaming of cowgirls everywhere.) Guides know the area, their horses, and how best to accompany experienced and inexperienced riders. End the tour with a sit by the fireside and some refreshments. Suitable for kids at least four foot ten (or fifty-eight inches tall). Riders must weigh less than 250 pounds. Wear long pants and long sleeves (trust me, I'm a cowgirl from way back).

Skagway Float Tours $$-$$$
P.O. Box 1321, Skagway, AK 99840
(907) 983-3688
www.skagwayfloat.com, info@skagwayfloat.com
Open May–September
Rafting, raft/hike, and raft/railroad combo tours start at $75/adults, $55/kids 12 and under. Check website for frequent specials.

A unique way to see the power of Mother Nature with respect to the gold rush days, Skagway Float Tours offers a pretty nice view from their stable rafts. A great trip with kids is the approximately two-hour Scenic River Float, a trip that takes passengers down the Taiya River, with a snack at journey's end. Look for wildlife. Two departures per day, 9:00 a.m. and 1:30 p.m. Suitable for all ages and stages. Prepare younger kids for at least twenty minutes of drive time to the put in and forty-five minutes of on-water time.

Hiking, Walking, and Parks
The Skagway Convention and Visitors Bureau has three maps to show visitors the way: a Broadway Street Map with fun facts and interesting buildings, a Trail Map showcasing the accessible trails from town and farther out, and a true Walking Tour Map for those who want to know more about the city's hot spots.

Our family enjoyed walking beyond the old rail yard to the **Gold Rush Cemetery,** where Soapy Smith and other notable (and not-so-notable) people are buried. It was a nice stroll and an interesting look at the community's history. Find it near Lower Reid Falls on any Skagway map.

Another nice walk takes visitors along Terminal Way (waterfront) to the Taiya Inlet bridge, adjacent to the little Skagway airport. Walk the bridge, then take a left onto the **Yakutania Point Trail,** hugging the coastline for almost seven miles, eventually ending up near Dyea.

Kids might like to use up a little energy at the **Molly Walsh Park and Playground** at Sixth and Broadway. It's a great place to relax (parents) and play (kids) after a busy day of sightseeing, and perhaps after one of those aforementioned cupcakes at Sugar Mamas.

The **Chilkoot Trail** begins along the road to Dyea. If you wish to day hike, take plenty of water, snacks, extra clothing, and bug spray and remember bear-aware tactics. Hike this historic trail along the Taiya River, noting the difficult tread, and talk about how tough it must have been for gold seekers to do this with a year's worth of "outfit" (food and supplies required by the Canadian government), horses, and terrible weather. Find more information and permits for camping at the National Park Service Trail Center on First and Broadway (www.nps.gov/klgo).

Haines (HNS):
Family Adventure away from the Crowds

Haines is one of those Alaska destinations that immediately captures the soul, even if you're staying only a few hours. Culturally significant to the history of Southeast Alaska from both a Native and non-Native perspective and full of outdoor recreation, Haines is a very grounded community. But the charm of this town is its people, who know each other in a neighborly way many of us have forgotten. I highly encourage at least a few hours' time in Haines, if only to walk the streets and get to know its timeless character.

ARRIVING
Haines is one of the few Southeast Alaska cities accessible by car, either from the Skagway side or via the Haines Highway from the Yukon town of Whitehorse. *The Milepost* (www.milepost.com) is an excellent tool for driving to and from Haines, providing up-to-date information about road conditions and border crossings (there will be two).

GETTING AROUND
If taking the ferry to or from Haines, be aware that the ferry terminal is about six miles from the downtown area. If you've walked aboard, local shuttle drivers can make sure you connect with your lodging, and if you've driven, take a left upon arriving to head toward town.

VISITOR INFORMATION
Once you arrive in town, stop by the **Haines Convention and Visitors Bureau** (www.haines.ak.us, hcvb@haines.ak.us), a little building at 122

Second Avenue (conveniently located near a coffee stand). Here, local volunteers and staff will point you and your kids to all sorts of low-key family fun.

SHOPPING/GROCERIES

Mountain Market
151 3rd Ave., Haines, AK 99827
(907) 766-3456
www.mountain-market.com

Organic groceries, coffee shop, cafe. A one-stop shop and a nice place to take a break.

MEDICAL CARE

Southeast Alaska Regional Health Consortium Clinic
131 1st Ave., Haines, AK 99827
(907) 766-6335

Basic medical care and consulting for more serious injuries. Call ahead before visiting.

LODGING
Haines is full of bed and breakfast–type accommodations, but these two stand out for families.

Aspen Suite Hotels $$-$$$
409 Main St., Haines, AK 99827
(907) 766-2211
www.aspenhotelsak.com

Recently constructed, this is a new fifty-room property in downtown Haines. Kitchenettes, laundry, free Wi-Fi, and other amenities make this a solid option for visitors with kids.

Hotel Halsingland $$-$$$
13 Fort Seward Dr., Haines, AK 99827
(907) 766-2000
www.hotelhalsingland.com

Located on the grounds of what once was Fort Seward, Hotel Halsingland boasts a full restaurant and bar on-site. It also has great views

SOUTHEAST

of Lynn Canal and is within walking distance to downtown. Listed on the National Historic Register, it's creaky in a most charming, lovable way.

FEEDING THE FAMILY

Dining in Haines is as equally charming as lodging. There aren't a lot of choices, and visitors will be mingling constantly with residents, so for kids, eating out is an opportunity to get to know people.

33-Mile Roadhouse $$
Mile 33 (of course) on the Haines Highway
www.33mileroadhouse.com
Open daily 10:00 a.m.–7:00 p.m.

If you can, make your way out here for burgers the size of dinner plates, french fries, and big breakfasts, too. It's been around simply forever, this place, and locals love it as much as tourists.

Fireweed Restaurant $–$$
37 Blacksmith St., Haines, AK 99827
(907) 766-3838
Open March–September 11:30 a.m.–2:30 p.m. for lunch, 4:30–9 p.m. for dinner

One of my favorites, featuring fresh-baked pizza, bread, and dessert, not to mention some great seafood. I also like that there's beer and wine for the grown-ups. It's located on the grounds of Fort Seward, so those staying up on the hill have easy access.

In May 2015 a mechanical difficulty kept the MV *Malaspina* from picking up nearly a thousand participants of the annual Great Alaska Craft Beer and Home Brew Festival in Haines. Apparently attendees took the twenty-four-hour delay in stride, some making arrangements via small planes, and others deciding to wait it out with another cold one or two. Or more.

FERRY FACT

FAMILY FUN IN HAINES

A great way to become acquainted with Haines is to explore on your own, either on foot or by bicycle. Visitors bureau staff will provide a great map of interesting sights. Rent bikes from **Sockeye Cycle Company** (www.cyclealaska.com, sockeye@cyclealaska.com, 1-877-292-4154, 907-766-2869) and pedal around Portage Cove and along Front Street, stopping at the fantastic **Tlingit Park** and the community playground, an awesome place to picnic. Walk along Front Street to Mud Bay Road and explore the historic **Fort Seward** grounds, where the US government established a military presence in 1902 to counteract ongoing border disputes between Canada and the United States. Decommissioned in the mid-1940s, the fort buildings are now private homes, an inn, restaurant, and a few shops and art galleries. Super views can be had from the upper grounds, making the uphill ride worth it.

Alaska Fact

The largest concentration of bald eagles in the United States is found near Haines, usually in the late fall months as they gather to feast on dead salmon along shore of the Chilkat River near town. People come from all over the world, usually via ferry from Juneau, to see our national bird in its natural habitat each November at the annual Haines Bald Eagle Festival.

MUSEUMS AND CULTURAL EXPERIENCES

Hammer Museum $
108 Main St., Haines, AK 99827
(907) 766-2374
www.hammermuseum.org
Open Monday–Friday 10:00 a.m.–5:00 p.m. (May–September)
$3/adults, free for kids 12 and under

Housed in a little white house in the downtown district, this museum features hammers big, small, old, and modern. It's pretty interesting to ponder the importance of the hammer over the past thousand years or so.

American Bald Eagle Foundation Center $$
113 Haines Hwy., Haines, AK 99827
(907) 766-3094
www.baldeagles.org, info@baldeagles.org
Open daily 9:00 a.m.–5:00 p.m. (May–September)
$10/adults, $5/seniors and kids 8–17, free for children 7 and under

Look into the life and habits of the state's most majestic raptors and a few of their smaller friends as well as the natural history of Southeast Alaska. This is a must-do for kids, if only to meet founder Dave Olerud, a passionate voice for the facility's museum and cultural center. Located within walking distance of downtown.

Sheldon Museum and Cultural Center $
Corner of Main and First St., Haines, AK 99827
(907) 766-2366
www.sheldonmuseum.org, director@sheldonmuseum.net
Open Monday–Friday 10:00 a.m.–5:00 p.m., Saturday–Sunday 1:00–4:00 p.m.
$5/adults, free for children 12 and under

Just up from the small boat harbor, this is a great place to capture an overall view of the Chilkat Valley's history and culture. Full of Native art, fascinating photographs from Haines's early days, and lots of local information about the geography of Haines, the Chilkat Valley, and Lynn Canal. I like this museum for kids age eight and up; some of the exhibits are not as interesting for little ones. Allow about an hour.

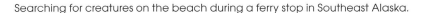

Searching for creatures on the beach during a ferry stop in Southeast Alaska.

Outdoor Recreation

Hiking is fantastic in Haines. The combination of water and enormous evergreen trees means lots of great views and some pretty fantastic terrain upon which to ply your boots. Most trailheads require transportation, but if you stop in at the visitors bureau for a map and a "Haines Is for Hikes" pamphlet, staff can direct you toward appropriate means.

Battery Point Trail is just right for kids. At 1.2 miles each way, this trail wanders the shoreline to a lovely beach that also provides access to the more challenging Mount Riley summit trail. Follow Beach Road south around Portage Cove to the end of the road. Park at the Mount Riley trailhead junction to Kelgaya Point picnic area. Watch for humpback whales feeding near the shoreline. **Note:** The trail, while mostly level, is

Hoonah (HNH)

In the past several years, the tiny Tlingit village of Hoonah has worked hard to bring tourism across Chatham Strait. Located about thirty-five air miles from Juneau, Hoonah lies on Chichagof Island and is a centuries-old home of the Huna Tlingit tribe. Originally settled in what is now Glacier Bay, the tribe moved south as glaciers advanced, eventually creating a new settlement they called Gaawt'ak, "village by the cliff."

Skilled craftsmen and navigators, the Huna Tlingit paddled the waters of Chatham Strait and nearby Cross Sound in hand-hewn canoes, hunting, fishing, and gathering the bounty of Southeast Alaska's shorelines and forests. As was the case up and down the coast, the arrival of explorers led to future settlements, including in the eventual village of Hoonah (also called Xu.naa), so-named due to its position "where the wind doesn't blow."

Salmon fishing and logging became primary sources of income for white settlers, and some Alaska Natives as well, as the construction of the Hoonah Cannery led to a fairly prosperous lifestyle. Women worked in the cannery, and men spent their days fishing in Chatham Strait and surrounding bays.

uneven and may be tough for little legs, although our son did this hike when he was three and loved it. Bring back or front packs for little ones.

Mount Riley is a longer trail and offers some fabulous views if the weather cooperates. For those who love to hike, this is a great option from the same trailhead as Battery Point. Kids should be decked out in hiking boots and have extra water, clothing, and food. Allow several hours for this seven-mile round-trip hike. Be bear aware.

Chilkoot State Recreation Site is located ten miles northeast of Haines and five miles past the Alaska ferry terminal (a right turn for those driving directly from the ferry). Situated at the south end of Chilkoot Lake at the mouth of the Chilkoot River, this is a peaceful location to kayak, canoe, fish, and watch bears enjoy the bounty of salmon spawning in the river.

Due to its location, Hoonah was also in an excellent position to serve as a rest stop for US troops and supplies transitioning between the West Coast and Hawai'i. During World War II, the US government built several "war houses" in downtown Hoonah that still stand today. In fact, when a disastrous fire nearly destroyed the village, some of those homes were offered to residents as a goodwill gesture.

Today Hoonah is on a twice-weekly schedule for the Alaska Marine Highway and has also become a stop for several large cruise lines, thanks to the reconstruction of Icy Strait Point, the original site of the salmon cannery. After millions of dollars in renovation efforts and buy-in from the Huna Totem Corporation members, Icy Strait Point and the Hoonah community now see several thousand visitors on a regular basis between May and September. For those arriving via ferry during a simultaneous cruise ship port call, a shuttle bus will transport tourists between the docks and Icy Strait Point, where tours, restaurants, and walking paths provide hours of entertainment (www.icystraitpoint.com).

SOUTHEAST

It's also a great campground. **Note:** During the summer months, be very aware of bears, especially along the riverbed, in dense brush, and near the mouth of the river. They are everywhere.

Guided Tours

If you have only a short time to spend in Haines and want to see as much of rugged Southeast as you can, it might be prudent to take a guided tour. **Rainbow Glacier Adventures** (www.tourhaines.com, joe@tourhaines.com, 1-877-766-3516, 907-766-3576) has a variety of tour packages, from kayaking to hiking to exploring the gold-mining community of Porcupine, home to the Discovery Channel's *Alaska Gold Rush*.

CROSS GULF ROUTE

Juneau—Yakutat—Whittier

Linking Southeast to Southcentral

While many passengers on board Alaska ferries choose one section of the state to explore, others decide to sail the length of Alaska's available Marine Highway coastline. The Cross Gulf route, as it is known, is a seasonal run for those wanting a longer ferry experience, or, as is the case with many people moving to or from Alaska, a way to get in or out of the state with their household goods, pets, and kids. Established in 1998 as a service route connecting the Southwest, Southcentral, and Southeast routes, the Cross Gulf is an important link in the AMHS chain, and without it, service would be much more difficult.

Truly created for transportation and not necessarily sightseeing, the Cross Gulf route is nonetheless a valuable experience for those itching to see as much of Alaska's waterways as possible. Connections to other routes are available in Ketchikan, Juneau, and Whittier, too, and options for recreation are abundant.

For most families not in the process of moving, however, the Cross Gulf route is not nearly as exciting from a scenic standpoint as the slower-paced trips using Southeast-route ferries. That said, depending upon your desired length of stay, port calls you'd like to make, and dates of travel,

AMHS reservations staff may recommend the Cross Gulf ferry aboard the MV *Kennicott*.

ADVANTAGES OF THE CROSS GULF ROUTE
- Access to Southcentral Alaska (Whittier), Prince William Sound, and miles and miles of rugged coastline and wild Alaska ocean water.
- One ferry ride means kids can have a single "home base" for the duration of their trip.
- Passengers can see the transition of environmental landscape, from rain forest to glaciers to boreal forestland.
- Depending on the time of year, passengers may spy humpback whales, shorebirds, sea lions, and orcas making their way to and from feeding grounds.

DISADVANTAGES OF THE CROSS GULF ROUTE
- A long trip with fewer stops may make for restless kids. Parents should bring plenty of games, toys, books, and electronic charging cords for this trip.
- The gulf can be rough on tummies. If you aren't sure your kids (or you) handle motion well, consider avoiding the long trek across this section of exposed ocean and opt for shorter stints between ports of call.
- Once the ferry arrives in Whittier, if passengers are not transferring to another ferry route, they will need to figure out transportation to Anchorage or other Southcentral Alaska cities. See chapter 7, Southcentral Route, for ideas.

THE VESSELS
As of this writing, the MV *Kennicott* is the vessel assigned to the Cross Gulf route, traveling between Bellingham, Washington, (see the section about Bellingham in chapter 5) and the Alaska port town of Whittier. Making fewer stops than the MVs *Columbia* or *Malaspina*, the *Kennicott*

makes calls in Prince Rupert in British Columbia, Ketchikan, Juneau, and Yakutat before crossing the Gulf of Alaska. At nearly six days, this is the longest route of the Alaska Marine Highway System.

WHERE YOU'LL GO

The Cross Gulf ferry route sails north along the same navigational points as the Southeast route between Bellingham and Ketchikan. From Ketchikan, however, the ferry picks up steam and sails north to Juneau, where it picks up passengers and vehicles making the trip across the Gulf of Alaska. Passengers will see the same charming sights as Southeast route cohorts, but with fewer minutes spent in port. From Juneau, the ferry prepares for its multiday trip to Whittier.

Only one stop is made between Juneau and Whittier—the tiny town of Yakutat, known for fishing and a seasonal influx of shorebirds that fill up Yakutat Bay. After that, it's nearly twenty-four hours of sailing before the ferry heads into scenic Prince William Sound and the funky port town of Whittier.

WHAT YOU'LL SEE

Sailing north from Juneau, passengers aboard the Cross Gulf ferry are likely to witness landforms seen by their nineteenth-century counterparts who arrived in Alaska via the steamships of old. What a thought! As the vessel swings right from Cross Sound and along coastlines of the last miles of Tongass National Forest, glaciers, and towering mountains in Canada, ask kids to imagine how the scene must have looked to those sailing this route in the late 1800s. This is wild, untamed wilderness full of unknowns, but it is the adventure of a lifetime for children, and many adults, too.

The Gulf of Alaska teems with life, ranging from small plankton and krill to enormous marine mammals like whales. It is also one of the most productive fisheries in the United States, thanks to extremely strong currents of cold water and abundant feeding grounds in bays and estuaries. Depending upon the ferry's location and the time of year, passengers may see humpback and orca whales, stellar sea lions, harbor seals, sea otters, and a wide variety of birds like puffins, cormorants, and the majestic bald eagle.

As mentioned earlier in this book, while ferry crew are not wildlife-spotting professionals per se, most of them enjoy looking for critters as much as the passengers and will eagerly point out a feeding whale or a floating sea otter mama and her pup. Bring binoculars and a camera, and take this opportunity at sea to create your own wildlife checklist. Bigger kids may enjoy browsing the NOAA Fisheries website (www.alaska fisheries.noaa.gov) for information about this unique and fragile habitat.

CULTURE

An interesting aspect of the Cross Gulf route is the opportunity to experience several distinct Alaska Native cultures. We've talked about the Tlingit, Eyak, Haida, and Tsimshian tribes of Southeast, but these groups also live as far north as the Copper River delta toward the north end of Alaska's panhandle. Similar in culture to the Pacific Coast tribes of British Columbia, Washington, and parts of Oregon, these Native groups have thrived for centuries on a sea-based, subsistence lifestyle that continues today. Sadly, the Eyak, who occupied the lands closest to the Copper River delta, were linguistically represented by one living Native speaker, Marie Smith Jones, until 2008 when she passed away, even though the tribe itself has more than five hundred registered members. Today, the Eyak Preservation Council is actively creating e-learning opportunities and hosts an Eyak Culture Camp for young people and adults who wish to bring back this culture and language before it is lost forever (www .eyakpreservationcouncil.org/eyak-culture/eyak-langauge-project/).

Closer to the terminus of the Cross Gulf route, passengers will enter the domain of Unangax (pronounced "u-nan-gan") and Alutiiq ("ah-lut-ik") maritime Native groups. These are seafaring people whose connection to the earth creates a distinctive relationship among land, weather, and water. Stretching from Prince William Sound to the end of the Aleutian Islands (more about this remote, rugged archipelago is in chapter 8, Southwest Alaska Route), the territory of the Unangax and Alutiiq are further divided into three subgroups, each ending in the suffix -*miut* meaning "the people of." Chugachmiut, or Chugach, live in the Prince William Sound area and were adept at crossing the isthmus between the Kenai Peninsula and Portage Valley and Passage Canal, where they lived for part of the year. The other groups are Unegkurmiut of Lower Kenai Peninsula, and Koniagmiut, or Kodiak people, of the Alaska Peninsula and Kodiak Island.

The Unangax and Alutiiq were masters of the *qayak* or *iqyax* (kayak), a watercraft known to sports enthusiasts around the world today. Sleek and set low to the water for speed and stealth, the qayaks of Prince William Sound and the Gulf of Alaska were made not of fiberglass and wood but of whale bone and seal skin, stitched together with gut thread and as watertight as any modern boat. While hunters would venture out into the wild waves of the gulf and beyond with others from their tribe, kayaking is primarily a solitary task, taken as a relational experience together with the sea and sky. Alone, bobbing on the waves, a hunter and his boat were in perfect harmony with the ocean, stars, or sun, speaking to one another as weather changed or as hunting grounds prospered or waned.

Yakutat (YAK): A Gulf Coast Wilderness Haven

The town of Yakutat sits between the Gulf of Alaska to the south and high mountain peaks void of any road system to the north. Oh, and glaciers tower to the east and west. About as remote as any Alaska community could be, Yakutat is a wilderness lover's dream. Surrounded by Wrangell–St. Elias National Park (the largest national park in the United States) and the Tongass National Forest, Yakutat is 220 miles southeast of Cordova and 225 miles northwest of Juneau, the closest major centers of commerce.

Yakutat is home to the annual Yakutat Tern Festival, held each year during the first weekend in June. Well-known among avid birders, the festival is full of opportunities to spy the Aleutian tern as the species makes its way to the area's breeding colonies.

Alaska Fact

With a history involving fur trade, a cannery, the timber industry, and even a bit of gold mining along black sand beaches, Yakutat today draws visitors who come to fish, hunt, and explore this rarely crowded area near Hubbard Glacier and Yakutat Bay.

The Alaska Marine Highway stops in Yakutat a few times per month on the Cross Gulf route, so ask about a port call here while making reservations, or check current ferry schedules for arrival and departure information to best fit your trip plans. If remote kayaking, fishing, and hiking appeal to your family, Yakutat may be a destination worth exploring. The **Yakutat Chamber of Commerce** (www.yakutatalaska.com) provides a comprehensive listing of lodgings and activities.

Whittier (WTR): Built for Function

Whittier is located on the northeast shore of the Kenai Peninsula, at the head of Passage Canal. Although only sixty miles from Anchorage, Whittier remains remote and elusive, thanks to high, craggy mountains preventing any sort of viable highway through the rocky expanse. The Chugach Natives would simply climb up and over these peaks, but in 1943 the surveyors of World War II built an engineering marvel: Anton Anderson Tunnel, the only highway-railroad structure of its kind, which persists as a throughway for people and materials between Whittier and Anchorage.

ARRIVING

The Alaska Marine Highway Cross Gulf route terminates in Whittier, and passengers have the option of catching a separate ferry to other destinations on the Marine Highway or traveling through the tunnel toward communities in Southcentral Alaska.

If you're beginning your ferry adventure in Whittier, there are two options to reach the terminal. You can rent a vehicle in Anchorage and drive south along the Seward Highway to Whittier, a distance of only sixty miles (one-way rentals are available). Or you can climb aboard the **Alaska Railroad**, leaving from downtown Anchorage's historic depot around 9:00 a.m. and arriving in Whittier by 11:30 a.m. Be sure the ferry

Mountains loom behind the blue waters of Prince William Sound near Whittier.

schedule jives with the train schedule, as you wouldn't want to miss the boat, literally.

If you arrived in Whittier via the ferry and without a vehicle, the same options outlined above are available to transport your family and gear to Anchorage, where most people continue their Alaska vacation or head home. The **Alaska Railroad** offers service via its Glacier Discovery Train, but only on specific dates. Check the railroad's website (www.alaska railroad.com) or call reservations agents at 1-800-544-0552 for assistance.

Avis provides one-way car rental between Whittier and Anchorage, but reservations must be made well in advance of your trip to ensure a vehicle on busy cruise ship arrival days (www.avisalaska.com/whittier, 907-440-2847).

Salmon Berry Tours (www.salmonberrytours.com, 907-278-3572) provides a Whittier to Anchorage transfer for ferry passengers, complete with a bit of touring time in between. The six-hour tour takes a trip to the Alaska Wildlife Conservation Center in Portage, stops for lunch in the quaint ski town of Girdwood, and includes a tram ride up Mount Alyeska before traveling the remaining forty-five miles to Anchorage. At $199 per person, it's an excellent introduction to Southcentral Alaska, and Salmon Berry Tours guides are well versed in accommodating children.

VISITOR INFORMATION

Whittier's location affords amazing views of glaciers, wildlife, and green forests. Most activities revolve around water: glacier and wildlife cruises, fishing, kayaking, and the like. Visit the **Greater Whittier Chamber of Commerce** website (www.whittieralaskachamber.org) for a complete listing of activities that might appeal to your family, including a tunnel access schedule and accompanying regulations.

LODGING

Hotel

Should you decide to stay in Whittier and enjoy its world-class kayaking, fishing, and off-grid exploring, there is one property that rises above all others.

The Inn at Whittier $$-$$$
5A Harbor Loop Rd., Whittier, AK 99693
(907) 472-3200
www.innatwhittier.com

Located near the entrance to the small boat harbor and cruise ship docks and within full view of the marine traffic for which Whittier is famous. Featuring a full-service restaurant, bar, and comfortable rooms, the inn is a delightful place to stay and belies the rest of this somewhat drab town.

Thumbs-up: Location, on-site restaurant

Camping/RV

Camping is available on the opposite side of the Anton Anderson Tunnel from Whittier.

Both **Williwaw** and **Black Bear Campgrounds** are operated by the Chugach National Forest and between the two offer tent and RV sites in beautiful Portage Valley. They are also well appointed with miles of biking and hiking available via the Trail of Blue Ice, a five-mile gravel path that winds around the forest and along Williwaw Creek. Be prepared for variable weather conditions any time of year, and watch for bears. These are popular campgrounds, so reservations are a must. Find out more at www .forestcamping.com/dow/alaska/chuginfo.htm.

FEEDING THE FAMILY
Whittier has a number of small establishments that serve coffee, hot chocolate, and such (and other things for adults), but listed here is our favorite.

Lazy Otter Café $-$$
Lot 2, Whittier, AK 99693
(800) 587-6887
www.lazyotter.com

Located on the boardwalk of Whittier's waterfront, the Lazy Otter offers sandwiches, wraps, soups, and boxed lunches, and they are committed to quality food, fast. They also have fabulous ice cream and milkshakes. Find them near the ferry dock, to the east, and look for a big green roof. This is the same family that owns Lazy Otter Charters, and they can box up a delicious lunch for your road trip or kayak adventure, too.

An interesting characteristic of Whittier is its approach to housing. With little infrastructure beyond the highly industrial docks and boat harbor, and due to steep mountains at their front and back doors, most residents live in the 196-unit Begich Towers (www.begichtowers.com), a tall condominium building that also houses the local school, medical clinic, post office, police department, and grocery store. During the harsh winter months, children walk through an underground tunnel, beneath a parking lot, to school.

Alaska Fact

FAMILY FUN IN WHITTIER

Phillips Cruises and Tours $$-$$$
Cliffside Marina, 100 W. Camp Rd., Whittier, AK 99693
(800) 544-0529
www.phillipscruises.com
Tours available May–September
Rates range from $123.95/adults, $13.95/ kids 2–11

CROSS GULF

Phillips offers unforgettable access to Alaska's famous glaciers and abundant wildlife through its trips from Whittier. The 26 Glacier Tour takes passengers 145 miles in five hours, showing off the glaciers by name and number, as the name suggests. A Chugach National Forest ranger is on board all ships to provide narration and help kids through the fun Junior Ranger program. Lunch consisting of chicken strips or cod fillets is also provided.

The shorter Glacier Quest tour is completed in just under four hours and takes passengers to two glaciers in Blackstone Bay and Shotgun Cove—perfect for families with smaller children or those with time constraints. Forest ranger narration and the kids' Junior Ranger program is on board this tour as well.

Lazy Otter Charters $$-$$$
East Boat Ramp, Whittier, AK 99693
(800) 587-6887
www.lazyotter.com
Tours offered March–September

A family-owned kayaking business with a solid reputation for providing quality experiences in this remote and rugged area of Alaska. Take a guided paddle or use their rental boats and explore on your own.

FERRY FACT

"It's wetter in Whittier." Or, if you prefer, "It's prettier in Whittier." Okay, maybe that's more of a statement, but both phrases apply to this unique community, and as ferry passengers, you'll want to remember rain gear so you can stand in comfort on the outer decks, watching the waterfalls, glaciers, and wildlife of Prince William Sound.

Prince William Sound Museum $
100 Whittier St., Whittier, AK 99693
(907) 472-2354
www.pwsmuseum.org
Open daily 9:00 a.m.–7:00 p.m.
$5/person

This new addition to the community, housed in the Anchor Inn Hotel, pays tribute to the valuable contributions of Whittier, past and present. It's quite fascinating to see the military port take shape in photos and witness the absolute dependence upon the railroad for delivery of goods. A new exhibit will feature explanations of the US Coast Guard's role here, all the way back to an 1898 rescue of the US whaling fleet. Definitely worth a stop while waiting for your boat or even if you're simply curious about the history and texture of this interesting port city.

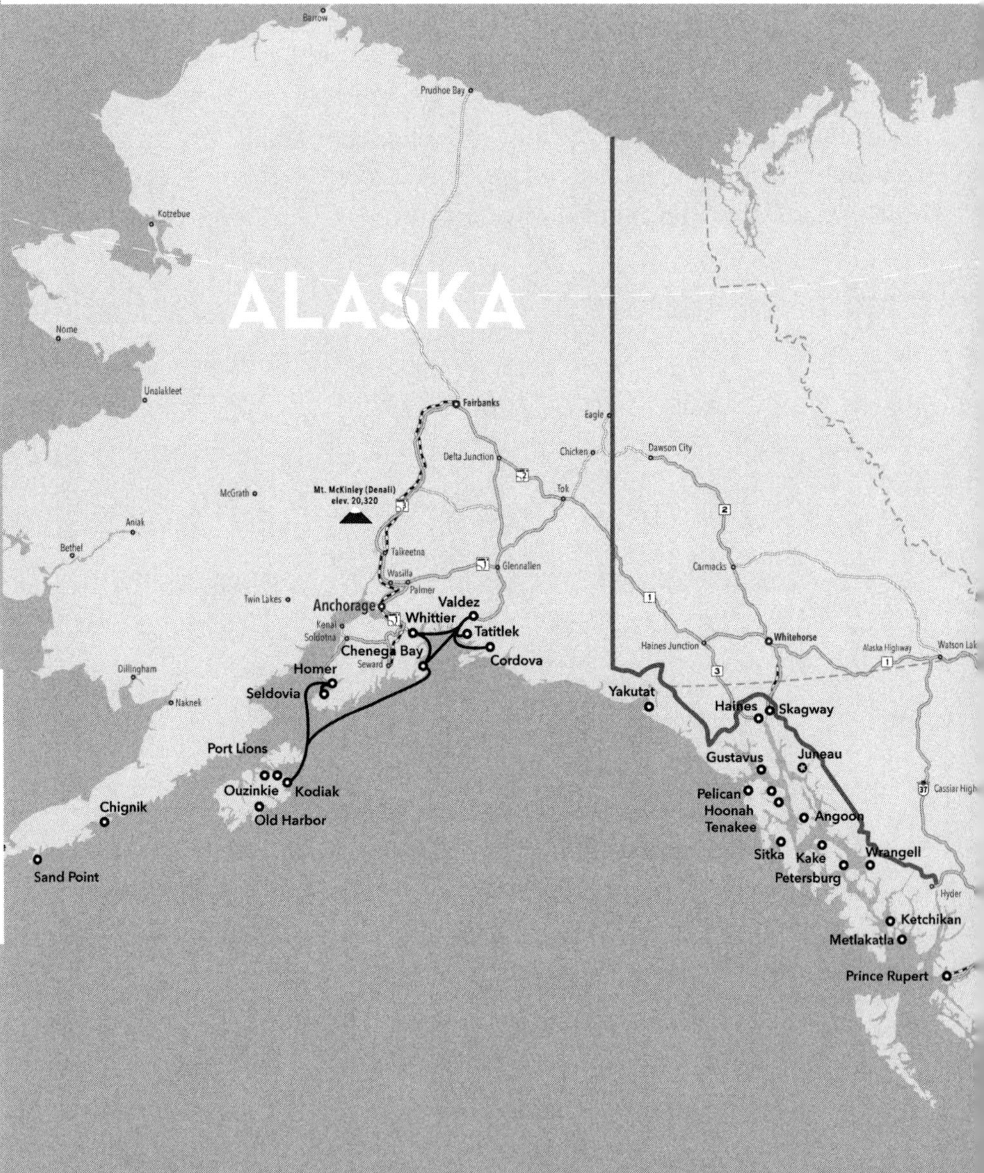
ALASKA
Barrow
Prudhoe Bay
Kotzebue
Nome
Unalakleet
Fairbanks
Eagle
Chicken
Dawson City
Delta Junction
Tok
McGrath
Mt. McKinley (Denali)
elev. 20,320
Aniak
Bethel
Talkeetna
Glennallen
Carmacks
Wasilla
Palmer
Twin Lakes
Anchorage
Valdez
Whittier
Tatitlek
Kenai
Soldotna
Chenega Bay
Seward
Cordova
Haines Junction
Whitehorse
Alaska Highway
Watson Lake
Dillingham
Homer
Seldovia
Naknek
Yakutat
Haines
Skagway
Port Lions
Gustavus
Juneau
Ouzinkie
Kodiak
Pelican
Hoonah
Tenakee
Cassiar Highway
Chignik
Old Harbor
Angoon
Sitka
Kake
Wrangell
Petersburg
Hyder
Sand Point
Ketchikan
Metlakatla
Prince Rupert
1
2
3
37

SOUTHCENTRAL ALASKA ROUTE

Homer—Seldovia—Valdez—Cordova

*We came to this new land, a boy and a man, entirely
on a dreamer's search; having had vision of a Northern
Paradise, we came to find it.*
—Rockwell Kent
Wilderness: A Journal of Quiet Adventure in Alaska

Population and Recreation

As scenic as Southeast Alaska, the Marine Highway's Southcentral route combines the beauty of Prince William Sound's glaciers and massive mountains with up-close opportunities to view wildlife, thanks to sweeping panoramas of the sound and the Gulf of Alaska. The Southcentral route also benefits visitors through a connecting road system that allows for passengers traveling with alternative transportation to combine driving with sailing, thus expanding the Alaska experience exponentially. Access to major highways linking to the rest of the state can be found in Valdez and Whittier, making the Southcentral route an excellent option for those who wish to diversify their ferry rides with road tripping and independent land touring.

THE VESSELS

Several AMHS vessels serve this busy route and often include the MVs *Tustemena*, *Chenega*, *Aurora*, and *Taku*, depending upon the season and route you choose. It is important to check with reservations agents for stateroom availability, as summer season travel in Southcentral, like Southeast, can be crowded. The MV *Chenega* is one of two Alaska Marine Highway "fast ferries" (the other is the MV *Fairweather* between Juneau and Skagway along the Southeast route), meant to shave off a few hours of travel between Whittier, Valdez, and Cordova. It is more expensive to travel this way, but if time is of the essence, the *Chenega* is a beautiful vessel that can speed along at a brisk 32 knots per hour (regular ferries travel between 17 and 20 knots).

WHERE YOU'LL GO

Unlike the Southeast route, riders of the Southcentral route generally use the ferry as a mode of transportation rather than a vacation experience. Flying between communities like Kodiak Island and the mainland is prohibitively expensive for many residents, and the ferry provides a cheaper, albeit longer, way to travel. As Southcentral ferry riders have the convenience of riding and driving, many families choose circuitous routes for vacation itineraries, looping between destinations like Valdez and Anchorage, or Homer and Kodiak, taking advantage of seasonal specials and the extra space a vehicle affords.

Families who have traveled the Cross Gulf route and wish to go even farther may pick up ferries in Whittier and continue to Valdez or Cordova along scenic Prince William Sound (necessitating a bit of backtracking, but worth the ride), or charge ahead to the island of Kodiak, and eventually the remote Aleutian Chain.

Southcentral Alaska is by far the most populated section of the state. Anchorage, Alaska's largest city, is approximately sixty miles from Whittier and houses half the state's population, and it shows during the busy summer season. Along the bustling Seward Highway connecting the Kenai Peninsula to Anchorage, cars, tour buses, RVs, and all manner of wheeled conveyances can be found along this head-turning drive north or south.

This population of residents and visitors also means that while making up your itinerary may have worked well for other ferry routes, it won't

here. Lodging reservations in nearby towns of **Seward** (www.seward
.com), **Anchorage** (www.anchorage.net), and **Homer** (www.homeralaska
.org) are a must, even for those who are camping. And arranging transportation for walk-on passengers who are disembarking is even more
important. Carefully read the recommendations in chapter 6, Cross Gulf
Route, for Whittier suggestions, and ask the visitors bureaus mentioned
here for assistance.

Seward is a former port of call for the Alaska Marine Highway, but service to this Kenai Peninsula town was discontinued at the end of 2004
due to ferry decision-makers who saw Homer and Whittier as more
than adequate.

FERRY FACT

For those sailing between Homer and Kodiak, open water dominates
the ten-hour journey. This is definitely a route upon which to consider
your family's sea legs before making reservations, as swells can be high
and weather rough. That said, a one-way trip, with a few days in the town
of Kodiak and a flight back to Anchorage, can make for a lovely long
weekend. Our favorite route? Whittier to Valdez (or reverse), driving one-
way through the scenic Glenn and Richardson Highway areas. A great
way to avoid the round-trip blues so many kids experience on a five-hour
ride anywhere, the ferry-drive combination is fantastic, and it offers lots
of fun both ways.

WHAT YOU'LL SEE
Within the Prince William Sound and Kenai Peninsula areas, the
Southcentral route teems with marine life ranging from black cod (sable-
fish) to humpback whales, the occasional fin whale, and puffins. Scenic
from every vantage point, passengers aboard the ferry have multiple
opportunities to see wildlife, marine traffic, and mountains that take the
breath away.

Sailing out of Homer means several hours cruising the final stretch of
the Kenai Peninsula from Kachemak Bay, often stopping by the tiny town
of Seldovia (www.seldovia.com), a destination unto itself. Halibut and

SOUTHCENTRAL

salmon charters as well as kayak and mountain bike enthusiasts often cross Kachemak Bay to indulge recreational pursuits in this quiet, quaint community, and a summer day often brings a rush of boats crossing paths with ferry traffic. The week of the Fourth of July, in fact, is quite the spectacle in Seldovia, making for a fun overnight adventure if you've got the time.

CULTURE

Southcentral Alaska is home to a number of Alaska Native groups, including the Dena'ina and Athabascan People, the first residents to settle around upper Cook Inlet near Anchorage during the last Ice Age of AD 500–1000. Finding the area much to their liking for communication and trade with other Native groups, the Dena'ina enjoyed their location between land and sea, living off the bounty of both. While the Southcentral region encompasses parts of the Kenai Peninsula, it was not determined that Dena'ina ventured much farther than Cook Inlet, and for the purposes of this section of the book, not into the realm of the Alaska Marine Highway's Southcentral route. It is, however, important to distinguish among this group, one of the largest in the area, from others.

As mentioned in the Cross Gulf chapter, the area of Prince William Sound and south along the Aleutian Islands is home to the Unangax (pronounced "u-nan-gan") and Alutiiq ("ah-lut-ik") tribes. Heavily influenced by Russian explorers and fur traders, the Orthodox Church holds an important cultural element to daily life, with food, worship, and even vocabulary taking on a distinct Russian-Native note.

These are people of the sea, knowing the moods of the ocean, moon, and stars and how they relate to a subsistence lifestyle. Paddlers used their kayaks for hunting, transportation, and exploration. It was the perfect man-sea connection and enabled hunters to secure food and pelts for the entire village. Today's Unangax and Alutiiq work hard to teach a younger generation about this rhythm of the ocean by which all life moves by offering culture camps to area youth.

The Unangax and Alutiiq did trade with their Dena'ina-Athabascan neighbors, along with the Yup'ik of Bristol Bay to the north, and sometimes with Ahtna Athabascans of the Copper River near Prince William

Sound, and even the Eyak and Tlingit. Research has shown that often trades were made to augment a diet rich in marine mammals, shellfish, and salmon.

As you ride the ferry through Southcentral, and perhaps toward the Southwest route, take note of the swells beneath your feet, the salty wind that shifts direction with little warning, and the position of the moon and sun overhead. Imagine paddling a kayak across this vast stretch of cold water, and take a moment to thank Mother Nature for her gift of the sea.

Homer (HOM): The End of the Road

Homer, on the southwest side of the Kenai Peninsula, is the terminus for the Sterling Highway and one of our family's favorite Alaska getaways. The Dena'ina and Alutiiq used ice-free Kachemak Bay for fishing, clamming, and transportation. When homesteaders began arriving in the 1800s and made newfound coal deposits a boon to the community after World War II, Homer established itself on the territory's map. In fact, many original homesteads are still owned and occupied by longtime Homer families, signaling a reluctance to give way to more modern dwellings. Surrounded by mountains and water, this tranquil yet busy Alaska Marine Highway

Homer
Population: 5,400 (2010 US Census)

Founded: In 1889 as a coal distribution center, but it wasn't named Homer until 1896, when Homer Pennock tried to establish the Alaska Gold Mining Company.

Known for: Halibut charters, early homesteading, and the famous Homer Spit.

Interesting fact: Storyteller and former Homer resident Tom Bodett rose to fame through his folksy tales of life at "the end of the road."

port shows off fleets of fishing boats, curious tourists, and legions of kids. It's eclectic, liberal, and a really fun place to spend time.

Besides linking to Whittier around the proverbial peninsular corner, Homer provides a gateway to Kodiak and the Alaska Marine Highway's Southwest route. Most people who travel ferries to or from here are folks with someplace to be, whether home, work, or other connections in Anchorage. Fishermen connect with seasonal jobs in Whittier or Kodiak, government employees kick off summer research projects across the gulf, and families make plans to visit relatives in other communities, toting purchases from the larger shopping communities of Homer, Soldotna, or Anchorage. It's fun to watch.

ARRIVING

Homer's ferry dock is located at the end of Homer Spit, where taxis can be found for transportation into town, or if you've brought your own vehicle,

Homer sits at the tip of the Kenai Peninsula and Kachemak Bay, and the ferry deck provides a great viewing platform.

SOUTHCENTRAL

the busy roadway awaits, especially if you'd like to connect to the rest of the Kenai Peninsula.

GETTING AROUND

Kostas Taxi Service (907-399-8008) provides ample transportation to and from the greater Homer area, and **Pioneer Car Rentals** is located at the Homer airport, a good choice for those wanting to spend time exploring this section of the peninsula (www.rentalcarhomeralaska.com, 3720 FAA Rd., #123, Homer, AK 99603, 907-235-0734).

VISITOR INFORMATION

The **Homer Chamber of Commerce** (201 Sterling Hwy., www .homeralaska.org, info@homeralaska.org, 907-235-7740) is located at the entrance to town. The chamber offers a wide range of information about lodging and activities, as well as current tide tables and fishing regulations. It is a must-stop before embarking upon further Homer adventures.

SHOPPING/GROCERIES

Homer Farmers Market
Ocean Drive, across from the laundromat
(907) 299-7540
www.homerfarmersmarket.org
Open Saturday 10:00 a.m.–3:00 p.m. (May–September), Wednesday
3:00–6:00 p.m. (July–September)

A great place to discover the treasures of this seaside town, at the farmers market you can sample homemade soup and bread or stock up on fresh veggies for your stay, all while listening to local musicians perform on a makeshift stage. The market is also a great place to buy gifts for those back home and savor the flavor of this beachside community. We dig it a lot.

Safeway
90 Sterling Hwy., Homer, AK 99603
(907) 226-1000

Find groceries, camping necessities, and deli and pharmacy items here. They also have a coffee shop and attached liquor store, and one can secure a fishing license as well.

SOUTHCENTRAL

MEDICAL CARE

South Peninsula Hospital
4300 Bartlett St., Homer, AK 99603
(866) 235-0369, (907) 235-8101
www.sphosp.com

Emergency room, pharmacy.

LODGING

Lodging options in Homer range from funky to fantastic and everything in between. Choices lie in accommodations on and off the spit and depend upon your family's tolerance for crowds and noise (usually found on the spit). Summer travelers should book well in advance, especially when traveling with children, as the most popular places fill up fast.

Hotels/Motels

Best Western Bidarka Inn $$
575 Sterling Hwy., Homer, AK 99603
(866) 685-5000
www.bidarkainn.com

Nothing fancy here but the Best Western name for quality stands true in Homer. Bidarka Inn has seventy-four rooms, with free Wi-Fi, a microwave and refrigerator, a seasonal restaurant, and year-round bar and grill. A free shuttle can transport you to and from the Homer Airport, the ferry dock, and some activities; inquire when making reservations. Children seventeen and under stay free with a paying adult, and the hotel has a free continental breakfast every morning. **Note:** This is not a smoke-free establishment, so ask about air quality management before booking if this is a concern.

Thumbs-up: Free stay for kids, shuttle service, restaurant on-site

Land's End Resort $$$
4786 Homer Spit Rd., Homer, AK 99603
(800) 478-0400
www.lands-end-resort.com

Located directly on the Homer Spit at the very end of the Sterling Highway, with an unobstructed view of Kachemak Bay and surrounding mountains. Land's End is the only lodging available on the spit and makes the most of its location with higher prices than other properties. The property is also mere steps away from the ferry dock, which is nice for families with kids who need to get to the room, stat. It is a little dated but clean and comfortable, and kids will be able to fully enjoy beachcombing or fishing from the shore.

Six different room layouts are available, including suites, so larger families will appreciate the space. Land's End rents high-end luxury condos next door. The property also features a restaurant, bar, espresso counter, and gift shop. Ask about seasonal specials.

Thumbs-up: Beachside access, great views of Kachemak Bay and boats

Driftwood Inn $-$$$
135 W. Bunnell Ave., Homer, AK 99603
(907) 235-8019
www.thedriftwoodinn.com, driftwoodinn@alaska.com

The Driftwood is located in Old Town Homer and is a favorite. This historic little inn offers clean rooms at affordable prices with the decided bonus of easy access to nearly every kid-friendly amenity one would want in a beach town. Rooms are tiny, I warn you, but you'll be too busy playing on the beach, eating, or enjoying the Driftwood's own playground to spend much time indoors anyway. Ask about early- or late-season specials, too.

Thumbs-up: Little playground, proximity to Bishop's Beach, and Old Town Homer

Cabins/Cottages
Homer boasts a wealth of opportunities for families wanting their own space combined with a little Alaskana. The **Homer Cabins and Cottages Cooperative** (www.cabinsinhomer.com, 1-888-364-0191) offers a complete listing of available places to rent for a day, a week, or longer. Some offer every luxury of home, others not so much, but you'll have to decide what your family requires.

Homer Seaside Cottages $$-$$$
128 E. Bunnell Ave., Homer, AK 99603
(907) 399-7688
www.homerseasidecottages.com, lodging@homerseasidecottages.com

These cottages provide our family with a getaway at least once or twice a year. With a cluster of three cabins of varying size in Old Town Homer (just down the street from the Driftwood Inn), Homer Seaside Cottages offer prime access to all the aforementioned goodies of the Driftwood Inn, with a full kitchen and run-around room. Well stocked with essentials, the cottages are perfect for larger families or groups of friends who want their own space but need a central location for meals or playtime. A separate and larger home, Alaska by the Sea, sits five miles east and is perfect for those wanting to truly get away. **Note:** Dogs are welcome in the Garden Shed Cottage only.

Thumbs-up: Spacious, clean, charming decor; walking distance to bakery, beach, and Islands and Ocean Visitor Center

Accommodation Alternatives

The **Homer Bed and Breakfast Association** (www.homerbedandbreakfast .com, 1-877-296-1114) is a coalition of property owners who offer a wide variety of B&B opportunities for guests. Properties' amenities for families are ever changing, so it's best to contact them directly for a current listing.

Camping/RV

Camping is to Homer what music was to Woodstock, or something like that. At any rate, there are many folks who feel a trip to Homer wouldn't be complete without a night or two spent on the beach, listening to lapping waves and watching sea otters frolic in the surf. Below are a few options for those who wish to experience Homer the old-fashioned way. Campgrounds on the Homer Spit are also closer to the ferry terminal, so the convenience factor can't be beat.

Homer Spit Campground $
4535 Homer Spit Rd., Homer, AK 99603
(907) 235-8206
stay@homerspitcampground.com
$30–$50/night, depending upon site
Open May through September or October, depending upon weather

This campground has 22 tent and 111 RV sites located at the end of the Homer Spit and in full view of the glorious mountains and Kachemak Bay. Restrooms, showers, and laundry facilities complete the package.

Note: Can be noisy at night due to the general hubbub of Homer Spit activities and a fair amount of people staying up way, way too late.

Heritage RV Park $
3550 Homer Spit Rd., Homer, AK 99603
(800) 380-7787
www.alaskaheritagervpark.com, HeritageRVPark@alaska.net
$68/night, $65/night for Alaska residents
Open mid-May–mid-September

Near the fishing lagoon and bike path, this clean, orderly, and well-managed park offers up 107 RV-only sites. A half mile of private beach makes for family memories of beachcombing and evening chats around the fire pit. Power, water, dump station, and pull-through sites. Nice gift shop and activities desk. **Note:** Ask for a beach site. Views are great, but reserve early!

Karen Hornaday Park $
Fairview Ave. and Hornaday St., Homer, AK 99603
$8/night tents, $15/night RV

Away from the beach, Karen Hornaday Park is located in the foothills of Homer, about a mile from downtown. It's quiet with a nice view of town and the surrounding neighborhoods. A bonus is the nearby playground featuring creatively designed play structures to be enjoyed by both little tykes and older kids. Adults must wait their turn to use the hand-operated backhoe in the sand pit. It's for the kids, after all. **Note:** Black bears occasionally wander through the wooded area, so heed bear safety rules and keep a clean camp.

FEEDING THE FAMILY
Homer is a culinary delight, in my opinion. From locally harvested fish, clams, and oysters to locally grown produce, Homer seeks to satisfy everyone.

Two Sisters Bakery $$–$$$
233 E. Bunnell Ave., Homer, AK 99603
(907) 235-2280
www.twosistersbakery.net
Open Monday–Friday 7:00 a.m.–6:00 p.m., Saturday–Sunday 7:00 a.m.–4:00 p.m. Dinner served Wednesday–Saturday 6:00–9:00 p.m. Winter hours vary, so call ahead.

It's hip, Two Sisters is, with wholesome food and an atmosphere of cheer to keep customers returning. Two Sisters is a stone's throw from popular Bishop's Beach, and families can enjoy a stop for hot chocolate, fresh baked goods, and excellent service. Not just about sweets, either, the establishment also offers counter-style breakfast, lunch, and dinner on Wednesdays through Sundays. A small play area off the rear porch entertains kids, and customers can watch the food being baked in brick ovens from the bar seating. Wine served at dinner.

Alaska Fact Homer's town motto is "Where the land ends and the sea begins."

Cosmic Kitchen $$-$$$
510 E. Pioneer Ave., Homer, AK 99603
(907) 235-6355
www.cosmickitchenalaska.com
Open Monday–Friday 9:00 a.m.–6:00 p.m., Saturday 9:00 a.m.–3:00 p.m.

Located on Homer's main drag, Cosmic Kitchen serves a nice variety of menu choices. Burgers, hand-cut fries, sandwiches, soups, and a great breakfast lineup satisfy even the hungriest sightseer. A fresh salsa bar nicely complements the breakfast burrito, by the way. Beer and wine. Seating is indoor or outside on the deck.

Fresh Sourdough Express Bakery and Restaurant $-$$$
1316 Ocean Dr., Homer, AK 99603
(907) 235-7571
www.freshsourdoughexpress.com

One of the most popular spots for breakfast, lunch, dinner, or a quick snack in between, Sourdough Express is on the way to Homer Spit in a small hollow that would easily be missed if it weren't for the hordes of people gathering on the front porch waiting for a table. Opened more than twenty-five years ago by a couple who wanted to create a sustainable restaurant using fresh, local foods, everything here is homegrown and homemade, from the chocolate syrup in your mocha to the raspberry jam

SOUTHCENTRAL

served with huge biscuits. Seafood is local, too. Kids will enjoy a menu just for them and the sandbox out front.

Captain Patties Fish House $$-$$$
4241 Homer Spit Rd., Homer, AK 99603
(907) 235-5135

Who comes to Homer and doesn't try fish at least once? Captain Patties is fish galore. Fried or grilled, their fish is great and the service is pretty fine, too. French fries are crisp and portions are adequate. With kids, eat lunch at Captain Patties, since dinner menu prices go way, way up. **Note:** Chefs will cook your own catch of the day if you bring it to them cleaned.

FAMILY FUN IN HOMER
It took us a while to make the most of our visits to Homer, though the community clearly welcomes children with open arms. Try the following with your crew.

Museums and Cultural Experiences

Pratt Museum $-$$
3779 Bartlett St., Homer, AK 99603
(907) 235-8635
www.prattmuseum.org
Open daily 10:00 a.m.–6:00 p.m. (May–September); Tuesday–Saturday 12:00–5:00 p.m. (October–April)
$8/adults, $6/seniors, $4/kids 6–18, $25/family of four, free for kids under 6

The only natural history museum on the Kenai Peninsula, Pratt Museum features both indoor and outdoor attractions, including the historic Harrington homestead cabin, where kids can see firsthand how folks lived without television, electric lights, and DVR. Also committed to Native culture and marine ecology, the museum provides a true understanding about who has inhabited the peninsula, when, and where. Check out the fascinating (and sobering) exhibit about the *Exxon Valdez* oil spill of 1989; older kids in particular can grasp the impact of the event on all Alaskans. Suitable for children five and older; younger kids may become restless. Ideal for school-agers and tweens and teens.

Islands and Ocean Visitor Center FREE
95 Sterling Hwy., Homer, AK 99603
(907) 235-6961
www.islandsandocean.org. info@islandsandocean.org
Open daily 9:00 a.m.–5:00 p.m. (Memorial Day–Labor Day); Tuesday–Saturday
9:00 a.m.–5:00 p.m. (Labor Day–Memorial Day)

This beautiful building overlooking Kachemak Bay Research Reserve and Beluga Slough is a must-see and is full of interesting, hands-on opportunities for kids. Better still, it's free! (Although donations are greatly appreciated.) The facility is accessible indoors and out, with restrooms, a gift shop, and many free programs throughout the year, thanks to staff from the offices of state and federal fish and wildlife agencies. Start by admiring the bronze sea lion near the entrance, then move into the interpretive exhibits, including a night and day perspective from nearby Gull Island. Embark on a short walk outside and spot sandhill cranes, moose, eagles, and a plethora of shorebirds. Volunteers can assist you with maps and other information about local flora and fauna, too. Fun for older preschoolers on up.

Center for Alaskan Coastal Studies $-$$
708 Smokey Bay Way, Homer, AK 99603
(907) 235-6667
www.akcoastalstudies.org, info@akcoastalstudies.org
Open year-round

Since 1982, the center has guided thousands of visitors toward a more intimate relationship with nature through experiential learning. While the main office is in downtown Homer, the real gems are located at Carl E. Wynn Nature Center off Skyline Drive (up on the bluffs) and across Kachemak Bay at Peterson Bay Field Station, where everyone can garner an appreciation for the unique plants, animals, and environments of the Kenai Peninsula. During the summer months, the center also opens a small yurt on the Homer Spit, where daily activities and programs are held for those who may be on a tight schedule or perhaps cannot navigate the landscape of Wynn Nature Center or Peterson Bay. Appropriate for the whole family, infants to grandparents.

Outdoor Recreation

HIKING, WALKING, AND PARKS

Kachemak Bay State Park (dnr.alaska.gov/parks/units/kbay/kbay.htm) lies across the bay from Homer. Alaska's first state park and its only wilderness park, the area features miles and miles of hiking and camping opportunities if you're willing to take an extra step to get there. With no road system, the park is accessed via floatplane or boat, easily arranged for a fee from Homer. Look for views of glaciers, wildlife, and sparkling water from the trail, but be aware that the solitude and scenery also come at a price: you are in a wilderness area with no services, so you must carry everything you need. That said, trails like China Poot, Halibut Cove Lagoon, and Grewingk Glacier are stunning reminders of the reason you came to Alaska in the first place. **Note:** Dress kids in hiking boots and layered clothing and bring plenty of snacks and water. Practice bear safety at all times. Find information about transportation to and from the park from the Homer Chamber of Commerce (www.homeralaska.org).

The **Carl E. Wynn Nature Center** (www.akcoastalstudies.org, 907-235-5266) has five miles of marked trails, ranging from boreal forest to mountain meadow, and features spectacular views of Homer, Kachemak Bay, and mountains beyond. A little log cabin acts as visitor center where you can pick up maps as well as information on plants and animals of the area. Admission fees of $7/adults and $5/kids under eighteen help keep the center maintained and beautiful for visitors. Suitable for all ages. **Note:** Mosquitoes can be fierce during the summer, so bring plenty of bug repellent and a net for stroller-bound babies.

> **PARENT PRO TIP**
>
> Visit the Wynn Nature Center. Even on a rainy day, our family enjoyed hiking the trails and exploring the log cabin. It's totally worth it.
>
> —Kathy, Wasilla resident and mom of two

Bishop's Beach is located in Old Town Homer. Popular with locals, this beach is level and accessible, and we never miss an opportunity to play here. Hike anywhere from ten minutes to two hours, exploring tide pools, interesting rocks, and the marsh from nearby Beluga Slough. The best time to visit Bishop's Beach is during low tide, when all sorts of interesting things appear and walking is easier near the waterline. **Note:** Keep track of time since tides that go out also come back in, and you wouldn't want to be stuck without a way to return to your car. (Pick up a tide table almost anywhere on the spit and at the Center for Alaska Coastal Studies.) To reach Bishop's Beach, take Sterling Highway to Main Street, turn toward the ocean, and take a left on Bunnell Avenue. Take a right on Beluga Avenue (Two Sisters Bakery is just ahead) and park in the small lot. Portable toilets and a small picnic shelter are available.

Peterson Bay Field Station (www.akcoastalstudies.org, 907-235-6667) is operated by the folks at the Center for Alaskan Coastal Studies in Homer. The field station is located across Kachemak Bay and is accessible only by boat. Built as a living laboratory, Peterson Bay features extreme low tides and thus a plethora of marine plant and animal life waiting to be explored with the help of knowledgeable staff. Daily guided hikes and natural history tours are offered Memorial Day through Labor Day with prior arrangement. Wildlife, marine mammals, and crustaceans are possible sights to see during a day spent playing at the bay. Tours range from $80 for kids 13 and under to $120 for adults and include transportation to the field station. Best for kids preschool and up, including teenagers, who will appreciate staff who challenge and engage them with great science activities. The organization also offers family camps for those wanting an overnight adventure.

FISHING CHARTERS

Halibut fishing is a bit different than salmon fishing, because halibut, unlike their active salmon counterparts, are bottom fish and are flat and funny looking. To catch a halibut requires heavy weights, a large pole, and deep water. Usually halibut charters operate under a half-day (four or five hours) or full-day (up to eight hours) schedule, which means your children will be on a boat, in potentially rough water, for a long, long time. Generally, kids ages ten and up can handle a halibut charter, but be forewarned that boats tend to leave very early in the morning and offer nothing in the way of food or beverages for clients; you're on your own for making sure kids are warm, well fed, and comfortable.

A halibut trip can be a fun bonding experience for those traveling with older kids. It's pretty neat to have your fish caught, cleaned, processed, and frozen for transport back home, and nothing says "Alaska vacation memories" quite like pulling a self-caught fillet out of the freezer come January.

Charter companies have their own rules when it comes to kids. Some are patient and willing to help children catch their limit (after all, you are the customer), but others are strictly grown-up oriented. How do you know? Ask, ask, ask. Do they have life jackets for children? What is their policy about kids on their boats? How about a canceled charter—will you get your money back? How many passengers do they allow? Can you bring toys?

BANK FISHING

The Homer Spit is ideal for saltwater fishing sans boat. Kids flock to the Nick Dudiak Fishing Lagoon, managed by the city of Homer, to reel in salmon. The lagoon has an accessible ramp, picnic tables, a fish-cleaning table, and a small restroom facility. This area can be incredibly crowded during the summer, but it's always fun. Find the Fishing Lagoon midway along the Homer Spit.

The end of the Homer Spit, near Land's End Resort and the Alaska Marine Highway System ferry docks, can also provide exciting fishing opportunities for kids. Flounder, cod, and the occasional salmon can be caught, depending upon the day.

FLIGHTSEEING AND WILDLIFE VIEWING

For some, a visit to Alaska is not complete until they've seen as many wild animals as possible. Of these, bears usually rate number one on the checklist. While it is possible to spy a brown or black bear along a salmon stream or (more likely) wandering through a neighborhood in search of an unsecured garbage can, the best way to experience a bear in a natural habitat is through a guided viewing excursion. While expensive, bear viewing and flightseeing is nonetheless a popular attraction and well worth the investment in this bucket-list experience.

Note: Flightseeing is done in a small plane that can seat up to five passengers. These planes are not equipped with any frills or fluff for families, and passengers must sit still for the duration of the flight. Wildlife viewing, too, is full of rules, and children under ten may have difficulty. It is crucial to gather information from a flightseeing company before booking. That said, older kids and teenagers generally consider flightseeing to be a highlight of an Alaska vacation.

Our favorite company is **Hallo Bay Bear Camp** (www.hallobay.com, 1-888-535-2237, 907-235-2237), a longtime company with impeccable outdoor manners for such a delicate operation as viewing bears, mountains, and seasides up close. A five-hour adventure that includes the flight over and back from Hallo Bay, located along the shores of Katmai National Park, is going to cost around $600 per person, but the experience itself is priceless. (I know; I've been several times.) Anyone participating in this trip will need to be at least ten years old, be able to walk on uneven terrain for up to two hours, and have the gumption to sit perfectly still and quiet for at least that long while bears live, work, and play in the meadows and on the beaches of their home.

Seldovia (SDV): A Place to Savor

With a mere three hundred full-time residents, Seldovia is a laid-back collection of artists, fishermen, and folks who don't want to live in the fast lane. But that doesn't mean people are lacking in the fun department. A trip to Seldovia means great hiking, biking, and exploring the ocean's treasures.

ARRIVING

Nestled in a cozy little cove, Seldovia is across Kachemak Bay from Homer. Inaccessible by car (remember, the highway ends in Homer), part of Seldovia's charm is in getting there. Pick up the ferry from Homer to Seldovia at least twice a week in the summer (once a week in the winter).

GETTING AROUND

Many people simply walk around Seldovia, as the community's size makes it easy to amble down the quiet streets and local trails. Bikes and ATVs are also common modes of transportation on the dirt roads of town. Spending the night in Seldovia? Ask your hosts about bikes to borrow or transportation to and from trailheads. Or rent a bike in Homer at Cycle Logical (3585 East End Rd., Homer, AK 99603, 907-226-2925, www.cyclelogicalhomer.com) and bring it with you to Seldovia.

VISITOR INFORMATION

Start by visiting the **Seldovia Chamber of Commerce** website (www.seldoviachamber.org) for detailed descriptions of activity ideas. We usually take the ferry and spend a few hours and return in time for a late dinner. If Seldovia is part of a larger ferry itinerary, you may or may not have time to spend in town. If you do, try a few places listed below for a bit of small-town Alaska.

LODGING

Across the Bay Tent and Breakfast Adventure Company $$-$$$
Jakolof Bay Rd., Seldovia, AK 99663
(907) 350-4636
www.tentandbreakfastalaska.com

Choose a cozy cabin or rustic wall tent and enjoy the beauty of Kachemak Bay from your doorstep. Transportation provided from the ferry. Kayak, do yoga, or simply allow the kids to play on the beach. Relaxation is guaranteed.

Seldovia Boardwalk Hotel $$-$$$
239 Main St., Seldovia, AK 99663
(907) 234-7816
www.seldoviahotel.com

With twelve private rooms near the lagoon area of town, this is the perfect place to stay if you wish to walk among the historic homes and local trails of Seldovia. Free Wi-Fi and coffee. Access to and from the ferry dock is convenient for families.

SOUTHCENTRAL

FEEDING THE FAMILY

Tide Pool Café $$
257 Main St., Seldovia, AK 99963
(907) 234-7502

Tidepool Café overlooks the harbor and is a nice place to grab some grub before heading off for other adventures. Sandwiches, fish and chips, salads, and soups are mainstays here, so kids should do just fine. The decor is fun and an adjacent bookstore makes for a nice stop pre- or post-meal.

FAMILY FUN IN SELDOVIA

Our favorite activities include a fabulous two-mile hike along the **Otterbahn Trail**, near the Seldovia school, that travels into an old-growth spruce forest, along a meadow, and ends up on a rocky, secluded beach where we've spent hours viewing otters, whales, and seabirds. Take a picnic, water, and your bear-aware behavior.

> **KIDSPEAK**
>
> I like the boat ride to Seldovia and hiking that Otter (Otterbahn) trail."
>
> —Owen, age eleven
> Southcentral route

Back in town, there is an old section of the village where homes are built over the water and you'll feel as if you've been transported back in time. A great way to experience Seldovia is via bicycle. If your lodging doesn't borrow them out, rent a bike in Anchorage or Homer or bring your own and ride miles and miles of packed dirt roads. In Anchorage: **Downtown Bicycle Rentals**, http://www.alaska-bike-rentals.com, 907-279-5293. In Homer: **Cycle Logical**, http://www.cyclelogicalhomer.com, 907-226-2925.

Small children will also find the small playground next to the boat harbor a winner. Make sure you watch for rafts of otters, humpback whales, and puffins, too.

Valdez (VDZ): Prince William Sound's Playground

Our family loves Valdez, both for the friends we've made over the years and for the amazing variety of activities we enjoy. Located in a natural fjord eleven miles from the vast waters of Prince William Sound, Valdez was originally home to the Chugach Eskimo people, who found the area's abundant wildlife and food sources to be perfect for their maritime and hunting lifestyle.

With the rush of gold seekers in 1898 pushing travelers from Port Valdez over the Chugach Mountains via Valdez Glacier, the city flourished and gradually increased in size and importance as a fishing and trade route to Interior Alaska. When black gold was discovered in the North Slope area of Prudhoe Bay in the late 1960s, Valdez was recognized as an ice-free deepwater port, and in the late 1970s, it became the endpoint for that eight-hundred-mile-long Trans-Alaska Pipeline.

Valdez has had its share of tragedy. A devastating tsunami hit Valdez after the great earthquake of 1964, a 9.1 temblor that shook almost the entire state and caused what is now Old Town Valdez to be wiped from its foundation. Then, in 1989, the infamous *Exxon Valdez* oil spill caused millions of dollars in damage and took the lives of as many fish and marine mammals. The city regrouped after each of these events and is a testament to both the human spirit and hard work.

This community would be a lot more remote if not for the benefit of access by both road and water. Alaska Marine Highway ferries stop in Valdez on a regular basis to drop off and pick up eager hikers, anglers, and road trip enthusiasts. Blessed with the Richardson Highway leading all the way to the Interior Alaska community of Fairbanks 360 miles away, Valdez is a hotspot for local and out-of-state visitors.

ARRIVING

If you'd like to make this a ferry-drive combo from Anchorage, you have two options. The first is to drive the Glenn Highway from Anchorage and follow it to the junction of the Richardson Highway in the town of Glennallen, a distance of 180 miles. Make a right onto the Richardson Highway, taking in the spectacular snowy peaks and other mountain scenery and stopping to look at wildflowers or hike several trails along the roadway. Travel the highway 120 miles south to Valdez, where you can either settle in for a few days prior or embark on your ferry adventure right away.

The second option is to drive to Whittier and take the ferry to Valdez, then drive back to Anchorage via the route explained above (just backward). Choose either the fast ferry *Chenega* (more expensive and not always running, especially in bad weather), which will get you to Valdez in about three hours, or what we call the slow boat, either the *Kennicott* or *Matanuska*, which will dock in Valdez five or six hours after departing Whittier, depending upon how much ice from Columbia Glacier gets in the way or how many whales are spotted (ferry captains love to point out cool things). Either way, you're in for a treat, for a ferry trip through Prince William Sound is akin to your own personal day cruise with a special sort of Alaskan panache. The ferry crosses right in front of the outwash of Columbia Glacier, a rapidly retreating wall of ice that calves (sheds ice) with regularity, causing bobbing bergy bits (smaller pieces of ice) and outright icebergs to float into the ferry's path.

Sea otters and harbor seals love the larger icebergs and medium-sized bergy bits, as both provide a measure of protection for pups and a cool place for a little sunbathing when the weather permits. Often ferry passengers will see eagles perched on the bluish tracts of ice waiting for something interesting to pass by, like hordes of people on a boat. Humpback whales frequent the area, too, waiting for herring and krill and providing a breathy whoosh of air as they surface before diving down for up to twenty minutes of feeding.

The ferry will stop in Valdez to offload and load up with passengers, goods, and gear and then depart for the small town of Cordova, located across the sound at the mouth of the Copper River.

GETTING AROUND

If you're disembarking the ferry and would like to see Valdez and its outlying areas or get to Anchorage and beyond, car rentals can be found at **Valdez U-Drive** (www.valdezudrive.com, 907-835-4402), located at the Valdez Pioneer Field Airport. The ferry dock is within easy walking distance of the downtown core, but many visitors wish to explore beyond this area.

VISITOR INFORMATION

The **Valdez Convention and Visitor Center** (www.valdezalaska.org) is a good first stop to pick up literature. It's located on the corner of Fairbanks Drive and Chenega Avenue.

LODGING

Valdez is a town that thrived on the Alyeska Pipeline construction, and as a result, several options to spend the night are located near the ferry dock downtown.

Hotels/Motels

Best Western Valdez Harbor Inn $$$
100 N. Harbor Dr., Valdez, AK 99686
(907) 835-3434
www.valdezharborinn.com

Sits at the entrance to the small boat harbor, with great views, a restaurant, free Wi-Fi, a free continental breakfast, and access to many of Valdez's activities.

Thumbs-up: Accessibility to all sorts of kid-friendly fun, plus an on-site restaurant makes for easier meals

Valdez Downtown Harbor Inn $$
113 Galena Dr., Valdez, AK 99686
(800) 478-2791, (907) 835-2791
www.downtowninn.com

Only one block from the small boat harbor, this cozy little inn is a nice way to settle in after a day of ferry travel, driving, or exploring the sound. It is just the place for quiet, comfortable, and affordable rooms. I love this place for the attention to details all parents love.

Thumbs-up: A coin-op washer and dryer, free continental breakfast, and group rates for larger families

Robe Lake Lodge $$-$$$
5325 Lake View Dr., Valdez, AK 99686
(907) 831-2339
www.robelakelodge.com

If you're willing to drive the six miles from town, this is a beautiful place to absorb the gorgeous scenery of the greater Valdez area, including nearby Keystone Canyon. Rent either the entire lodge or a single room, but either way, you'll be charmed by the log construction and warm, comfortable surroundings. Owners Josh and Tabatha are also parents, and they get that kids like to be active and busy. A full kitchen is available for your use for an additional daily charge, and it might be worth it for a night or two if you're planning to stay a while.

Thumbs-up: Location, decor, and friendliness

Camping/RV

Due to its position as a prime fishing destination, Valdez has plenty of camping options for weary travelers.

Eagle's Rest RV Park $-$$
139 E. Pioneer Dr., Valdez, AK 99686
(800) 553-7275
www.eaglesrestrv.com

Here you can park your RV or trailer or rent a cozy little cabin on wheels. No kidding, the park rents fake log cabins that feature two beds, a bathroom, and efficiency kitchen. Our son loved it.

Bear Paw RV Park $-$$
101 N. Harbor Dr., Valdez, AK 99686
(907) 835-2530
www.bearpawrvpark.com

Bear Paw is located next to the Valdez small boat harbor and is within a few minutes' drive from the ferry terminal. Park almost at water's edge and watch fishing boats, charters, and the glacier cruise vessels come and go. Walk to restaurants, the local park, and many attractions, too. Nice for those who are tired of parking the rented RV over and over.

FEEDING THE FAMILY

Ernesto's Taqueria $$
328 Egan Dr., Valdez, AK 99686
(907) 835-2519
Open daily, year-round

Located near the visitor center, Ernesto's was always a hit with our son, who often prefers Mexican dishes over anything else. Find traditional

SOUTHCENTRAL

tacos and burritos but also be sure to sample the fresh seafood dishes made with just enough spice to liven up your day. A great place to stop on a rainy Valdez afternoon or evening.

Fat Mermaid $$
143 N. Harbor Dr., Valdez, AK 99686
www.thefatmermaid.com
Open daily during the summer, generally Memorial Day to Labor Day

Looking for sandwiches and some outstanding pizza? We like to sit in this kitschy place with a microbrew and people-watch while our kid enjoys a slice or two of pie.

FAMILY FUN IN VALDEZ

Museums and Cultural Experiences

Remembering Old Valdez Exhibit $
436 Hazelet Ave., Valdez, AK 99686
(907) 835-2764
www.valdezmuseum.org
Open by appointment only
Admission by donation.

Stop in to see the scale model of the city before the earthquake and tsunami and an interesting video about the earthquake itself. Then, if you have time, drive out to the **Old Town Valdez site** and walk the gravel grid of streets at the head of Port Valdez. A few interpre-

> **PARENT PRO TIP**
>
> Visit the Old Town Valdez museum before walking the Old Town Valdez site. It's easier to comprehend the scale of the tsunami and better map the streets as you walk around the town site.
>
> —James, Anchorage resident and dad of one

tive signs posted at the entrance to the site provide photo documentation of the former town, and it's quite sobering to stand on the foundations of homes and businesses that were wiped away. To get to the site, follow the Richardson Highway six miles out of town, and turn right just past the flashing yellow light. Follow the gravel road to the first set of interpretive signs to roadside parking.

SOUTHCENTRAL

Valdez Museum $
217 Egan Dr., Valdez, AK 99686
(907) 835-2764
www.valdezmuseum.org
Open daily 9:00 a.m.–5:00 p.m. (Memorial Day–Labor Day); Tuesday–Sunday
12:00–5:00 p.m. (Labor Day–Memorial Day)
$8/adults, $6/seniors, $5/students, free for kids 13 and under

Offers some insight into the oil spill and is better suited for older children. The antique fire truck is pretty cool, though, as are some of the old photos.

Maxine and Jesse Whitney Museum FREE
303 Lowe St., Valdez, AK 99686
(800) 478-8800
www.mjwhitneymuseum.org
Open daily 9:00 a.m.–7:00 p.m. (May–September)
Donations welcome

Located on the Prince William Sound Community College campus, this museum showcases the collections of this intrepid couple who enjoyed collecting Alaska Native arts and crafts so much they opened their own gift shop. Maxine Whitney eventually became owner of the Eskimo Museum in Fairbanks, and in the 1990s the entire collection was donated to Prince William Sound Community College, where school officials quickly realized its value. Don't miss the amazing mounted animals, beadwork, and art.

Ocean Adventures
For a glimpse into the rich marine life near Valdez, try these guides and outfitters.

Stan Stephens Glacier and Wildlife Tours $$–$$$
112 N. Harbor Dr., Valdez, AK 99686
(866) 867-1297
www.stanstephenscruises.com
Open May–September
Rates vary

One of the oldest day cruise companies in Alaska and an excellent choice for families. Choose from a 6.5- or 9.5-hour cruise (lunch is included), and see wildlife, glaciers, and the stunning scenery of Prince

William Sound. Our son enjoyed the shorter cruise as a preschooler and did fine a year later on the long cruise. Bring plenty to amuse kids, though, since wildlife is not a given.

Pangea Adventures $$-$$$
107 N. Harbor Dr., Valdez, AK 99686
(800) 660-9637
www.alaskasummer.com
Open May–September
Rates vary

Kayaking is excellent in and around Valdez. Pangea Adventures offers day and overnight kayak trips for all ability levels, and they welcome kids six and up. Our favorite is the Duck Flats paddle, an easy three-hour tour that cruises around the harbor area near town.

Anadyr Adventures $$-$$$
225 N. Harbor Dr., Valdez, AK 99686
(800) TO-KAYAK
www.anadyradventures.com
Open May–September
Rates vary

Another day and overnight kayak outfitter, Anadyr Adventures has the addition of multiday "mother ship" tours that provide yacht accommodations and daytime paddling. Kids age six and up are welcome on these adventures, and no experience is necessary.

Solomon Gulch Fish Hatchery FREE
1455 Dayville Rd., Valdez, AK 99686
(907) 835-1329
www.valdezfisheries.org/the-hatchery/

Fishing is big in Valdez, either from the banks or aboard a boat. A great place to toss in a line is the hatchery, where people and bears share a common goal—fish. Pay attention to the rules, fish only where allowed, and watch for those bears! Find the hatchery near the Alaska Pipeline Terminus, about ten total miles from downtown Valdez, across the harbor. Even if you don't fish, it's fun to watch thousands of pink or coho salmon jostle their way upstream to spawn. The hatchery is open when salmon are spawning, but the viewing area is always open.

Hiking, Walking, and Parks

Valdez has some excellent family-friendly trails, including the twelve-mile paved trail from city center near the small boat harbor out the Richardson Highway. We walk to the Forest Service Visitor Center, known as Crooked Creek, just outside of town to see salmon spawning and hear the busy creek next door. Pick up a trail map here, or grab one at the Valdez Convention and Visitor Center (see above). This is a stroller-friendly trail, but do watch for the occasional black bear feeding near Duck Flats.

FERRY FACT

The Alaska Marine Highway ferries played an integral role as support for the 1989 *Exxon Valdez* oil spill. Acting as floating offices and overnight accommodations, ferries had skiffs tied up to booms around their hulls, like horses at hitching posts, as workers took a break, held meetings, or grabbed a fast meal.

Cordova (CDV): Alaska's Hidden Treasure

The Copper River delta is home to the small fishing town of Cordova, where outdoor recreation packs a punch for families with adventurous spirits and independent travel styles. Sweeping shorelines, glacial ice, and miles of boating and paddling await those who give Cordova more than a passing glance.

Located seventy-eight nautical miles from Valdez, Cordova is not always on the itinerary of visitors, but it should be. Shaped by dramatic landscape and true Alaskan hospitality, the cultural heritage and history of this town with only twenty-three hundred full-time residents is very much alive. Known for both commercial and sport fishing, Cordova also features world-class hiking and biking trails and is the site of the famous Copper River Shorebird Festival each spring.

ARRIVING

Between May and September, the Alaska Marine Highway System serves Cordova on a daily basis, and four times per week the rest of the year. Those wishing to fly one way and ferry the other have options in the form of **Alaska Airlines** (www.alaskaair.com, 1-800-252-7522) and **Ravn Alaska** (www.ravnalaska.com, 1-800-866-8394). Both offer twice-daily service.

SOUTHCENTRAL

Ferry travelers will be happy to know that year-round service is available to Cordova via the MV *Chenega*, a fast ferry that strips the trip down to a manageable three hours and fifteen minutes from Valdez (as opposed to five hours) to maximize fun in this outdoor community. During the busy spring and summer months, be sure to make reservations, especially if bringing a vehicle, as the *Chenega* is much smaller than the other, slower vessels.

Note: As of this writing, the Alaska Marine Highway was in the middle of a severe budget crisis, and the future of the fuel-guzzling fast ferries was in jeopardy. Check the AMHS website for current scheduling and ferry assignments before you begin planning.

GETTING AROUND

Rent a car at **Chinook Auto Rentals** (www.chinookautorentals.com, 1-877-424-5279) at the Cordova Airport. Delivery can even be made to the ferry dock or back at the airport with prior arrangement.

VISITOR INFORMATION

The **Cordova Chamber of Commerce** (www.cordovachamber.com, 907-424-7260) is located at 401 First Street in downtown Cordova, and they can assist with lodging, dining, and activities.

LODGING

Hotels/Motels

Reluctant Fisherman $$–$$$
407 Railroad Ave., Cordova, AK 99574
(907) 424-3272
www.reluctantfisherman.com

If immersing yourself in the fishing culture of Cordova is your goal, then stay here. Watch boats arrive and unload their catch while feasting on fresh seafood in the restaurant. Enjoy Wi-Fi and a balcony room. Kids will enjoy the scenery and action just as much as the grown-ups.

Thumbs-up: On-site restaurant, views, access to downtown

SOUTHCENTRAL

Orca Adventure Lodge $$$
2500 Orca Rd., Cordova, AK 99574
(907) 424-7249
www.orcaadventurelodge.com

Orca Adventure Lodge is a full-service property that also has room-only accommodations for those who want to explore on their own. Kayaking, fishing, hiking, and remote getaways are but a few options offered at this lovely property, and kids six and under stay free. Ask about the Junior Angler program, too. An on-site dining facility keeps everyone fed and full with local specials and to-go lunches available seven days a week.

Thumbs-up: Packages and specials, kids' program, dining options

Camping

Childs Glacier Campground $
End of Copper River Highway
www.reserveamerica.com/camping/childs-glacier-recreation-area

A US Forest Service–maintained facility with access to fishing and hiking near its nine campsites. As of this writing, the highway bridge is under construction, and access is unavailable by private vehicle, which also means no RVs or trailers—but Orca Adventure Lodge can help transport tent campers. Camping near the glacier comes with its own rewards: stellar up-close views of the glacier and its frequent calving, sometimes so loud you need to cover your ears.

Note: As of October 2016, the campground is closed due to a bridge closure along the Copper River Highway. Orca Adventure Lodge will take guests in for a fee for walk-in camping.

FEEDING THE FAMILY
In addition to the **Reluctant Fisherman** and **Orca Adventure Lodge**, Cordova has some good options when it comes to kid-friendly dining.

Picnic Basket $–$$
170 Adams St., Cordova, AK 99574
(907) 424-4337
Open April–October, hours vary

Set up in a little white trailer, this local food stand serves up soups, sandwiches, pie, and fish and chips. Great for take-out, but call ahead. If staying, be prepared to eat outdoors in potentially chilly weather, especially on the shoulder months.

The Baja Taco (look for the bus) $
(907) 424-5599
www.bajatacoak.com
Open April–September, hours vary

Famous thanks to its funky school bus exterior and fresh, locally sourced ingredients. Salmon tacos are the signature dish here, along with a hearty menu that features breakfast and lunch. Relax with a microbrew from either Alaska or Mexico, and enjoy the lively conversation at this popular restaurant.

FAMILY FUN IN CORDOVA
People visit Cordova for outdoor adventure, be it fishing, hiking, boating, or simply sitting by the water and observing glaciers or birds. Kids who love being outside will thrive in Cordova, as long as they are dressed for adventure.

Museums and Cultural Experiences

Cordova Historical Museum $
622 1st St., Cordova, Alaska 99574
(907) 424-6665
www.cordovamuseum.org
Open Monday–Saturday 10:00 a.m.–6:00 p.m., Sunday 2:00–4:00 p.m. (Memorial Day–Labor Day); Tuesday–Friday 1:00–5:00 p.m., Saturday 2:00–4:00 p.m. (Labor Day–Memorial Day)
$1/adults over 18

Trace both the centuries-old traditions of Eyak and Chugach Native groups and the more recent settling of the city of Cordova at this wonderful little museum. Kids have a wealth of programs at their fingertips, so call ahead or visit the website to see what's coming up during your visit.

The **Cordova Historical Society** also publishes a great printed map suitable for walking tours of the town and surrounding areas. Pick one up at the Cordova Chamber of Commerce and let the kids lead you on a tour.

SOUTHCENTRAL

Hiking, Walking, and Parks

Make no mistake, the trails and forests of Cordova are world-class examples of wilderness, and the opportunity to stand at the face of a glacier is a special one, indeed. Cordova is in the middle of the enormous Chugach National Forest, and miles of trails crisscross the area. Visit the USFS website (www.fs.usda.gov) and find the Cordova District for assistance with everything from campsites to trails to public use cabins.

Best bets for families include the **Saddlebag Lake and Glacier Hike** (3.1 miles) or **Childs Glacier,** where kids can walk short or longer distances around this scenic and popular glacier area. Short on time? We love the **Haystack Trail** and boardwalk, a short 1.6-mile round-trip walk. Great views and bird-watching are your rewards on this trail.

More adventurous hikers may want to try **Crater Lake Trail** or **Heney Ridge**. Be sure to bring food, extra clothing, and pepper spray. Cordova is known for its fishing bruin friends, and you won't want to be caught unaware here. Be bear aware and stay safe.

Fishing

As Cordova provides so much bounty from the sea, fishing is a very popular activity among locals and visitors. Try **Orca Bay Charters** for a day trip (www.orcabaycharters.com, 907-830-7158) or **Orca Adventure Lodge** (above) for overnight or longer fishing trips that include the kids.

SOUTHWEST ALASKA ROUTE

Homer—Kodiak—Port Lions—Chignik—Sand Point
King Cove—Cold Bay—False Pass—Akutan
Unalaska/Dutch Harbor

The sea was full of fish, the beaches were full of sea lions, the hot lava and air were full of birds. Thus life and deadly volcanism lived together.

—Volcanologist Thomas Jagger, upon inspection of
Bogoslof Volcano in 1906 as it smoked from a recent eruption

Sailing the Chain

The most remote of the Alaska Marine Highway routes, and by far one of the most unique, is Southwest Alaska—rugged, wild, and far off the beaten path for the average Alaska visitor. Originating in the Kenai Peninsula town of Homer and ending almost a thousand miles away in the city of Unalaska and the port of Dutch Harbor, the Southwest route is at least four solid days of sailing across open water, along the Alaska Peninsula, and between the islands that make up the Aleutians. Known as "the Chain" to regular ferry passengers, residents, and the legions of seasonal workers who risk life and limb to fish these rich waters, the Southwest is windswept, treeless, and prone to storms that toss the MV *Tustemena* like a toy in a child's bathtub. It is also breathtakingly beautiful,

ALASKA

Barrow

Prudhoe Bay

Kotzebue

Nome

Unalakleet

Fairbanks

Delta Junction

McGrath

Mt. McKinley (Denali)
elev. 20,320

Aniak

Talkeetna

Bethel

Wasilla
Palmer

Glennallen

Twin Lakes

Anchorage

Valdez

Kenai

Whittier

Tatitlek

Soldotna

Chenega Bay

Dillingham

Seward

Cordova

Homer

Naknek

Seldovia

Port Lions

Ouzinkie

Kodiak

Chignik

Old Harbor

Cold Bay

King Cove

Dutch Harbor

False Pass

Sand Point

Akutan

Nikolski

featuring emerald-green hills, 120 varieties of wildflowers, bald eagles, and endless opportunities for exploring.

WHERE YOU'LL GO

The Southwest journey begins in the small town of Homer, located at the end of Southcentral Alaska's Kenai Peninsula (see chapter 7, Southcentral Alaska Route). Typically, the MV *Tustemena* departs late in the evening for an overnight Gulf of Alaska crossing, arriving in the city of Kodiak early the following morning. From Kodiak, the ferry proceeds across Shelikof Strait toward the Alaska Peninsula before reaching the Aleutian Islands proper.

Serving ten total stops between Homer and Unalaska/Dutch Harbor, the Southwest route's value lies in its ability to provide essential service during the summer months to communities along the Alaska Peninsula and Aleutian Islands chain. While some towns like Kodiak, Sand Point, or Cold Bay do have air service, prices are high and service is sporadic, thanks to challenging weather patterns. The *Tustemena*, on the other hand, is well known for her ability to plow over and through all but the worst weather, connecting people to other Alaska communities and delivering supplies, vehicles, and critical links to bush Alaska survival. Operating between May and September, the route transports families to fish camps, seasonal hires to jobs, and a dedicated force of ardent bird enthusiasts for the rare species and excellent photo opportunities. It is important to note that not all communities will be port stops during all sailings. On our first trip down the Aleutian chain, we skipped all Kodiak Island communities except the city of Kodiak. Depending upon the sailing, your ferry trip may or may not include places like Port Lions.

The terminus of the Southwest route is the fishing hub of all Alaska: Unalaska/Dutch Harbor. Given two names that actually mark the city proper (Unalaska) and the port through which the state's largest number of commercially caught fish arrives and is packed and shipped (Dutch Harbor), this is actually two islands making up one community.

Amaknak Island is smaller, more condensed, and the site of the Unalaska Airport and Dutch Harbor proper. It is also where the Alaska Marine

SOUTHWEST

Highway ferry docks and offloads passengers and supplies before sailing back up the chain to Homer. Surrounded by steep Mount Ballyhoo to the northwest and bays with names like Unalaska and Iliuliuk, Amaknak possesses a deep connection to World War II history and current industry.

Unalaska Island is reached via the "bridge to the other side" (really) from Amaknak, and it is the center of the community's commerce and government. It, too, is full of physical reminders connecting the Aleutian Islands to World War II (see "Family Fun in Unalaska/Dutch Harbor" later in this chapter).

Practical, unfussy, and exciting, both in history and Alaska culture—that's the Southwest route, and that's how it will stay, even though plans are on the table to build a new, larger ferry to replace the *Tustemena*. Our family sailed the trip down the Aleutian Chain by embarking in Homer, but, if time is a factor, you can also catch the ferry in Kodiak, since the ferry spends most of the day there before departing for the rest of the route. I'd recommend beginning the trip sailing south and west rather than reversing direction; the impact on kids will be far greater as the ferry moves from a fairly populated environment to hardly inhabited, at all.

FERRY FACT

The MV *Tustemena*, also known as the *Trusty Tusty*, has been in service since 1964 and is one of the original vessels in the AMHS fleet. She may be old, but the *Tusty* continues her hardscrabble completion of the Southwest route with success, even after all these years. However, the *Tusty* does break down quite often, so riders should always check AMHS alerts to ensure a timely departure. Or not.

WHY SAIL THE SOUTHWEST ROUTE?

In my first book, I discussed the merits of exposing children to areas of Alaska other visiting families might miss in favor of better weather and more access to kid-friendly activities. That said, for the independent traveler, Alaska's remote sections offer opportunities to explore cultural and recreational opportunities unique to a particular area, not to mention some pretty amazing adventures.

SOUTHWEST

Southwest Alaska, with its centuries-old Native traditions and significant role in World War II, provides families with more than the typical vacation. It is a chance to live among residents, if only temporarily, in one of the state's most distinctive areas. Underutilized as a tourist destination in my opinion, Unalaska/Dutch Harbor deserves attention if history and culture are to be preserved for future generations.

Ports of call along the Alaska Peninsula and Aleutian Islands chain often are the only link to "big city" living, including restaurants. When the *Tustemena* pulls into harbor, long lines of area residents are already in place, not waiting for people arriving, but for the chance to come aboard for a burger and fries, a ferry specialty.

FERRY FACT

WHAT TO KNOW

For those with a keen interest in history and independent travel, the Alaska Marine Highway's Southwest route presents an unforgettable vacation opportunity. However, even the savviest among us should consider the following when planning a nine-hundred-mile journey to an area that is likely more remote than anything we've ever encountered before.

Children should be comfortable on boats in all sorts of weather. The Southwest route is rough and unpredictable, and often very stormy. Families who do not travel by boat often enough to recognize seasickness should perhaps take a shorter, calmer ride to gauge kids' readiness for a trip of this length.

Families should know that forethought is imperative when traveling along the Aleutian Islands chain with kids. Unlike other AMHS routes, outside sleeping is exponentially more difficult due to weather and heavy seas, and tents are not allowed due to high winds. Common area sleeping space is at a premium, too, so the best piece of advice I can offer is to book a stateroom a year in advance of your trip, if at all possible.

Be prepared for heavy rain, wind, waves, and drippy, dense fog during the journey and upon arrival in Unalaska/Dutch Harbor. Bring

SOUTHWEST

A bald eagle takes stock of the landscape atop an old signal post in Unalaska.

high-quality rain gear, rain boots, waterproof gloves, a warm hat and a hat with a brim, and non-cotton layers to add or subtract to the clothing equation as conditions change. **Note:** No one cares what you wear, unless it's clothing that looks more suited to an afternoon in a downtown mall than the dusty roads of Unalaska Island. In this case I promise people will stare.

The *Tustemena*'s dining room is small and open only for one hour, three times per day. Snack opportunities are limited to candy, chips, soda, and water in vending machines. Families can and should bring non-perishable foods that are able to be stored in tight quarters. Very few if any opportunities exist for shopping along the route, with the exception of Kodiak, and prices will be significantly higher.

WHAT YOU'LL SEE

Straddling the Bering Sea and the Pacific Ocean, the Aleutian Islands and Alaska Peninsula are products of geologic activity that shaped everything from human migration to a wide variety of plants, birds, mammals, and fish. Volcanoes—some steaming, some dormant—are present along nearly every mile of the Southwest route. Seabirds paddle and soar by turn above foaming waves, and orca, humpback, pilot, and fin whales make their way to summer feeding grounds farther north.

SOUTHWEST

The Aleutians are also a mainframe of Alaska's commercial fishing and crabbing industries, including the famous king crab fishery, subject of the Discovery Channel program *Deadliest Catch*. While ferry riders won't be experiencing the wild winter weather and waves of boats upon the Bering Sea, passengers can and do witness the power of Mother Nature's weather patterns. In each port community, starting with Homer, you'll be able to watch boats being cleaned, refurbished, and stocked for their respective fishery or repaired after a particularly rough week or two at sea. Some are floating processors; others, tiny in comparison. But all have names and stories and people keeping the fishing industry alive in Alaska.

CULTURE

From Chignik to Unalaska/Dutch Harbor, the sea plays not just an important role in work and daily life, it is the cornerstone of each village's identity, albeit in different ways. Be it establishing a summer fish camp or managing city government, residents of the Aleutians are dedicated to home and heritage, no matter their individual place of origin, in this place sometimes referred to as the "Cradle of Storms."

The human story of the Aleutians begins nearly nine thousand years ago when the Unangax (pronounced "u-nan-gan") people settled the islands of the chain, traveling among the rocky shorelines in order to maintain what eventually became a thriving subsistence lifestyle dependent upon both land and sea. The Unangax (also known as Unangan or Aleut) made good use of hillsides to build underground dwellings that shielded them from harsh winds, and they used every bit of the animals they hunted for food, clothing, shelter, and often all three. Archeological dig sites a short distance from the Unalaska/Dutch Harbor Airport prove the existence of village sites all around Amaknak and Unalaska Islands, not just surviving, but thriving as Mother Nature sought to throw her best and worst at these tenacious people. But tough times were afoot.

When the business of hunting sea otters for their luxurious pelts arrived in the Aleutian Islands in the late 1700s, the Unangax/Aleut found themselves victims of shady operations and less-than-subtle demands for their hunting expertise. Eventually treated for all intents and purposes as slaves, the Unangax̂/Aleut were thrust into the original pyramid scheme. They did the work, lots and lots of it, harvesting sea otters as fast as the creatures reproduced, and fur traders and buyers reaped the benefits, while one of the Aleut's main sources of warmth and tradition faced extinction. Careful and respectful harvest of the sea's raw materials had always been the basis for existence among the Aleut, but now, with nearly all tribal members engaged in the pursuit of natural resources on behalf of European traders, cultural traditions were in jeopardy.

As Unangax̂/Aleut struggled with the burden of being both responsible for the loss of marine life and representation as stewards of its future, the Russian Orthodox Church arrived in Unalaska with the construction of a chapel in 1808 for the benefit of fur traders from Russia. Up until this time, the Russian monarchy had attempted to manage the fair treatment of the Aleut with varying degrees of success. In 1825 Father John Veniaminov became priest of the church that would eventually be known as the Cathedral of the Holy Ascension of Christ. Father John, as he was known, established a relationship that would carry forth for decades of worship at the church and an unfailing commitment to the Russian Orthodox religion, no matter what tragedies or tribulations befell the Aleut People.

When World War II emerged as a global crisis, the Aleut were not exempt from harm. As the US military began a frenetic buildup of airstrips, forts, and bunkers, the Alaska Natives of the Aleutian Islands found themselves under the watchful eye of the government and, subsequently, were evacuated without warning from their homes to unfamiliar and certainly substandard settlements in Southeast Alaska. Suddenly the Aleut population of all villages, beginning with Attu at the end of the chain, found themselves refugees. Many Aleut died in these camps, which were often nothing more than abandoned canneries with no heat, light, or insulation, and the toll the war's effort took on the culture was devastating. In all, 881 people were evacuated from nine villages and herded onto crowded transport ships with one suitcase per person. They watched in disbelief and horror as their homes, churches, and outbuildings were sometimes set fire to prevent the Japanese from overtaking their community. For nearly three years, families clustered together in the dense rainforests of Southeast Alaska, struggling to remain alive when afflictions like tuberculosis and pneumonia wiped out the very old and very young.

> In 1942, my wife and our four children were whipped away from our home . . . all our possessions were left . . . for mother nature to destroy . . . I tried to pretend it really was a dream and this could not happen to me and my dear family.
> —Bill Tcheripanoff Sr., Akutan Aleut evacuee, quoted
> in an exhibit at the Museum of the Aleutians, Unalaska

Today, thanks to the efforts of federal, state, and tribal organizations, the descendants of the Aleut people are being offered a chance at cultural restoration and preservation through hands-on opportunities. Culture camps, workshops, and art classes for all ages seek to bring back the rich traditions and valuable oral storytelling skills so generations to come will be able to know and experience this "birthplace of winds."

Kodiak (KOD): Alaska's "Emerald Isle"

Many visitors to Kodiak are surprised that the term refers not to just one island, but an archipelago of islands located 158 miles across the Gulf of Alaska from Homer. Kodiak Island itself is 177 miles long, and at five thousand square miles is roughly the size of Connecticut. Most Kodiak Island Borough residents live in Kodiak proper. With six thousand full-time residents, it holds its own against other rural Alaska towns, but many smaller communities are accessible only by boat or airplane. Alaska Marine Highway passengers are fortunate to have nearly an entire day to spend in Kodiak, getting to know this close-knit community and exploring its network of trails, beaches, and Alaska Native history. Take advantage of the opportunity; it's the longest stop along the Southwest route and an excellent introduction to the low-key lifestyles of residents who live in this part of Alaska.

Kodiak's history and culture revolve around its island location and the people who have made their living from the land and surrounding ocean.

SOUTHWEST

The Alutiiq people have etched a living from the ebullient marine- and land-based bounty, continuing those traditions today, but it was the settlement by Russian fur traders in the 1700s that shifted the tide for Kodiak's place in Alaska commerce, first as the capital of Russian America, then as a major sea otter pelt distributor for many years. Today, Kodiak's prime means of support is through a vibrant fishing industry, and visitors are able to reap the benefits, enjoying halibut, salmon, and crab straight from the ocean. Kodiak is a wonderful place to explore with children, full of interesting World War II artifacts and Alaska Native culture, with miles and miles of beach and trails to explore.

As a ferry passenger, you'll most likely enjoy almost an entire day in Kodiak before moving across the Gulf of Alaska and the Alaska Peninsula. The *Tustemena* docks in a most convenient location, at the Kodiak Island Convention and Visitors Bureau in the downtown core and within walking distance of several attractions with appeal for families.

Alaska Fact

In 1912 Kodiak was nearly buried by the eruption of Mount Novarupta, which spewed two feet of ash upon town and brought three days of darkness to the entire island.

ARRIVING

Some ferry passengers prefer to skip the Homer to Kodiak segment of the Alaska Marine Highway's Southwest route, knowing they'll save nearly a day of transit if they opt to fly instead. If this is you, Kodiak does have more access than other ports along the chain, thanks to a regional airport with regular service from Anchorage and Seattle. Kodiak is an easy hop from Anchorage aboard **Alaska Airlines** (www.alaskaair.com, 1-800-252-7522) or **Ravn Alaska** (www.flyravn.com, 1-800-866-8394, 907-266-8394). But just a heads-up, while air service to Kodiak sounds fairly straightforward, Kodiak's weather patterns tell otherwise. Weather here is unpredictable and slightly frustrating if you're on a tight schedule. As we've mentioned in previous sections, pack patience along with your rain gear. Prepare for

SOUTHWEST

weather delays by supplying kids with books, toys, and movies if you get stuck at the airport.

GETTING AROUND

Since the island is rather large, and with many adventures located beyond the scope of town, it is handy to have access to wheels when visiting Kodiak. **Avis** (www.avis.com, 907-487-2264) and **Budget** (www.budget .com, 907-487-2220) are located at the Kodiak Airport for car rentals.

Taxi service is available through **Kodiak City Cab** (907-486-5555) or **Kodiak Island Taxi** (907-486-2515) for those who want to take a quick jaunt across town for an activity.

VISITOR INFORMATION

The **Kodiak Island Convention and Visitors Bureau** (www.kodiak.org, 907-486-4782) is located at 100 Marine Way, at the ferry dock. Pick up maps and brochures or plan a guided tour.

SHOPPING/GROCERIES

Kodiak Safeway
2685 Mill Bay Rd., Kodiak, AK 99615
(907) 481-1500

Groceries, bakery, pharmacy, coffee shop, and deli. It's a bit out of the downtown area, but taxis are glad to take you there and wait while you shop.

MEDICAL CARE

Providence Kodiak Island Medical Center
1915 E. Rezanof Dr., Kodiak, AK 99615
(907) 486-3281
http://alaska.providence.org/locations/pkimc/Pages/default.aspx

LODGING

If you do arrive in Kodiak ahead of the ferry, or if you choose to disembark here, the city has a number of options in both the downtown core or slightly on the outskirts. Depending on your preference and budget, the visitors bureau can assist with a list of accommodations for your family.

SOUTHWEST

Hotels/Motels

Best Western Kodiak Inn $$-$$$
236 E. Rezanof Dr., Kodiak, AK 99615
(907) 486-5712
www.kodiakinn.com, info@kodiakinn.com

Most folks stay at this Best Western near the downtown area with an on-site restaurant and convenient amenities, including cribs and roll-aways, a complimentary breakfast, and a hot tub. Kids under seventeen stay free in parents' room.

Thumbs-up: Proximity to downtown shops, restaurants, and activities

Russian Heritage Inn $-$$
119 Yukon St., Kodiak, AK 99615
(907) 486-5657
www.russianheritageinn.com

The Russian Heritage Inn, while dated and a bit thin on upgrades, has twenty-five rooms with suites, full kitchens, or kitchenettes. It's the access to cooking facilities that might appeal to families, however, and the property managers are very accommodating and responsive to guest needs. It's affordable too, with prices depending upon room size and time of year.

Thumbs-up: Location near downtown, kitchenette access

Bed and Breakfast

Cliff House B&B $$-$$$
1223 Kouskov St., Kodiak, AK 99615
(907) 486-5079
www.kodiak-alaska-dinner-cruises.com/kodiak-bed-and-breakfast.html, mygarden@alaska.net

The Cliff House B&B, owned and operated by Marty and Marian Owen, is a great place to spread out with a larger family or group. Located above Kodiak's boat harbor, the Cliff House receives rave reviews for hospitality and decor. Kitchen facilities are always fully stocked, even if you only stay in one room. Marty and Marian also own Galley Gourmet Dinner Cruises and can arrange harbor tours and other Kodiak adventures. Marty is the former Kodiak harbormaster, too, and he knows history, boats, and nearly every fisherman in town.

Thumbs-up: Hospitality of charming hosts, amazing food, views

Camping

Fort Abercrombie State Historical Park $
Miller Point, Kodiak, AK 99615
Directions can be found at dnr.alaska.gov/parks/aspunits/kodiak/fort
abercrombieshp.htm

Fort Abercrombie is a fantastic location for camping, with miles of trails, awesome scenery, and a lake in the middle of the park. With only thirteen campsites, though, you must get your hustle on to secure a spot for the night.

FEEDING THE FAMILY
When it's eating time after a busy day of hiking, boating, or inspecting museums, dine at Kodiak's favorite establishments.

Henry's Great Alaska Restaurant $$-$$$
512 Marine Way, Kodiak, AK 99615
(907) 486-8844
www.henrysalaska.com
Open Monday–Saturday 11:30 a.m. for lunch and 4:30 p.m. for dinner, Sunday
12:00 p.m. for lunch and 4:30 p.m. for dinner

The only place in Alaska where you can get a true crawfish pie, Henry's is a friendly, honest place that serves up good food on a consistent basis. Children have their own menu of favorites, and adults can find craft ales and a pretty extensive cocktail list. Also located within walking distance of the ferry dock.

Noodles $$
1247 Mill Bay Rd., Kodiak, AK 99615
(907) 486-2900
Open for lunch and dinner Monday–Saturday, call for hours.

Sometimes it's nice to have Thai food, and Noodles lives up to its name with plenty of options for bowls, platters, and curry combinations served with wonderful, slithery Thai noodles, or rice if you prefer. Fresh rolls are really fresh, too. Plus, I like to say "noodles" to my kids, because they laugh, no matter how old they're getting.

SOUTHWEST

Java Flats $$
11206 Rezanof Dr., Kodiak, AK 99615
(907) 486-2622
www.javaflats.com
Open Wednesday–Sunday 7:00 a.m.–3:00 p.m.

Located thirteen beautiful miles from downtown Kodiak, and worth every minute of transit time, Java Flats is a unique little coffee shop and bakery that just happens to serve gourmet soups, sandwiches, and loose-leaf teas. Situated on Bells Flats, where bears roam freely and people breathe deeply of the salty mountain air, Java Flats is destined to become a family favorite. Read the backstory of this little place on their website, too; it's rather endearing. For ferry passengers, Java Flats is a bit out of the way, but it's worth the taxi ride or car rental as it's also on the road to hiking trails and beaches.

FAMILY FUN IN KODIAK

Kodiak has plenty to keep kids hopping, indoors and out, so hit the streets and beaches for a little island exploring. Remember to bring the rain gear, hats, and mittens for outdoor adventures. Kodiak's wild weather can pop up at any time, and you'll want to be prepared.

Museums and Cultural Centers

Kodiak Wildlife Refuge Visitor Center FREE
402 Center Ave., Kodiak, AK 99615
(907) 487-2626
www.fws.gov/refuge/Kodiak/visit/visitor_activities.html
Open daily 9:00 a.m.–5:00 p.m. (Memorial Day–Labor Day); Tuesday–Saturday 10:00 a.m.–5:00 p.m. (Labor Day–Memorial Day)
Free admission

Be sure to stop by the visitor center and see the wonderful exhibits showcasing the wildlife and ecosystems of the Kodiak area, including a complete skeleton of a gray whale and a family of fishing bears. Summer hours bring regular interpretive programs and guided hikes, and visitors can also catch a short movie about the refuge, available on demand. Suitable for the entire family, with elementary and older kids a target audience.

SOUTHWEST

Baranov Museum $$

101 Marine Way, Kodiak, AK 99615
(907) 486-5920
www.baranovmuseum.org
Open Monday–Saturday 10:00 a.m.–4:00 p.m. (May–October); Tuesday–
Saturday,10:00 a.m.–3:00 p.m. (winter)
$5/adults, free for kids 12 and under

The Baranov Museum got its start in a Quonset hut downtown and now occupies the old Russian American building known as the Erskine House. This is a history museum, for sure, so little kids might find the weapons, kayaks, and artwork to be a bit boring, but the facility is excellent for older children who are beginning to learn US history and geography. Lots of military and early Alaskan artifacts can be found here, as well as fishing implements and flotsam and jetsam collected over the years. **Note:** Behind the museum is a swing made of an old fishing float if anyone needs a little playtime.

Alutiiq Museum $$

215 Mission Rd., Kodiak, AK 99615
(907) 486-7004
www.alutiiqmuseum.org
Open Monday, Wednesday, Friday 9:00 a.m.–5:00 p.m., Saturday–Sunday 9:00 a.m.–3:00 p.m. (June–August); Tuesday–Friday 9:00 a.m.–5:00 p.m., Sunday 12:00–4:00 p.m. (September–May)
$5/adults, free for kids 16 and under

Providing insight into seventy-five hundred years of Alaska Native culture, heritage, and tradition, this museum ranks high on the list of Alaska must-sees. A real winner with families, the museum features a *wamwik* (a place to play) just for younger visitors, offering dress-up clothing, traditional toys, games, and puzzles.

Kodiak Fisheries Research Center FREE

710 Mill Bay Rd., Kodiak, AK 99615
(907) 486-9300
www.kodiakak.us
Open Monday–Saturday 8:00 a.m.–4:30 p.m. (Memorial Day–Labor Day); Monday–Friday 8:00 a.m.–4:30 p.m. (Labor Day–Memorial Day)

Stop by the interpretive center and catch some info about marine life, commercial fishing, and fisheries research throughout the Kodiak

SOUTHWEST

Archipelago. The best part is a huge cylindrical aquarium and touch tank to do your own tidepooling.

Hiking, Walking, and Parks

Start in downtown Kodiak and explore the paved 3.5-mile trail to Fort Abercrombie. Strollers are great for this trail, but keep an eye out for joggers and bikers. The **Kodiak Island Convention and Visitors Bureau** (www .kodiak.org) has a very nice listing of walks, hikes, and scenic drives. If you brought a bicycle on board the ferry, this is a great ride with an excellent historical endpoint at the fort.

Fort Abercrombie State Historical Park (dnr.alaska.gov/parks/aspunits/ kodiak/ftaber.htm) is 221 acres of forestland, trails, and beaches. During the summer, rangers offer interpretive walks and tidepooling activities. Nearby Lake Gertrude is great for canoeing or kayaking. When World War II ended, the military left its gun emplacements behind, and you and your family can check out the interesting artifacts dug deep into the hillsides. Stop by the **Kodiak Military History Museum**, a short distance from the park's main parking lot. Allow at least a few hours to explore the many trails and visit the museum, as it's time well spent.

Buskin River State Recreation Site (dnr.alaska.gov/parks/units/kodiak/ buskin.htm) is another area with connections to World War II. Located a short drive from the Kodiak Airport, the area offers picnicking, camping, and hiking along old roadbeds and river areas. See if you can find the old structures left behind at the end of the war, part of Fort Greely, which was meant to protect the United States against Japanese invasion. The area is actually owned by the US Coast Guard but leased to the state of Alaska, so be respectful of artifacts found—and always be bear aware.

Fossil Beach lies along Pasagshak Road, about forty-five miles from downtown Kodiak and a super place to look for shells and fossils. Also find **Surfer Beach** here, where extreme surfers can be found taking advantage of the big waves (and often freezing cold water).

Chignik (CHG)

This primarily Alaska Native community is the first stop along the Southwest route that truly captures the essence of just how far removed rural Alaska villages can be. Chignik is a fishing community, busy during the summer months as crews ply the cold waters of Shelikof Strait in search of salmon, cod, pollock, and other Alaska fish. Families have fished here for years, and often adult children will return via the ferry each summer to help their parents, an important intergenerational tradition.

The *Tustemena* stays in Chignik long enough for you to take a walk down the muddy pathways leading to town, a rather sparse collection of homes clustered around tiny Chignik Lagoon. If this is your first taste of rural Alaska, smile as you step off the ferry and be welcomed into the community of hardworking people whose lives revolve around the tides. Stroll across the dock and take a right, following the handmade signs proclaiming "Doughnuts, 500 feet!" Whether you follow the signs or your nose, find homemade doughnuts and fresh coffee at the end of the path before turning back to the ferry dock and continuing your journey.

Alaska Marine Highway crew members always stop at the doughnut stand, often buying a few boxes to last them the remaining days of their shifts.

Sand Point (SDP)

Known to most locals as Qagun Tayagungin, the city of Sand Point is located on the northwestern side of Popof Island, off the Alaska Peninsula. A true salmon fishing village, Sand Point is one of the largest commercial fisheries along the Aleutian Chain, and visitors will see evidence in the form of a crowded harbor, moored tenders, and a general summertime hustle and bustle.

About half of the town's residents are of Aleut descent, and many work in the fish processing industry at a plant owned and operated by seafood giant Trident Seafoods. Peter Pan Seafoods also manages a support facility in Sand Point to keep up with a busy fishing season that processes

SOUTHWEST

millions of pounds of fish every year. Rich in Russian Orthodox history, Sand Point's residents cling to traditional and cultural resources, and they live a quiet lifestyle on this mostly treeless island.

The *Tustemena* stops in Sand Point only briefly, but you'll be able to see fishing boats and perhaps a tender or container ship, too, as the port is a vital link for shipping and receiving goods from the Pacific Northwest. Whales can also be seen from the entrance to Sand Point.

Sand Point has a small airport that does a brisk business, operating flights to and from Anchorage daily via PenAir for the 550-mile trip (www.penair.com, 1-800-448-4226) if this is as far as you want the ferry to take you.

Cold Bay (CBY)

Located on the tip of the Alaska Peninsula, Cold Bay is the hub for other Aleutian villages and has previously played an important role in military operations, especially during World War II, when fighter planes were stationed on its airstrip at Fort Randall. The scenery in Cold Bay is striking, especially on a sunny day, when two volcanoes, Pavlof and Cold Bay, provide a snowy, conical backdrop to the landscape.

This former home to the subsistence-living Aleut was visited by Russian merchants and trappers during the late 1800s, often to find shelter in the bay from the ocean's wild storms. It was the war, however, that turned Cold Bay into a strategic defense location after the Japanese invasion of the Aleutian Islands in 1942. Today it is still possible to find remnants from Fort Randall near the dump and as you walk the dirt roads of this intriguing and remote little town.

The *Tustemena* stops in Cold Bay for a few hours, long enough, certainly, to don your rain gear and warm clothing for a walk through town and down along the interesting shorelines. The dock itself is fun for kids, as it's a straight, narrow path that seems to go on forever. Watch for traffic, as the dock driveway is wide enough for only one vehicle at a time.

The Alaska Marine Highway stewards often arrange for a small bus tour of beautiful **Izembek National Wildlife Refuge**, one of Alaska's smallest refuges, but certainly one of the most diverse (www.fws.gov/refuge/izembek). Primarily a stopover for migrating birds, the refuge does receive quite a bit of attention from visiting brown bears. This two-hour tour is free of charge, so if offered the opportunity, take it. No services are provided, so bring extra clothing, food, drinks, and your camera.

For those wanting to stroll around town, head across the dock driveway and follow your nose to any one of the several dirt roads that meander into town. The grassy meadowland and sharp wind provide a rugged, lonely sort of atmosphere, and one in which we felt very, very small. Watch for bears. About a mile from the ferry dock, the local school's playground provides a few rusty swings and a slide for kids who want to test out this remote equipment. The shoreline near the ferry dock is a treasure trove of all sorts of washed-up flotsam and jetsam. Be careful of rusty metal and such, but the shells, glass, and rocks can be fun to hunt.

False Pass (FPS)

Situated midway between the Bering Sea and the Gulf of Alaska on the eastern edge of Unimak Island, False Pass, or the Pass as it's known to locals, is also the name for the stretch of water called Isanotski Strait, where boats making their way between the two bodies of water must travel. Called "false" by early ship captains who thought the passage was too shallow for their enormous vessels, the name stuck and is how most people refer to the area today.

Not a large community at all (perhaps a hundred people call False Pass home), the town nonetheless sees quite a bit of traffic as fishing vessels and, yes, the ferry, transit back and forth. Traffic also comes in the form of gray and humpback whales on their way to or from rich feeding grounds farther north. Brown bears like to roam the beaches and hillsides in search of food, too, and can often be seen from the ferry's upper decks.

The *Tustemena* will stop in False Pass for a bit of wandering time. While there isn't much in the way of shopping or commerce for ferry travelers, it is a nice time to explore the beach, look for interesting sea glass or shells, and ponder the windswept landscape as a year-round home for

SOUTHWEST

the hardy few who live here. This is also an excellent venue through which to take photos of the ferry, with the dramatic mountains as a backdrop.

Unalaska/Dutch Harbor (UNA)

Welcome to the end of the line! Pulling into Dutch Harbor early in the morning, you may feel like the early explorers did upon reaching distant shores. Relieved. But truly, the adventure is just beginning. So much history, geography, and culture await in this Aleutian Island community that you'll be wanting to get right to it after disembarking the ferry.

HISTORY

For nine thousand years or more, the Unangax people have inhabited this windy, green, and rocky swath of land midway down the Aleutian Chain. Traveling around the islands in search of homesites that offered shelter, food, and options for clothing and tools, the Unangax developed a complex society that thrived in the islands for centuries. Today's visitor can

The Unalaska/Dutch Harbor community is undoubtedly dedicated to the fishing industry.

SOUTHWEST

see areas of archeological investigation, including the unearthing of tools used to survive in this seemingly inhospitable landscape.

Really two islands supporting one community, as mentioned before, Unalaska and the Port of Dutch Harbor are unique testaments to Alaska industry and culture. Located on Unalaska Island, the city's administration offices, schools, and community organizations provide the business side of things, while Amaknak Island is home to the industrial, with an airport, a port, and a long-defunct US Army base. Created in this way to take advantage of natural geological landforms creating the harbors and bays, Unalaska/Dutch Harbor has proven time and time again its value to fishermen, military operations, and import and export industries.

World War II history buffs may be interested in myriad opportunities to hike among discarded and abandoned bunkers, a fort, and foxholes created in anticipation of a Japanese attack, which eventually arrived in June of 1942. Also prevalent are emotional reminders of the massive relocation of Alaska Native families to camps in the Southeast region of Alaska. In short, there is more to Unalaska and Dutch Harbor than simply the endpoint of a ferry trip. Stay. Learn.

ARRIVING
A one-way ferry trip necessitates transportation in to or out of Unalaska/Dutch Harbor, easily achieved in theory at the airport, where **PenAir** (www.penair.com, 1-800-448-4226) currently provides service to and from Anchorage. Alaska Airlines has in the past provided jet service, and might once again, but at the time of this writing, negotiations were still underway.

GETTING AROUND
To adequately explore the islands, you need a vehicle. Two rental options are available at the airport, **BC Vehicle Rentals** (907-581-6777) or **North Port Car Rentals** (907-581-3880). Be forewarned that availability can be limited, so securing a reservation in advance is a must. Know, too, that vehicles are typically older-model trucks, SUVs, or vans, depending upon what is hanging around the parking lot that day. The upside? These rigs

SOUTHWEST

are used to the rough gravel roads of this area, so go for it and explore every inch of Unalaska/Dutch Harbor.

Several taxi companies also do a brisk business in Unalaska/Dutch Harbor. Try **Aleutian Taxi** (907-359-1750) or **Blue Checker** (907-581-2186). Most will hang out near the airport and be available to schlep you and your family around town but will not normally trek up and around the far roads too much. If you think you might want a longer drive, better to rent a vehicle.

VISITOR INFORMATION

The **Unalaska/Dutch Harbor Convention and Visitors Bureau** does a fantastic job of informing current and potential travelers of their options for lodging, dining, and activities. Stop in their office while in town for current events and insider tips, and long before you travel be sure to carefully read their excellent website, www.Unalaska.info. Additionally, volunteers from the bureau and community make sure to meet every single ferry (and the occasional cruise ship) and hand out maps and visitor guides and provide direction to taxis and car rentals. They make the visit sparkle, and we were impressed by their helpful nature and friendliness.

SHOPPING/GROCERIES

Safeway
2029 Airport Beach Rd., Unalaska, AK 99685
(907) 581-4040
http://local.safeway.com/ak/unalaska-1834.html

Find groceries, a deli, bakery, and movie rentals.

MEDICAL CARE

Illiuliuk Family and Health Services
34 Lavalle Ct., Unalaska, AK 99685
(907) 581-1202

LODGING

Finding lodging is a fairly simple process in Unalaska/Dutch Harbor, since there is but one option. Yes, one.

SOUTHWEST

Grand Aleutian Hotel and Harbor View Inn $$-$$$
498 Salmon Way, Unalaska, AK 99692
(866) 581-3844
www.grandaleutian.com

This complex of three restaurants and more than one hundred rooms is both budget-friendly and not (depending upon your choice and availability). Find simple rooms with a television and amenities like a coffee maker and hair dryer. A limited supply of cribs may be available upon request. There is a massive fee for Internet use, and it doesn't work well anyway, so better to save your money and go to the public library instead.

Thumbs-up: Clean accommodations, on-site dining, King crab brunch

FEEDING THE FAMILY
Unalaska and Dutch Harbor residents and seasonal workers know that one of the top ways to entertain themselves during a crummy weather day or evening is through dining out, so the community has a surprising number of options for food, although parents should note that unlike other places in Alaska, Unalaska/Dutch Harbor bars do not admit anyone under twenty-one, no matter how family-friendly the place might seem.

The Chart Room at Grand Aleutian Hotel $$$
498 Salmon Way, Unalaska, AK 99692
(907) 581-3844, ext. 7120
www.grandaleutian.com

As fancy as you'll find in Unalaska/Dutch Harbor, the Chart Room is nonetheless worth a visit because of two events: Seafood Buffet night, usually held on Wednesday, and Sunday Brunch, held each Sunday morning and afternoon. King crab is, well, king of the menu during these days, and I can still taste the freshness of this Aleutian specialty. Everything else is good, too, but at the high end of most family price points. But hey, you're only in Unalaska/Dutch once, right?

Amelia's Restaurant $$
Biorka Dr., Dutch Harbor, AK 99692
(907) 581-2800

A funky little place in Dutch Harbor, Amelia's is where the locals go for a diverse menu that offers a little bit of everything, with a leaning

SOUTHWEST

toward Mexican food. Kids like it for the simplicity of items, and parents like it for the atmosphere that appeals to their youngsters.

Harbor Sushi $$
Gilman Road, Unalaska, AK 99692
(907) 581-7191

Part of the Grand Aleutian ownership, Harbor Sushi is a delightful place to nibble sea-themed sushi and enjoy the service of very kind, very thoughtful servers. Truly fresh and truly delicious, we stayed in the restaurant longer than we'd planned, but with warm sake for us and a teriyaki chicken bowl for our son and a view outside, it was a nice place to land after a busy day.

FAMILY FUN IN UNALASKA/DUTCH HARBOR
For outdoor families, this is the place to roam, exploring as much of the bear-free, grass-laden hillsides as possible. Often we found ourselves simply stopping the car and climbing into the landscape, listening to the sounds of water and screeching eagles as we pondered life on this chunk of rock. The Unalaska/Dutch Harbor Convention and Visitors Bureau has an interesting list of **52 Things to Do** (www.unalaska.info/visitors/see-do) that kids may find helpful when planning a trip or to fill spare moments.

Unalaska Public Library FREE
43 Raven Way, Unalaska, AK 99685
(907) 581-1251
www.ci.unalaska.ak.us/library
Open Monday-Friday 10:00 a.m.-9:00 p.m., Saturday-Sunday 12:00-6:00 p.m.

One of the only places to find free and reliable Internet service in the Aleutians, the public library in Unalaska is a nice place to sit down, relax, and spend a rainy day. A kids' area features a variety of periodicals, books, and quiet activities. To use the Internet, you'll have to sign in at the front desk, but librarians understand the needs of visitors and are very accommodating.

Unalaska City Aquatic Center $
55 E. Broadway (within the Unalaska City School building), Unalaska, AK 99685
(907) 581-1649
Open Monday-Friday 6:00 a.m.-10:00 p.m., Saturday 8:00 a.m.-10:00 p.m.,
Sunday 12:00-7:00 p.m.

The center was renovated in 2011 and now has a sauna, six-lane swimming pool, water slide, and warming pool. Use the pool for $5/adults, $2/kids ages six to eighteen, free for kids five and under.

Museums and Cultural Experiences

Museum of the Aleutians $$
314 Salmon Way, Unalaska, AK 99685
(907) 581-5150
mota@aleutians.org
Open Tuesday–Saturday 12:00–6:00 p.m.
$7/adults, $3/kids 4 to 12, free for kids 3 and under

Located near the Grand Aleutian Hotel, the museum should be one of the first stops you make upon arriving in Unalaska. Dedicated to telling the story of human history throughout the Aleutian Island chain, this facility packs a lot into its small building. Look for collections of early settlers, Alaska Native groups, and explore the rich cultural legacy of those who made a life living and working on these barren islands. Of particular interest to many is the exhibit showcasing the archeological dig sites scattered throughout the islands, many within reach of town. Kids can see in real time the value of archeology as a science and discuss finds with local experts.

Aleutian World War II National Historic Area, Ounalashka Corporation $
400 Salmon Way, Unalaska, AK 99692
(907) 581-1276
www.ounalashka.com
Open 9:00 a.m.–5:00 p.m.

In 1996 the US Congress designated the thirteen-acre Aleutian World War II National Historic Area as a partner area of the National Park Service to interpret history of the Unangax (the Aleut people) and explain civil defense of the Aleutian Islands and the United States during World War II. The Aleutian campaign involved the removal of Alaska Natives from their traditional homelands to squalid camps in rainy Southeast Alaska. Subsequently, the US military burned homes and built a number of installations, many of which are visible today, for protection against Japanese attack.

SOUTHWEST

The Ounalashka Corporation owns the majority of this land surrounding Unalaska and Dutch Harbor, but they are willing to permit access upon these grassy hills with the purchase of a recreational land permit that ranges from $10 to $50 per family. See "Walks and Hikes" below for more information about specific hikes and walks around Unalaska, but for now, realize that you will be treading on sacred land that has housed several generations of residents.

Aleutian World War II Visitor Center $
Unalaska Airport, Unalaska, AK 99692
(907) 581-9944
www.nps.gov/aleu/planyourvisit/visitorcenters.htm
Call first, but generally open Wednesday–Saturday 1:00–6:00 p.m. (summer);
Wednesday–Saturday 11:00 a.m.–6:00 p.m. (winter)
Donations accepted

Located near the Unalaska Airport runway, this World War II museum is a fascinating glimpse into life in the Aleutians during the campaign to protect the islands from Japanese invasion. The facility is housed in a former theater, and the infrastructure of wood and high ceilings makes for an atmosphere befitting the 1940s. While many of the exhibits are for readers, smaller kids will also enjoy the uniforms, machinery, and an upstairs viewing area with a recording of air traffic. Several World War II–era films are also shown in the vintage theater. Allow about an hour to explore the museum.

The Extra Mile Tours $$
P.O. Box 332, Unalaska, AK 99685
(907) 581-1859
www.unalaskadutchharbortour.com
Two-hour tour is $50/adults, $45/kids 12 and under

There are not many people who know Unalaska/Dutch Harbor better than Bobbie Lekanoff, so if given the opportunity to spend a few hours on her van tour, do so. Bobbie's route takes visitors from Amaknak to Unalaska, basically one end of the community to the other. Or at least as far as the roads go. Tours are two or four hours in length and are reasonably priced. From birding to World War II history, Bobbie knows every inch of the islands and the people who call them home. If you are limited on time

SOUTHWEST

or need an overview of Unalaska and Dutch Harbor before embarking on independent adventures, start with Bobbie and get your trip off on the right foot.

Walks and Hikes

Don't let the Aleutians' stormy weather deter your family from hiking or walking along the miles of trails or scenic beaches that crisscross Unalaska and Amaknak Islands. Whether wartime history is your area of interest or you just need a few hours of free time with the kids, this is one place that piques curiosity.

Amaknak Island hikers can access the **Spit Trail** across from Dutch Harbor proper, where excellent views of Iliuliuk Bay and town are visible, along with a healthy population of birds and sea otters. **Bunker Hill** is a steep climb from Airport Beach Road and rewards hikers with a number of concrete emplacements where gunners would lie in wait for an impending Japanese attack. The trail can also be accessed from Captain's Bay, to the right of Airport Beach Road, and although it's a more gradual climb with many bunkers to see, it's also longer. Kids may enjoy this more on a sunny day. Hardy hikers will like the **Mount Ballyhoo** climb from Ballyhoo Road, a nearly straight-up trek that tops out at sixteen hundred feet for great views of town. **Fort Schwatka** can also be accessed from Mount Ballyhoo, although most people take the switchback road from the Dutch Harbor entrance. Here, an entire fort was left after World War II, with building remnants to explore in a most desolate space. Watch for foxes, rabbits, and bald eagles as you wander the pathways. Heed the steep cliffs.

Unalaska Island features longer trails that are suitable for families with hiking experience. Since you'll be away from town a fair distance, make sure to bring water, extra food, and clothing to withstand the Aleutian elements. From the town of Unalaska, take Overland Drive (a dirt road) to find several trails. **Peace of Mind Trail** is a three-mile climb toward Beaver Inlet that crosses a few steams along the way to a now defunct sauna beyond a marshy lake area. Allow at least two hours each way. For a backpacking adventure, the **Agamgik Trail** departs from an unmarked trailhead just before the bridge at Humpy Creek, coming from Summer

Bay Road. While the trail is a relatively flat four miles, there is a steep gully and stream crossing that requires careful attention. Check with the Ounalashka Corporation for detailed maps and trailhead identification, as many trails are unmarked and can be difficult to find.

Parks

For a small community, Unalaska possesses a high number of outdoor parks and open spaces for public enjoyment. Stop by the visitors bureau for a map of town and local parks. **Sitka Spruce Park** is home to a small grove of spruce trees planted in the 1800s and is now a National Historic Landmark, with walking trails, a picnic area, playground, and restrooms. **Town Park** is located in the downtown area and features a gazebo, playground, picnic area, and restrooms and is a nice place to burn off some energy after exploring museums. **Memorial Park** is located near the entrance to Summer Bay Road and showcases the area's commitment to the US military. Flags, monuments, and an excellent view of Dutch Harbor can be found along the short boardwalk and park. The city of Unalaska has a complete listing of all community parks on its website, www.ci.unalaska.ak.us/parksrec/page/parks-trails.

ACKNOWLEDGMENTS

Writing about a subject as fluid as travel can be frustrating at best, especially during a tumultuous season of Alaska's statewide financial uncertainty. This book would not have been possible without the ongoing support of the Alaska Marine Highway System and the Alaska Department of Transportation, whose staff tirelessly answered my questions, provided information, and allowed our family to sail every AMHS route. We learned a lot about Alaska and where we fit in as residents tasked with promoting such a valuable thread in the tapestry that is our home state.

This second *Alaska On the Go* book also required meticulous editing, and Joanne Haines cheerfully stepped in to make sense of ferry schedules, passage details, and my somewhat casual writing style. I am grateful for her professionalism and unending attention to detail.

Additional gratitude is due to the staff and board of the University of Alaska Press, who recognized my passion for travel and children and embraced the idea of a family travel guide series.

Finally, my thanks go out to the legions of readers, friends, and family who convinced me that writing a second book was a pretty good idea after all. Maybe, just maybe, one of the children who sail aboard an Alaska Marine Highway System ferry will become as entranced by the experience as we were, and grow up to become an advocate for this very special way of traveling the state. Wouldn't that be amazing?

INDEX

Note: Italicized page numbers indicate illustrations.